5/11/47

For:

Mrs Mary L. Stidham,
with the compliments of

THE PURDUE EDITION

Signed by the Author

FOR THE FRIENDS OF

PURDUE

GEORGE ADE, *Warmhearted Satirist*

GEORGE ADE

George Ade

WARMHEARTED SATIRIST

BY FRED C. KELLY

THE BOBBS-MERRILL COMPANY

Publishers

INDIANAPOLIS • NEW YORK

First Edition

To the
memory of
WILL D. HOWE

Acknowledgments

THE author expresses his thanks to the following publishers for permission to quote from sources mentioned:

Doubleday & Co.: for material from the story, "Effie Whittlesy" from Ade's book *In Babel,* and for quotations from *Single Blessedness and Other Observations;* Julian Messner, Inc.: for excerpts from Ade's *The Old-Time Saloon;* Dodd, Mead & Co.: for material from *Fables in Slang* and *Bang! Bang!;* The Macmillan Co.: for material from Hamlin Garland's *Roadside Meetings.*

Cosmopolitan magazine: for material used from a series of reminiscences by Ade, published during the years 1925, 1926, 1927; *The Twainian,* published by George Hiram Brownell, of Elkhorn, Wisconsin: for material from Ade's "Revived Remarks on Mark Twain" and "One Afternoon with Mark Twain"; *American* magazine: for paragraphs from "They Simply Wouldn't Let Me Be a Highbrow"; *Liberty* magazine: for the quotation from the Ade article on football at Purdue; *The Magazine of Sigma Chi:* for excerpts from the Ade memorial edition, October-November 1944.

M. Witmark & Sons: for verse and chorus of "Remorse," from *The Sultan of Sulu.*

John S. Knight, owner of Chicago *Daily News,* for material from the old *Record;* New York *World-Telegram:* for the T. E. Powers cartoon in the old *Evening World.*

Author's Preface

I BEGAN to read George Ade in 1893. A youngster in knee pants, I went with my mother to the World's Fair in Chicago. We had hoped to stay for a couple of weeks, but in the afternoon of the fifth day our money gave out and we were obliged to start back to Ohio. To console me in my disappointment, my mother said she had noticed in a morning paper, the *Record,* a daily department, "All Roads Lead to the World's Fair," delightful little stories of happenings at the Fair. She would subscribe for that paper and we at least could read about some of the things we had missed seeing.

After the Fair was over, and "All Roads Lead to the World's Fair" was succeeded by "Stories of the Streets and of the Town," we continued to take the *Record.* So far as I know, no other copy came to our little town. I was entertained by the stories for years before I knew who wrote them. Then when the "Fables in Slang" began to appear in the same department on the paper's editorial page I was one of the countless number to whom George Ade was a hero.

I first met him in 1906. By that time I was a columnist on a paper in Cleveland, and he came there with one of his plays. A little later, the Sunday editor of the New York *Herald,* for whom I had written some articles, asked me if I would go over to Indiana and write a Sunday feature about George Ade's farm and his way of life there. I jumped at the chance. When I wrote to Ade about the suggestion, he asked me to meet him in Chicago and said we would take the train to Brook, near the farm, together. On the way, he apologized for the slow train. "The stations are exactly eighty feet apart," he said, "and it stops at them all."

During that train ride and a week end at the farm, we formed a friendship. I saw him from time to time through the years, and I was glad that my son wanted to attend Purdue University, because when I visited him it would be easy to visit George Ade.

In the spring of 1944, I was writing the biography of David Ross, promoter with Ade of the Ross-Ade Stadium at Purdue. No one knew certain facts about Ross except George Ade, and he was too ill to receive callers. But when he chanced to hear of what I was doing, his first thought was to try to be helpful, and he sent word that I should come to see him. His smile had its old-time warmth as he said: "I'm not very ambidextrous or acrobatic, but the old bean is still functioning, and I think I can tell you some things you'll want to know." A month later he died.

From the first, in writing the present biography, it was evident that the best way to acquaint the reader with the character and individuality of George Ade was to use his own language. I have not hesitated to quote him at every opportunity. And the reader may be assured that in no quotation of consequence have I trusted to anyone's memory. Yet it has seemed unnecessary to give this biography the appearance of a scholarly treatise with footnotes or references to all the articles, books, speeches, unpublished manuscripts, and letters from which the quotations are taken.

So many scores of persons have been generous with their help that I shall not try to list them all. A few to whom I am especially indebted must be mentioned: George Ade's sister, Mrs. Ella McCray; his closest friend, John T. McCutcheon; James D. Rathbun, executor of the Ade estate, and for many years George's business manager, who turned over all the hundreds of Ade papers for my inspection; George Ade Davis, who inherited all the Ade copyrights; the late Booth Tarkington who in long conversations and in many letters gave me rich material; John Ade Plugge and Julian Street for valuable help; and the late Will D. Howe for priceless technical advice.

FRED C. KELLY

Contents

CONTENTS—*Continued*

Illustrations

ILLUSTRATIONS—*Continued*

GEORGE ADE, *Warmhearted Satirist*

1

The Ades Become Hoosiers

"BECAUSE I was born in a little Indiana town framed with cornfields," wrote George Ade, "and showed a criminal preference for the Midwest vernacular and the homely types blooming in the outer townships, those who took the trouble to write about me when I was busy as a playwright and story-teller always assumed that I came of the most abandoned and confirmed Hoosier stock."

He was not of Hoosier stock. Neither of his parents was a native of Indiana, his father not even of America. By only a narrow margin was George Ade a Hoosier. If his parents had settled four miles farther west, Illinois could have claimed him.

John Ade, his father, was born in England, at Lewes, near the famous seaside resort of Brighton, but came to America at the age of twelve for a peculiar reason. A tax had been placed upon the residents of Lewes and the country round to restore an ancient ruin. Any tax was vexation enough, but this was for the Church of England, and the Ades were Baptists. George's grandfather called the tax an outrage. Though he had a secure job as maltster in a brewery—a fact embarrassing in after years to George's father, a total abstainer—he told his family, "We shall go elsewhere." With his wife and five sons, of whom John was the eldest, he set out for London. In June 1840 they boarded a vessel which sailed down the Thames and, after a stormy six weeks, docked at New York. In mid-ocean the sailors celebrated the Fourth of July. The Ade youngsters, especially John, caught the enthusiasm and never forgot it.

After a week in New York the family headed west. By rail, canal, and flat-bottom river boats they made their way to Cincinnati. At every landing they met people who were debating the approaching campaign for President. When John Ade heard men shouting for William Henry Harrison, the hero of the Battle of Tippecanoe, he asked where the battle took place. In Indiana? And where was Indiana?

The Ades stayed near Cincinnati in the little town of Cheviot. For three months John went to school. Then he became a blacksmith. At nineteen he explored the new country to the west and passed the summer of '49 in Chicago, which boasted a population of nearly 22,000. A contractor for whom he worked as teamster offered him two plots of ground, near where Dearborn street now crosses the river, for $150 each, but Chicago seemed to John unpromising. The only water mains were bored-out logs and much of the city water supply had to be hauled to customers in carts from the lake. The town was a mudhole. Opportunities would be better, he decided, back in Cheviot. Besides, he knew a girl there. He returned, resumed his blacksmithing and became a tollgate keeper. When others of his family moved west to Davenport, Iowa, John stayed behind because of dark-haired Ohio-born Adaline Bush.

They were married in 1851 when he was twenty-three and she eighteen. Her mother was an Adair, and, as George Ade has said, "according to the genealogists, who can become excited over the various kinds of fruit hanging on family trees, the names of Ade, Adee, Adie, Adey, Aide, Ader, Yde, Ide, and others of phonetic similarity are all variations of the Scotch name of Adair. The name became variously twisted and abbreviated because no one, not even the authors, knew how to spell." Thus George could trace back to the Adairs in two directions. "The ancestry is all British," he wrote. "That is why I have always felt that I had a right to take

George Ade's parents at time of their marriage. Ade treasured these pictures and thought his parents "a fine-looking couple."

Birthplace of George Ade in Kentland, Indiana.

George Ade at the age of four, and as a "Historic Boy." (Cartoon from the old *Life* by C. Foster Lincoln).

liberties with the English language. .... The only celebrity I have been able to spot in the general ancestry is Robin Adair of the old English ballad. I hope that Robin was a relative."

John Ade, a trifle below average height, with dark blue eyes that took in everything, wore good clothes and looked romantic, a little suggestive of an actor. His wife was painstaking about her hairdress, liked earrings and pretty hats. She took life seriously and was not given to smiling; but she was amiable, and as time went on came to be known as the kind that neighbors could call upon at any hour of the night for help in illness or at the coming of a new child.

Two years after their marriage the Ades became true pioneers. Friends in Cincinnati persuaded John to go to Indiana to take charge of a store they were opening at Morocco, the only town in what was to become Newton County. With their baby daughter they journeyed down the Ohio River to Madison, then by rail to Lafayette, and by wagon, over corduroy roads or rutted trails, into the swampy prairie of northwestern Indiana. There the houses stood dismally far apart. Deer, fur-bearing animals, prairie chickens, waterfowl, and every form of wild bloom abounded, but the crudities of living were beyond anything that the Ades had ever heard of. It was the Indiana of Eggleston's *The Hoosier Schoolmaster*. "The men believed in whiskers, and the women sang old-fashioned hymns in high, piping tremolo." Men and women walked barefoot to church in favorable weather and put on their shoes when they got there. Adaline Ade was looked upon with suspicion because she wore not a homemade sunbonnet but a hat bought in a store.

The first white baby in the region was born only twenty years before the Ades arrived. Buggies and carriages had not yet appeared. Mail came once a week on horseback to Brook, a post office twelve miles away. Here and there a few families jointly built a log cabin to be used for a school, but there was not one public school. If a spelling bee or other meeting was held in the log school at night, those who came brought saucers of grease with rags in them to furnish light.

Furs of the mink and other native animals were the one cash crop, and the store in John Ade's charge was mainly a fur-trading center. He became also the first postmaster at Morocco, but after three years was removed for "offensive partisanship," because he had not supported the Democratic national administration. Meanwhile, he had quit storekeeping and returned to his blacksmithing.

Morocco had less than a dozen cabins, widely separated, was forty miles from a railroad, yet within a year after John Ade came the place had a bank. Under a new "free banking law" in Indiana, any person or persons depositing with the Secretary of State bonds of any state in the union, could issue currency for an equal amount.

Years afterward George Ade described the situation.

"The town was so small and remote and hard to find that a band of enterprising promoters down at Indianapolis decided that it was entitled to a bank."

"Those were the happy days of wild-catting. Morocco was in line for a bank because it would be impossible for the general public to visit any bank at Morocco. The idea was to have the banks so far away from the banking public that no one could drop in and draw out money.

"So the Bank of North America was founded. The founders might have called it the Bank of the Western Hemisphere or the Bank of the Solar System, but they preferred to be modest. They deposited certain collateral with the State Treasurer and then they floated seventy-five thousand dollars worth of notes, redeemable only at the bank of issue.

"A year had passed and, as yet, no one had been able to find the bank. But . . . a man down in Clinton county made a land trade and received, as boot, about $1,000 in notes issued by the Bank of North America. He tried to put these into circulation and found it difficult to do so. His only chance to get real money on these notes was to hunt up the Bank of North America and present them and demand specie.

"He went to Lafayette, bought a horse and started out across the lonely prairies on a search for the Bank of North America. The cabins were miles apart and not one of the surprised natives had ever heard of the Bank of North America. On the evening of the third day he saw a log house in a distant clearing and rode to it. A man was standing in the doorway. The horseman said, 'I am looking for the town of Morocco.' And the man in the doorway said, 'Stranger, you are there.' He was standing on one of the principal corners of Morocco, Indiana, and right in front of the Bank of North America. He dismounted and went in.

"It was only about seven o'clock in the evening and the bank was still open. The cashier examined the notes. There was only one thing to be done. He went to a potato barrel, took out a tin box and paid the man in gold coin. But that was the end of the Bank of North America. When the promoters heard of the disaster that had overtaken them, they called a meeting and decided to go out of business. The bankers said it was no use trying to keep a bank open if people insisted on coming in and asking for money on their wild-cat paper."

In 1860, seven years after the Ades arrived in Indiana, it was decided to take part of Jasper County, in which was Morocco, and form a new county, Newton, the last in Indiana to be organized. John Ade was elected recorder. He moved his family to the new town of Kent, afterward called Kentland, four miles from the Illinois boundary, and eighty miles south of Chicago. This place was made the county seat because it was the only settlement on the new railroad. As an illustration of the simplicity of the community, the courthouse, built in 1861, was a square frame building that cost only $974, and yet it continued to be used until 1906.

Up to the time Kentland was laid out settlements had always been in or at the edge of one of the few groves of timber. No one thought of building in the open prairie. "Land is good," a government report said, "but, owing to the scarcity of timber, can never support anything but a very sparse population." There were no trees at Kentland. John Ade planted some. People who drive through Kentland today, on the main highway between Indianapolis and Chicago, admire the little town's great shade trees. They were put there by George Ade's father.

The little one and one-half story frame house into which the Ade family moved, was the second dwelling built in Kentland. It faced the south side of the courthouse square. In that house on February 9, 1866, the year after the end of the Civil War, George Ade was born. The period was eventful in the annals of American humorous philosophers. Three months before George's birth, Mark Twain had first received widespread recognition for his story, *The Celebrated Jumping Frog of Calaveras County;* the next year marked the death of Artemus Ward.

George grew up in a family of three boys and three girls. Three sisters, one of whom had died in infancy, and two brothers, William and Joseph, had already arrived and another sister was born after George. Being next to the youngest of the six, he might have been spoiled by petting, or frustrated by nagging, but thanks to the good sense of his mother no such things occurred. John Ade left the bringing up of the children largely to his wife, and the household was happy and harmonious.

The mother has been described by George. "Her willingness to serve and help and comfort was so unbounded and her goodness was so efficiently directed by unruffled common sense and

entire lack of theatrical emotionalism that sometimes I marvel
at the fact that, from no merit of my own, I was privileged to have
such a remarkable mother. Of course, she was the best of house-
keepers and when it came to preparing food, all the best chefs
in New York City could have learned wisdom from her."

As far back as George could remember his father was cashier
of the Discount & Deposit Bank in Kentland. Those were the
days, George used to say, "when it was all right to be a banker.
The usual rate of interest was two per cent a month, with a lot of
fine print inserted between the 'promise to pay' and the long list
of signatures below. The country banker had to figure that if he
could get enough names inscribed on various parts of the note,
one of them might turn out to be good."

Being a banker did not mean high income for George's father.
He was an employee, not one of the owners of the bank. Many a
night George's mother washed the children's underclothing and
dried it by the stove while they slept, because there was no money
to buy each child more than one suit. It is doubtful if John Ade
ever possessed, aside from his modest house, more than $1,000. In
his personal finances, he was anything but the cautious country
banker. Money was something to give away, to the church or to
the needy.

He did not attend the same church as his wife. She was a
Methodist, but he liked more action in his religion and became
a pillar of the Campbellite or Christian church with communion
services every Sunday and baptism by total immersion. Sometimes he preached. Dutifully every Sunday morning he took his
wife to her church and then went on to his own; after services he
hastened back to the Methodist to walk home with his wife.

From the Ade home "it was only a short cut across fields to un-
broken prairie—a grassy jungle matted with flower gardens. . . . A
traveller leaving the beaten road found himself chin-high in a

rank growth of blue and yellow blooms. . . . The explorer could start from anywhere out on the prairie and move in any direction and find a slough. In the center an open pond of dead water. Then a border of swaying cattails; tall rushes; reedy blades sharp as razors, out to the upland, spangled with the gorgeous blue and yellow flowers of the virgin plain. A million frogs sang together each evening and a billion mosquitoes came out to forage when the breeze died away. The old-fashioned flimsy mosquito-netting would not keep out anything under the size of a barn swallow. . . . Chills and fever entered into the program of every life."

So plentiful were wild geese, prairie chickens and quail, that hunters brought in wagonloads. The Ade children "used to tire of quail potpie and long for meat from the butcher's."

Kentland had one watch repairer, one druggist, one blacksmith and four saloons. There were not four thousand people in the county, and the population of the town was less than six hundred. For a boy with an instinctive interest in people it was an ideal place in which to grow up, for here it was easy to observe human nature.

2

Life Is One Grand Sweet Song

ONE of George Ade's early recollections—"as far back as I can reach into the past"—was of sitting on a fence on an October night in 1871 looking at "a blur of illumination in the northern sky." Chicago was "burning up in a highly successful manner."

The city eighty miles away seemed as remote as another planet, not a place one would ever be likely to see. Few of the villagers ever went that far from home. For months they were held prisoners by mud. The soil was "a dead black layer of shoe-polish on a subsoil of yellow clay." Roads would be just about impassable except to horsemen who could thread their ways along the turfy sides.

"After a mushy road froze solid it was a small topographical duplicate of the Rocky Mountains. Our only respites came in the summer when each dirt highway dried out and worked down to a couple of dusty tracks, and also in the winter when a blanket of snow covered the rutty surface and heavy runners succeeded in opening a right of way. We were kept at home because we lived on an island which was crisscrossed by wooden sidewalks and entirely surrounded by mud or water or, during a few happy weeks each year, acres and acres of glistening ice bordered with fine white snow."

True, the Panhandle railroad went through the edge of town and one could bump along over soft iron rails behind a locomotive "mostly smokestack," but a train journey was a rare luxury.

People were still carrying lanterns when they went out at night, though there were a few street lamps in glass cages. One of George's first means of earning spending money was to light at dusk each night a lonesome coal-oil burner, for which he received twenty-five cents a month. "I had to climb a ladder and struggle with slow-burning brimstone matches to touch off the charred wick and eventually flood a few square feet with modified gloom."

For indoor illumination there was "simply the old-fashioned coal-oil lamp which threw out a weak yellow glare. After you had one lamp lighted, you had to start another one so you could tell where you had put the first one."

There were no base-burners in which a fire could be kept overnight, but only wood-burning stoves. Sometimes the children saw "large, hard, golden ears of corn being shoveled into the sheet-iron stove as fuel because it wasn't worth hauling to the elevator." Whatever the fuel the fire was out in the morning before getting-up time. Then came the struggle to pull on cold, damp, copper-toed boots!

"Architecture ran to cubes." But even a humble citizen was likely to "put on some scallops and jigsaw dingle-dangles. . . . The front of every cubical house was a sealed tomb, with lace curtains mercifully screening the gilt frames and varnished monstrosities." It was a period of wax flowers, and the twin bedroom chromos of Fast Asleep and Wide Awake. All this was concurrent with a firm belief in infant damnation.

"Just when everything was darkest, the cardboard motto and the professional elocutionist appeared, to complicate the general environment of yokelism." When the women began running yarn through cardboard, the front room that had been "gleaming with cold horsehair" began to brighten up with a framed "God Bless Our Home" in mottled colors. And elocution, "now prohibited by law in many of our states, was almost an epidemic in the seventies. Tall, brunette ladies of intense personality would travel from town to town and collect their victims into halls and goose-pimple them with 'Rum's Maniac,' or 'Curfew Shall Not Ring Tonight.'

"Poetry was ladled out with a spoon, and the story papers were soggy with highfalutin, impossible, stilted, romantic serials. . . . E. P. Roe was the favorite novelist."

In the field of music the favorite instruments were the jew's-harp, harmonica, melodeon and guitar. "Every young lady was supposed to sing if she could find someone to turn the music for her. The male quartet was everywhere, a hideous by-product of the Civil War. Hearing a throaty tenor, with oil on his hair, sing 'Juanita' was a common experience."

George yearned to play the cello and did learn chords on the piano. One of his elder sisters started to give him lessons on the melodeon, but his father put his foot down on such nonsense. There was a general distrust of any male who could make music.

It was a time when women carried much strange rigging. "The bustle, a rear extension from just below the waistline, something that looked like an aft-deck or a rumble-seat, was supposed to add to feminine charm. The bustle was the most unbelievable item in human history."

The more formidable beaux used hair oil—Macassar oil; and pinned to the backs of sofas and chairs to protect them were knitted covers called antimacassars. Beaux wore huge padded cravats, spring-bottom trousers and Derby hats with narrow brims and high crowns, "lined with puckery silk." It was a time, too, of congress gaiters. Among the luxuries were gold-mounted tooth-picks and watch chains made of human hair.

Youngsters wore garments made over from something the older relatives had discarded. Some of the winter caps which pulled down over the ears had peekholes for the eyes. If there was a suspected case of measles anywhere in town, school children reeked with "assifidity" carried in little bags worn next to the skin.

His Sunday garb made a deep impression on George Ade. "When the starched waist had been connected with the shapeless nether garment by an equatorial girdle of white buttons, and the suffocating collar had been lashed up with a large bow and the forelock had been securely gummed to the brow, then the proud little man was supposed to be all fixed up for Sunday-school."

Looking back, George wondered why any boy ever found an excuse for living. But not dreaming of future improvements, all supposed they were having a good time. "There were hickory nuts to crack, corn to pop, and taffy to pull, a Christmas tree every Christmas, once in a while an oyster supper at McCullough's Hall, a couple of theatrical 'troupes' every winter, an average of one circus per summer, the traveling medicine show, possibly the thrill and tingle derived from a panoramic lecture on the Holy Land, revival service at the M. E. church."

"The street fights between a couple of agricultural huskies who had trained on copper-distilled Kentucky sour mash was a free show, and the parade which trailed behind the town marshall and the combative drunk, up Main street toward the 'calaboose,' was a frequent spectacle not without educational value. . . . Was existence drab or the hours empty? No indeed! Life was one grand, sweet song."

When George went to school he used the McGuffey Readers, which exposed him to specimens of prose and poetry by recognized authors who were great boosters for honest toil, truthfulness and other virtues. He had already begun to read. Stretched out, face downward, on the floor—a habit he retained to young manhood—he got enough of the meaning of words to catch the main drift of stories in the *Youth's Companion* or *Harper's Young People,* and he liked to make out a word at a time the lines under the pictures in *Harper's Weekly*. At school it was not difficult for him to read in the Primer, "The dog ran at a cat."

Because he often became deeply absorbed in what he read, he was called a dreamer at an early age. His mother insisted that even when not reading, his thoughts were often far away. One day she asked him to bring in an armful of wood for the kitchen stove. George got the wood, carried it through to the parlor and put it on the floor beside him as he dropped into a chair and picked up a book. Until reminded by his mother, he thought he had left the wood in the kitchen.

From the habit of entertaining himself with his thoughts came one of the most vivid of George's recollections of his first year at school. The family had moved to a house about a mile from the school. There was a short cut if one followed the railroad track. As trains did not pass often, it was not considered dangerous for children to use the short cut. But one November afternoon the first snowstorm of the season came with a strong wind. As school was closing George's mother put on her cloak and hat and started on a run. She feared that George might walk backward, shielding his face from the snow, and would not hear the train. When she reached him just before the train came, he *was* walking backward. Some time afterward he wrote of his narrow escape in a school essay, "A Mother's Intuition."

The Ades kept a cow. During good weather George drove it from the barn to a near-by pasture each morning and back in the evening. One evening the cow was not in the pasture. George followed the fence all the way around to see if there was a break, but found none, asked the neighbors if they had seen a stray cow and finally had to report to his father that the cow had disappeared. John Ade himself inspected the fence and conducted further inquiries, but in vain. As he and George neared the house, the father heard the moo of a cow.

"It seems to come," he said, "from the direction of the barn. Maybe, wherever she's been, she decided to come home."

Then George remembered something. He had not taken her that morning to the pasture!

His father looked at him sadly and shook his head. "I'm afraid, George, you're always going to be a dreamer."

As time went on, John Ade worried more and more about George. The boy did not seem to be fit for anything except to sit around and read.

Once, though, George was a hero. A young nephew had disappeared. When last seen, he had been dipping water from a cistern and carrying it into the house to use with some toys. The top of the cistern was open. Probably the child had fallen in. George was picked to investigate. The water was over his head, and cold, but he did not shrink from what seemed to be his duty. Down the ladder he climbed and felt over the bottom with his feet. Then, with his teeth chattering, he reported that "so far as he could ascertain" no nephew was there. A few minutes later the boy was found under a bed. He had gone into hiding because he had spilled water on the floor and feared a scolding. While rejoicing over the lost one that was found, the family made a great to-do over George's bravery. "It wasn't anything," said George; "the water wasn't much below zero."

George got along well at school. He was especially good at spelling. His teacher said the time would come when it would be just about impossible to find an English word he could not spell correctly. Spelling matches were a form of public entertainment in which grownups as well as youngsters took part. Sometimes George would "spell down" a teacher. One night, though, when only he and a schoolma'am were left standing, and it looked as if he might be the winner, he failed on the word "bruit," meaning to noise about. That was a new one to George.

Only once did he have any serious embarrassment in school. A male teacher switched him with a hickory stick, and for no worse offense than making what the teacher said was too much noise when going to his seat. George did not think he deserved the punishment and he did not forget the humiliation.

George's problem was to find enough to read. Kentland had no public library, but on the bookshelves in the Ade home were a few of the novels of Charles Dickens. By borrowing, he was able to read all of Dickens; he read the books over and over. Their influence on him was great, probably more than that of any other author. He did not confine himself to the more approved kinds of literature. With other boys he resorted to an underground circulating library, named after Mr. Beadle, and the haymow was the chosen reading room. An advantage of this kind of reading was that it came in a form which could be secretly spread inside a school geography!

Another kind of reading was the old-time subscription book. George has told how the center table in the parlor was saved from utter dullness.

"Do you remember the center table of the seventies? In the dim front room—it seemed to harmonize with an apartment which was half sanctuary and half sepulcher. The marble top showed glossy in the subdued light that filtered through the lace curtains, and it was clammy cold even on hot days. The heavy mahogany legs were chiseled into writhing curves from which depended stern geometrical designs or possibly bunches of grapes.

"The Bible had the place of honor and was flanked by subscription books. In those days the house never became cluttered with the ephemeral six best sellers. The new books came a year apart, and each was meant for the center table, and it had to be so thick and heavy and emblazoned with gold that it could keep company with the bulky and high-priced Bible.

"Books were bought by the pound. Sometimes the agent was a ministerial person in black clothes and a stove-pipe hat. Maiden ladies and widows, who supplemented their specious arguments with private tales of woe, moved from one small town to another feeding upon prominent citizens. Occasionally the prospectus was unfurled by an undergraduate of a freshwater college working for money to carry him another year.

"The book-agents varied, but the book was always the same . . . many pages, numerous steel engravings, curlycue tail-pieces, platitudes, patriotism, poetry, sentimental mush. One of the most popular, still resting in many a dim sanctuary, was known as 'Mother, Home, and Heaven.' A ponderous collection of 'Poetical Gems' did not involve the publishers in any royalty entanglements. Even the 'Lives of the Presidents' and 'Noble Deeds of the Great and Brave' gave every evidence of having been turned out as piece-work by needy persons temporarily lacking employment on newspapers. Let us not forget the 'Manual of Deportment and Social Usages,' from which the wife of any agriculturist could learn the meaning of R.S.V.P. and the form to be employed in acknowledging an invitation to a levee.

"Nobody really wanted these books. They were purchased because the agents knew how to sell them, and they seemed large for the price and, besides, every well-furnished home had to keep something on the center table.

"Subscription books were dry picking for boys. . . . Let one glorious exception be made in the case of 'Dr. Livingstone's Travels in Africa,' a subscription book of forbidding size, but containing many pictures of darkies with rings in their noses.

"Just when front-room literature seemed at its lowest ebb, so far as the American boy was concerned, along came Mark Twain. His books looked, at a distance, just like the other distended, diluted, and altogether tasteless volumes that had been used for several decades to balance the ends of the center table. The publisher knew his public, so he gave a pound of book for every fifty cents, and crowded in plenty of wood-cuts and stamped the outside with golden bouquets and put in a steel engraving of the author, with a tissue-paper veil over it, and 'sicked' his multitude of broken-down clergymen, maiden ladies, grass widows, and college students on to the great American public.

"Can you see the boy, a Sunday morning prisoner, sidling toward the new book with a dull sense of foreboding, expecting a dose of Tupper's 'Proverbial Philosophy'? Can you see him a few minutes later when he finds himself linked arm-in-arm with Mulberry Sellers or Buck Fanshaw or the convulsing idiot who wanted to know if Christopher Columbus was sure-enough dead? No wonder he curled up on the hair-cloth sofa and hugged the thing to his bosom and lost all interest in Sunday School. 'Innocents Abroad' was the most enthralling book ever printed until 'Roughing It' appeared. Then along came 'The Gilded Age,' 'Life on the Mississippi,' and 'Tom Sawyer,' one cap-sheaf after another. While waiting for a new one we read the old ones all over again.

"The new uniform edition with the polite little pages, high-art bindings, and all the boisterous wood-cuts carefully expurgated can never take the place of those lumbering subscription books. They were the early friends and helped us to get acquainted with the most amazing story-teller that ever captivated the country boys and small-town boys all over America."

Thus George Ade came to know Mark Twain and "his miracle of making the subscription book something to be read and not merely looked at. He converted the Front Room from a Mausoleum into a Temple of Mirth."

George never ceased his hero worship of Mark Twain. After he had become thoroughly familiar with all the Mark Twain books, his favorite was *Life on the Mississippi,* because here the author was telling of a most interesting part of his own career "with shameless candor." Fiction was never so fascinating to George as autobiography. Again and again he re-read Dana's *Two Years Before the Mast. Robinson Crusoe* irked him somewhat, because he feared that it was not quite truthful.

No less than to books George was devoted to magazines, particularly those dealing with current events. It became a common saying among the young people in Kentland that if George Ade was invited to a party it would be well to hide all the magazines or he would pay no attention to anything else.

Yet George liked to go to parties, even though he never seemed to have difficulty in resisting the charms of young girls. There is no record of his going off his feed in his school days from an attack of lovesickness. One night he was to escort home from a social gathering a girl who lived three or four miles from town, and he would have the use of the Ade family surrey. When the party was about to break up, George got hold of a boy named Art Hawkins who was not taking any girl home and urged him to hide in the surrey behind the front seat. If he would throw the lap robe over him, George told him, no one would know he was there, but he must keep as quiet as a mouse. The boy, looking for an interesting adventure, did as asked. As they jogged along toward the girl's home, the boy overheard almost no conversation, because she was a quiet soul, "hard to talk to." When at last the boy joined George in the front seat for the return to town, he was full of curiosity. Why had he been invited to make the trip in hiding?

"She might have thought it was funny if she knew you were along," George explained. "That is, she might have thought I was scared of her. But I wanted to have company driving back."

Not all George's education was gained at school or from reading.

George Ade and Lillian Howard, the Purdue coed believed to be the one girl he ever loved.

George Ade and John T. McCutcheon in their college days.

Where the Ades lived in Kentland in 1885.

From the time he could run errands for his mother he was likely to loiter to listen to the talk of those about the stove in Pat Keefe's grocery, or in Eph Sell's hardware store. Sell was one of his heroes, for he was known to be a nephew of Peter Sell, head of the Sells' circus; but Keefe's grocery seemed to have the best talkers. Two of the regulars were Ory Six and Bluford Light— the latter known as "Blue." No matter how commonplace the subject might be, any kind of talk fascinated George. Even exchange of views about the weather seemed worth hearing. He was unconsciously storing in his memory bits of the talk:

"This is a terrible day, ain't it?"

"I believe it's the worst day I ever saw around here."

"Well, I don't know. We had an awful day on March 3, three years ago."

"Yes, that was a bad storm."

"It ain't really so cold today but that wind is damp and cuts right through your clothes."

"It sure does. I went out in the backyard this morning to dump the ashcan and I thought I'd freeze."

"Yesterday was such a purty day I felt sure we was goin' to get some good settled weather."

"I was sayin' to my wife last night that I thought winter was over, and now we're havin' the worst blizzard of the season."

"Well, that's the way it goes. I had my folks out for a ride yesterday and I told 'em it wouldn't be long 'til we'd see a robin."

"A man in Effingham, Illinois, claims he saw one last Thursday."

"You don't say."

"It was in the paper."

What possible good could come from a boy listening to that kind of chat!

A man whom George admired, Alexander Kent, founder of

Kentland, was sometimes at Keefe's. He owned the biggest grain elevator in northern Indiana and was a "character." A committee called upon him to ask for a donation of corn for stricken areas of Nebraska and Kansas where grasshoppers had destroyed the crops. Without looking up from his whittling, he said: "Go over to the elevator and take all you want." He was the biggest contributor to every church of every denomination for miles around. George remembered the day when Kent saw a preacher poorly dressed and "yanked him to a store and bought him everything from the hide out, including galluses."

Cool weather gave George another reason to go to Keefe's grocery. They might have oysters. If he went to ask his father for a quarter, his father knew it was for oysters. For everything else he earned his own spending money. It was always a proud moment for him when he reached home carrying a bucket of oysters for the family supper—a little pasteboard bucket with a wire handle. He liked ice cream, too, and only once in his boyhood did the supply seem even half enough. On the night that his eldest sister was married George and some of his friends discovered a huge freezer of ice cream parked on the kitchen porch and—there was not enough for the wedding guests to have any.

Whatever else was lacking, George's early environment was not without emotional excitement. "The famous orators were those who could cause jurors to weep. The popular preachers were those who could make the most noise while picturing hellfire. A really successful funeral could be heard a mile away.

"Religious convictions were vivid and concrete. Satan . . . devoted all his time to frying those who had failed to attend church." George would never forget one local campaign by the churches against the Demon Rum, strongly intrenched in the town's four saloons. He was one of a flock of youngsters, wearing blue ribbons (bearing the name of Francis Murphy, famous temperance crusader), who went to call on Louie Wildberg at his clothing store. "Louie was a useful citizen of mild demeanor who had been much respected until the community became worked into a frenzy. He became a marked man because it was rumored that he kept bottled beer on ice."

Louie was waiting on a country customer when George and the other earnest youngsters filed in and begged him to follow their example and line up against King Alcohol. He just looked at them over his glasses and said, "Run along to school, children." They felt sure he was a lost lamb.

Early in life George lost interest in church, and for a good reason. One night at a lecture in the Methodist church he sat alone at the rear. He had been out playing with other boys and dropped in at the church solely to join his mother and father as they started homeward. (His father saw no harm in attending a Methodist church for a nonreligious lecture.) No one had noticed George slip into a rear pew. The lecture did not end as soon as he expected, so he stretched out and tried to make himself comfortable. He was asleep when the sexton locked the doors. Along about 3:00 A.M. he fell off the narrow bench and suddenly awakened. The strange surroundings filled him with terror. He remembered with quickened heartbeats a recent funeral in this same church of a man who had died from having his throat slashed. Groping his way toward the front door, he overturned a coal scuttle that made an unholy racket. The door was locked. He crept to the nearest window which to his immense relief was unlocked and dropped the seven or eight feet to the ground. At home he found that his parents had been going from house to house inquiring if anyone had seen little George, and the search was about to extend over the whole township.

From that time George was ill at ease in church, and his understanding mother permitted him to attend devotional services less and less. He had the willing support of his brother Joe, who avoided sermons when he could. Brother Will, an enthusiastic churchgoer, was inclined to worry about the souls of George and Joe.

George did not quit church attendance before he had memorized every Methodist hymn he had ever heard. It was not that he made any effort to learn them by heart; the words and tunes just sank so deeply into his memory that they were there for keeps.

Shortly after his perilous escape from the church George attended a lecture, on woman suffrage, by Elizabeth Cady Stanton. Admission was free, so there was a crowd. George and his friends were in the front row. When about to begin Elizabeth Cady Stanton noticed many grownups standing in the rear, and her eyes fell upon the youngsters. She announced that her lecture was not for small boys and asked the janitor to remove the gang that had taken possession of the best seats. George and his friends had to file out amidst jeers and laughter. They held a meeting on the sidewalk in front of Noble's jewelry store and pledged themselves to oppose woman suffrage for all time. A little later George heard a native Indiana speaker for equal suffrage, Helen M. Gougar, who was so pleasantly persuasive that he decided to renege on his vow.

The theater had stirred George's curiosity before he was old enough to go to school. His first little stack of pennies went for a book of songs popularized by the team of Harrigan and Hart. He tried to know the songs that were hits on the stage, especially in minstrel shows. Once he blacked up and sang "The Skidmore Guards" in a school entertainment.

A theatrical "attraction" at McCullough's Hall was more likely to be a magic-lantern show or Swiss bell ringers than a regular dramatic troupe, but there were repertoire companies that worked

out of Indianapolis and played in small towns such stand-bys as
"East Lynne," "Lady Audley's Secret" or "Ten Nights in a Bar-
Room" with seats at ten, twenty and thirty cents. The Riley Company, the Graham Earle Stock Company and the Harry Hotto
Players sometimes came to Kentland. Occasionally there was
something special. Over at Brookston in near-by White County
lived a stage-struck young man named Seth Kent, to be known
later on Broadway as S. Miller Kent. He was a nephew of the
founder of Kentland, and at McCullough's Hall he made his first
costume appearance, in scenes from "The Lady of Lyons." George
Ade got in for passing bills. Another budding actor who en-
thralled George in Kentland grew up at Bennett's Switch near
Logansport, Richard Bennett—though his first name wasn't really
Richard—later to become a star and to have daughters famous in
motion pictures.

It was a bitter disappointment to eight-year-old George that he
was not taken to Chicago to see the Interstate Exposition where
the most talked-of exhibit was "Iolanthe, the Sleeping Beauty,"
done life-size in butter. Later his father did take him to Chicago
to see *Fanchon the Cricket* with a star named Lotte, the most
vivacious lady George had ever seen. On that trip George was
permitted to peek into the barbershop at the Palmer House where
silver dollars were used as centerpieces in the mosaic flooring.
When he was ten, he had another trip to Chicago where he saw,
again at McVicker's, the great Edwin Booth in *The Fool's Revenge*.
He was enough of a critic, he afterward insisted, to recognize that
he was seeing "real city acting."

Those two trips to Chicago gave George prestige among his
playmates. Not many had ever seen shows in a city theater, so he
had the standing "of a local Marco Polo."

George early became politically conscious, for everyone there-
abouts took politics "in huge, bitter doses."

"It was a time when one of the chief lunacies was the belief that voters could best prove the fervor of their political convictions and the high character of their patriotism by walking mile after mile carrying torches and permitting kerosene to drip on their clothing."

Newton County was a Republican stronghold and "the first lessons learned were those of political hatred. We studied our Nast cartoons before we tackled the primer." George believed, like many of his elders, that if the Democrats won "the whole solar system would be disarranged."

When he was seven years old, George went with his parents to Davenport, Iowa, to visit relatives, and he came back with two exciting stories to arouse the envy of his playmates. As the train was leaving Peoria, he had met and actually talked with Thomas Nast, the cartoonist, who was on a lecture tour, and Nast had given him an orange. George's father did not need to explain to him why Nast was considered a great man. On the same trip George was stirred by seeing in front of a cigar store in Davenport a gayly painted wooden Indian with a tomahawk in one hand and a bunch of cheroots in the other; but meeting Nast was the big event.

Before long he was meeting other celebrities. Albert G. Porter, governor of Indiana, afterward minister to Italy, and Schuyler Colfax, Vice-President under Grant, came to the Ade home when George was a spindly youngster and he liked them both because they were so amiable. He worked his way into a carriage ride with Porter and the carriage got stuck in the mud. Then he was "a little surprised to learn that a great and good Republican such as Albert G. Porter couldn't spread his wings and fly out of that mud-hole."

George did not forget the white plug hats and the oilcloth capes of the 1872 campaign, nor the campaign of '76 when he firmly believed that Samuel J. Tilden was a "snorting demon with eye-balls like coals of fire." It was during that memorable autumn of '76 that he rode across the prairie to a political rally seated along-side Benjamin Harrison, later President of the United States, who was running for governor against "Blue Jeans" Williams. Two things struck George as interesting about Harrison. One was that he wore gloves, and anyone who did that in those days—unless he were a pallbearer—was under suspicion; the other was that during the ride of twenty-five miles in the Ade family carriage, Harrison never once addressed a word to him.

One of the stories that George always cherished was of "an affecting incident" in '76. "In those days every voter went up an alley and prepared his ballot and tucked it into his vest pocket and fought his way to the ballot-box." Along about noon a respected farmer drove into town and delivered a load of oats at the elevator, receiving the usual check. He went to the Republican headquarters and received a straight ballot which he folded up and put in his pocket. Then he walked over to the polling place. A few minutes later he came into the bank, open as usual, and tried to cash a Hayes and Wheeler ballot. He had voted his grain check!

To show his open-mindedness during that same '76 campaign George "sat under the soft maples in the courthouse yard" and listened to the Democratic orator, Thomas A. Hendricks. "I knew that he was telling a pack of lies, but he was so ingratiating and earnest and plausible that finally I had to get up and go away. I felt myself slipping."

Before he was out of knee pants, George loafed around the office of the *Gazette,* the Republican weekly in Kentland, and did small chores "mostly for the glory of the Republican cause." One day during a hot campaign he drifted into the office of the rival paper and swiped some proof sheets he saw hanging on a hook.

He was able to give the Republicans advance information about the last-minute attacks to be made on some Republican candidates. He was warmly praised by those on his side, but the Democratic editor, unable to find out who the culprit was, said in the next issue that whoever had taken those proof sheets was "an infamous skunk" and "never again must the air of our sanctum be contaminated by the fumes emanating from his filthy carcass."

Naturally George felt much set up. "Any twelve-year-old boy who could get that kind of piece written about him was certainly making headway in politics."

3

The Dreamer Is a Problem

DURING high school years George Ade found himself removed in summer from even the little entertainment Kentland could provide. He worked on a farm. "I did not volunteer; I was drafted. My parents thought that if they kept me away from the gaieties and temptations of a village of eight hundred people I might grow up to be a good citizen."

George would never look back on these summers with pleasure. "The distrust with which I regarded horses at that time has never been overcome."

He began by pulling cockle-burrs out of the corn. "It was pretty hard to look over a field of cockle-burrs and find the corn. Sometimes the corn crop would fail and sometimes the oat crop would fail, but the cockle-burr crop and the mustard crop never failed.

"One of my earliest jobs was to sit on the front end of the corn planter and pull or push the lever so as to drop three grains of corn every time we came to one of the crosslines. I regret to say that very little of the corn I put in could be plowed both ways.

"The self-binder was just being tried out, but the makers had not yet solved the problem of having the machinery tie a knot in the twine. The first binders used wire which took a single turn around the sheaf and then was twisted and cut off, leaving two points projecting. We had to wear heavy gloves when we were shocking the grain and when I was promoted and became a band-cutter on an old-fashioned threshing machine run by horsepower, I had to cut each band with a hatchet. The wire bands got into the straw stacks and proved to be highly indigestible for cattle and horses.

"If the country boys got a town boy on the straw stack they put him at what was known as the 'tail end' of the machine where he would get all the dirt and dust and chaff and crickets. . . . There is no ordeal more unpleasant than that of breathing chaff all day, when the weather is hot, while several crickets, with spikes on their shoes, are walking around under your hickory shirt."

One day George was in charge of a horse-drawn hayrake. In the shade of a tree at the edge of the field, he saw a water jug and leaped off the machine to quench his thirst. Not wanting to risk leaving the team any longer than necessary, he tried to swallow all he could at one gulp. Too late he found that the water jug contained machine oil! That night he did not tell what ailed him and his mother treated him for what appeared to be a strange form of cholera.

George was feeling more and more sure he was never going to like farming. The sordidness of life on arms depressed him. Most of the farmers he met showed no interest in making life more comfortable, and they seemed to hate beauty. At threshing time there were "thirty or forty men and ten million flies, all reporting for dinner at the same time." One farm wife had put a vase of flowers on the table when the harvest crew came in. Her husband looked at the flowers in disgust and asked: "Can we eat them things? Take 'em away."

On a July day in 1881 fifteen-year-old George had what he considered the worst farm job yet, painting a picket fence. It was a blazing hot day and he was not working in the shade. He didn't see how he was going to stick at the job. Then someone brought news from town. A man named Guiteau had shot President Garfield. George immediately quit work—said he was too upset by the news to continue. He laid off for three days, one a legal holiday, July fourth.

John Ade shook his head in discouragement. What was to become of a boy in a farming community who did not like farming and had no talents or aptitude for anything else?

In October of that same year 1881 George gained distinction. The high school at Kentland in those days had only a two-year course and George was in his second or senior year. One afternoon the teacher told the seniors to write compositions on a subject she assigned. The subject, whatever it was, did not interest George and he dillydallied and got almost nothing on paper. That night he had to stay after school and he told the teacher he could write a composition if she would let him pick another subject. What he wrote bore the title, "A Basket of Potatoes." The teacher thought it was so good that, with the permission of George's father she sent it to the *Gazette,* the paper where George sometimes loafed and did small chores, and the editor put it in the paper.

Here it is, the first work of George Ade ever to be set in type and published:

A BASKET OF POTATOES

A very common subject and one on which it would seem as if little could be said. Just a common basket of potatoes composed of large potatoes, small potatoes and medium-sized potatoes. And yet by this basket of potatoes we can illustrate the great problem of success of life, of how men rise to the top of the ladder, and how men stay at the bottom and why men can never rise to high places. Now let us begin our investigations.

Here is a bushel basket and here is a bushel of potatoes. We pour the potatoes in the basket and now we will make our first comparison or supposition. Each one of these potatoes is a young man not yet entered on his life's great work. The large potatoes are large-minded, large-hearted, honest young men. The small potatoes are small-minded, small-hearted, mean, dishonest young men. The medium potatoes are a mixture of the good and the bad. As we have them now, the large ones and small ones are mixed all over the basket. There are large ones at the bottom and small ones at the top and vice versa.

Now let the battle of life begin. Let these young men be put upon a level footing and be put face to face with the stern realities of life. We will illustrate this with the basket of potatoes by lifting it up and jolting and shaking and tipping it very thoroughly for some time, and then when we stop we find to our surprise that the small potatoes have gone to the bottom and the large potatoes have gone to the top, while the medium-sized have stopped in the center and do not seem to go either way. Friends, remember this; in the tough, earnest battle of life the big potatoes will go to the top and the small ones will go to the bottom.

There are few rules which have no exceptions and it is thus with this rule, for here right on the top of the basket we find a small potato and we are puzzled accordingly, but it is soon clear, for upon investigation we find that it is held in its place by two large ones and from this we draw the following conclusion: Whenever you see a small potato in the top of the basket, somebody's holding it there.

And here are several more exceptions, for down in the bottom of the basket we find several large ones and again we are mystified, but it soon clears away and we know the cause when we discover projecting from each one several large knots or projections and in order that these potatoes may have a fair chance we break off these knots and discover that the most common knot is intemperance. The others are love of gain, inactivity and several other bad habits. And from this we draw the conclusion that if we would rise to the top we must break off our bad habits and vices and be as big a potato as possible.

What is true in one case is true in another and we find that small potatoes are kept on top by these projections and when these are examined we find that smooth tongues and lying words have put them on the level of the big potatoes.

And now when we have everything fixed to our satisfaction

and are satisfied with our examinations, we casually pick up the largest potato in the basket and look at it and discover something which we had not before noticed, viz.—a large rotten spot in its otherwise solid body. And from this we draw the conclusion that even the big potatoes are not all perfect and man is apt to be sinful in spite of everything.

And so it is everywhere, life is but a basket of potatoes. When the hard jolts come, the big will rise and the small will fall. The true, the honest and the brave will go to the top. The small-minded and ignorant must go to the bottom. And now I would like to say something to these young potatoes. Now is the time for you to say whether or not in the battle of life you will be a small or large potato. If you would be a large potato get education, be honest, observing and careful and you will be jolted to the top. If you would be a small potato, neglect these things and you will get to the bottom of your own accord. Break off your bad habits, keep away from rotten potatoes and you will get to the top. Be careless of these things and you will reach the bottom in due time. Everything rests with you. Prepare for the jolting.

While that composition did not suggest the humor that George was to write later, still it did anticipate the Ade Fables in that it pointed a kind of moral. And it showed that George was learning to express himself in good, straightforward English. One wonders how many second-year high school lads can write so clearly.

After that piece about the potatoes appeared, George's teachers took more note of what he was doing. Reports about him interested Mr. Hershman, the County Superintendent of Schools. Toward the end of George's senior year Mr. Hershman went to call upon John Ade. He wanted to tell him that he thought George ought to go to college. He was the kind, the superintendent said, who would gain from a college education.

It was a startling suggestion. John Ade had once proposed to his eldest son Will to pay his expenses if he wished to go to a theological seminary and prepare for the ministry, but Will had declined the offer. There had been no thought of sending Joe Ade to college, because he had scant interest in book learning. Nor had it ever before occurred to the father that George should go to college. The experiment would be costly and might only stiffen George's habit of dodging work. On the other hand, several professions were said to be open to college-bred men who could never hope to succeed at anything practical. John Ade promised to think it over. His business friends advised him not to waste his money.

If George did not go to college, John Ade reflected, what *could* be done with him? Gradually he made up his mind to send him, even though the expense would mean added household economies. Not many local boys had ever gone to college, but reports were that the cost might run to $250 a year, or $1,000 for the whole course, a lot of money to risk for an experiment.

What college should it be? Indiana University at Bloomington might do, but it was more than one hundred and fifty miles away. Some one remembered that less than fifty miles away was "that little agricultural school near Lafayette." It was called Purdue University, after the Lafayette merchant who had put up part of the money for it, John Purdue—in later years described by George Ade as "a portly bachelor, self-made and hard-boiled, who wore plain broadcloth, and whose plump jowls were supported by a Henry Clay collar."

John Purdue, while lacking faith in the practical value of Latin and Greek, had thought there should be a school to teach "agriculture and mechanic arts." That sounded good to John Ade. Perhaps Purdue University would be just the place for George. Maybe he would finally become interested in something useful.

The Commissioners of any county in Indiana could issue two scholarships to state colleges each year to young people of "good moral character." John Ade, on September 5, 1882, applied for one of those scholarships for George. No one questioned George's character, whatever the neighbors may have thought about his persistent avoidance of work, and no one else in the county wanted to go to Purdue, so George got the scholarship.

But George was not yet to begin his great adventure. His mother put her foot down on his going to college that year. Willing enough to make any financial sacrifices for him, she said he was still too young to be so far from home. He was only a few months past sixteen, to her a mere child. She could well imagine the temptations that could beset a boy in a city. Purdue University was within a mile of a city of 15,000.

So instead of entering Purdue George took special courses in high school. He would go to Purdue the next year. Surprisingly, George was not too disappointed over the delay. He had been pleased when his father proposed sending him to college, but at times he felt almost alarmed over the prospect of staying for many weeks at a stretch so far from home.

When finally in September 1883 George set out for Lafayette, there were much shaking of heads and clucking sounds with tongues by those who hated to see John Ade make a big mistake.

Perhaps John Ade was by no means sure he was acting wisely. Only two other boys in the county were going to college and George was the only one going to Purdue. It did seem a daring extravagance.

George himself did not look happy when the time came to start away. He was serious-faced as he stood on the station platform with his baggage. This consisted of a canvas "telescope" which contained his other suit, the one "kept for nice," and a change of both shirt and underwear. He also carried a neat package, three sandwiches and some cookies, his mother had prepared for his lunch. His father did not say much to him as he climbed aboard the early morning train. But George knew what was in his mind.

"I think the limit of his hopes for me was that eventually, somewhere, somehow, I would make a living."

4

College—and the Op'ry House

THE early morning train took George to a junction. With two changes and long waits he did not reach Lafayette until well into the afternoon. He wore a quiet blue suit and a narrow-brimmed soft felt hat with a band of watered silk and a buckle. A good observer would have noted a shrewd, slightly aquiline nose, long strips of dark eyebrows, serious light blue eyes, ears of liberal size extending outward, a prominent forehead, also an unusual development of the head rearward. A still better observer might have detected that one ear was slightly lower than the other and that his entire nose seemed to be aimed a wee trifle starboard.

Purdue was two miles from the station, and there were no street cars. To ride in a hack, it seemed to George, would be putting on airs. A man with a sullen-looking gray horse and big wagon offered to deliver his baggage. George asked to ride with him. He at once inquired about the local theater. The driver said there was a show at the Grand Opera House, he could not remember what. There was nearly always a show he said, and George began to lose something of homesickness.

"Yonder she is—the main building," the driver called as they reached the Purdue campus at the summit of Chauncey Hill. George got out and, carrying his bag, trudged along a gravel walk to register.

Purdue was more than ten years old—as George said, "the plaster was nearly dry." Four austere buildings stood somewhat far apart. About two hundred students were enrolled, nearly half in the preparatory department. Only thirty entered as freshmen in the college course, though almost anyone not known to be feeble-minded might have been accepted. There was no rigid insistence upon entrance examinations.

George was assigned to living space in the dormitory. His chamber, of "monastic simplicity," cost fifty cents a week. Most of the students lived at the dormitory. He noticed that some of the new arrivals had on their Sunday clothes. "The ready-made cravat was favored, and a full-sized Ascot was about the size of a lily pad. The horseshoe stickpin was regarded as a natty effect. The Derby hats with wide brim and low crown seemed to have been made in a foundry." Tight fitting, bell-bottomed pants were being worn. "Only the erudite and snobbish called pants trousers." The only suit of evening clothes in the dormitory belonged to a sophomore, Shrewsbury Beauregard Miller, of Charleston, West Virginia. (When its owner wore the suit, other students leaned out of windows to hoot.)

Board, on the lower floor of a "nondescript building of un-necessary scallops and unexpected and unoccupied turrets" known as Ladies Hall, would cost $2.50 a week; but a student could join a club and be fed for as little as $2. The manager of the club got his board free. George afterward commented, "Anyone who would take the responsibility of providing twenty-one meals for $2 to a hungry student, in return for his own meals, was entitled to an education." Even at $2.50 the meals were not elaborate. As George was to find, "when the waitress asked you if you wanted fruit and you said you did want fruit, you got dried currants with here and there a stem and some gravel."

That first afternoon he recalled what the driver had said and he inquired what show was on. The other students did not know. George began to move about and found that the play that night was *Juanita, The Puritan Girl*, with Minnie Maddern as the star.

He learned from a man at the lunch counter that Lafayette was one of the best "show towns" for its size in the country. It was a convenient place for theatrical companies to break the journey between Indianapolis, or Cincinnati, and Chicago, and nearly every company visited Lafayette. He was wondering if he could afford to go to *every* show.

A seat in the gallery cost only twenty-five cents and George was in the front row within a minute after the doors opened. One of the first comers, he had an opportunity to study the stage curtain. The scene on the curtain was supposed to be Lake Como. On a stone terrace leading down to the ultramarine lake stood a solitary goat. Within a few weeks he would acquire a growing prejudice against the dreariness of that scene and dislike for that goat as he waited impatiently for the curtain to rise. But on this night of September 7, 1883, he did not mind either the scene or the long wait. He was in a theater and happy. He felt sure this show would be good. And he knew he was going to like student life!

Other freshmen were impressed the next day when George told of seeing "an awful good show." Here was a man who was up and doing. Before many days George knew every boy in the dormitory and had a circle of friends, for in his quiet shy way he showed an interest in everyone. His room was soon a gathering place for all who sought moments of relaxation. George's conversation was interesting. He usually observed things in chapel or in classrooms that others had overlooked, maybe a curious mannerism of a professor, or a surprising item about a student's clothes. He simply stated facts unobserved by others, but they brought laughs.

Those who came to George's room began to have parties. "Throwing a party didn't involve anything more extravagant than concocting a raspberry punch worth at a liberal estimate ten cents a gallon." The boys sat around in stocking feet, played penny ante and smoked cigarettes—Richmond Straight Cut and Sweet Caporal.

One freshman George wondered about—Harry Cory, aged thirteen. To George it seemed that so young a lad should not be at college. Surely there were subjects in high school to occupy him until he was older. Later Harry Cory's brother came along, also at thirteen, and made a name for being the only student who had ever attended classes barefooted. Harry Cory became one of the foremost irrigation engineers in the United States, and his brother Clarence the Dean of Engineering at the University of California.

George had selected the scientific course, leading to the degree of Bachelor of Science, not because he craved a knowledge of the sciences, but because that course would permit him to dodge some of the higher mathematics. "By careful weaving in and out of the optional courses I managed, also, to avoid the ancient and modern languages." During one spring term he did take German. It was a choice between that and more mathematics.

Probably if he had known what he discovered later, he might even have taken Latin, because the Latin teacher, Annie Peck, was interested in mountain climbing. That might have convinced George that she was worth knowing for he liked anyone who did something unusual or well. Besides being a Latin teacher, she was the matron in charge of the Ladies Hall, with about twenty "prim and corseted co-eds of the most approved Victorian type," but mountain climbing was her means to international fame. At the age of fifty-eight Annie Peck reached the summit of a peak in Peru higher than Mt. McKinley, the highest point in the Americas yet attained by an American, and when she was eighty-four, in her biography in *Who's Who in America,* she still gave her occupation as mountain climber.

George felt relieved that just before he entered college, Emerson

E. White, author of a famous arithmetic textbook, had resigned as Purdue's president. He would have been uncomfortable sharing the same campus with the man whose book had tortured him in grammar-school days.

Mathematics had often darkened the skies over George in high school, and now college mathematics gave him night terrors. His sufferings stirred the sympathy of engineering students in the dormitory who took turns in supporting his faltering steps and his geometry mark for the second term was 100. But when he took higher algebra in the third term and tried to operate under his own steam his best mark was 60. He shuddered when he saw students in the engineering courses using textbooks that showed how to apply analytical geometry to practical problems, such as designing bridges or buildings. It was enough, he said, to worry through a mathematics textbook without having to think of using such lessons afterward.

George was regarded as a hard-working student for most of his first two years. Any college boy, he afterward said, who can establish a reputation for studiousness during his first year "may be pleasantly surprised at what he can get away with later on." He was good at drawing and history and at his best in English composition and literature. In three written tests in literature during one term he got marks of 100. His class essays were painstaking, better than most, but they showed no great originality. If he gave promise it was not exactly sensational. In his second year he became one of the editors of the only student publication, a monthly, the *Purdue;* but he served through only the latter half of the year and was never on the editorial staff again.

Nothing that he wrote was humorous. He was still the serious-minded lad who wrote "A Basket of Potatoes." In the first term as freshman his little essay on "Habit and Character," was printed in the *Purdue*. It began: "The person whose qualities form the ideal character will be truthful and high-minded. He will respect others and yet maintain sufficient self-respect or individuality to resent insults or encroachments upon his rights. He will be ambitious when it leads to some noble end; generous and charitable when it helps a worthy cause . . ."

Already he knew how to use semicolons!

Toward the end of his second year the *Purdue* devoted a page and a half to another of his classroom themes, an analysis of *Romeo and Juliet*. In his junior year the *Purdue* had an Ade editorial which attacked the crowding of children into upper classes and "putting them out into the world with a degree at the very age when they should be beginning college." Perhaps the editorial was inspired by Harry Cory, a freshman at thirteen.

In his junior year the *Purdue* published in two successive issues, his classroom essay on "The Literature and Learning of the Anglo-Saxons."

The only published item in which he figured that was not serious had been a personal in his freshman year: "George Ade 'walls his eyes' very comically."

The teacher of English composition, Mrs. Emma Mont McRae, formerly a high school principal in Muncie, had a strong influence on George Ade's future. She was "so learned, so gracious, so tactful and so enhaloed with kindly intentions that I have always felt sure she was one of the really 'great' women of her time." Still preserved is his notebook in which he recorded the rules for writing that he learned in her class. One of his notes says: "Concrete ideas render a composition beautiful by filling the mind with pictures. The abstract is dry and devoid of power over the imagination." Another: "A sentence may be constructed in accordance with the rules for concord, clearness and unity and still produce little effect. Something is wanting to fix the attention and sustain the interest." Then he added a line or two about the importance of "fitness of the words to convey the idea with force." His later writing shows that he retained those bits of guidance in his memory. However, among the notes is a rule that he later may have forgotten: "Avoid use of newly-coined words."

Purdue had two literary societies, deadly rivals, which met every Friday evening for recitations, orations and debates. One was named for Thomas Carlyle, the other for Washington Irving. George joined the latter and gave wholehearted support to his fellow members in detesting the Carlyles, most of whom "lived in Lafayette and wore scarf-pins!" When he was a junior, George became president of the Irvings and it was his job to arrange the programs. For a special annual entertainment he asked one of the boys in the dormitory to read an essay on any subject of his own choosing. The youngster agreed but he was slow getting to work. A week before the meeting George asked for a progress report and the boy confessed that he had not started his essay because he had not been able to think of a subject. He said he would get right at it.

On the night before the meeting he had not yet started. George was alarmed as he had the responsibility for the entertainment and the programs were already printed. He sat down to write an essay for the procrastinating member to read. The first subject that popped into his head was "Books Then and Now." He could not pause to think of impressive scholarly words, and so he used short easy words. The writing took less than an hour, and then he went back to putting a final polish on the oration he himself was to deliver. Local papers gave perfunctory commendation to all who took part in the entertainment but reported that the real hit of the evening was the essay, "Books Then and Now." In response to demands by subscribers who had attended the exercises, one of the papers wanted to publish it.

The boy who had read the essay was much embarrassed as

congratulations fell upon him. Almost in tears he declared to George that he was unwilling to sail under false colors and was going to announce the truth about the authorship. George insisted that he keep mum and treat the whole thing as a good joke. To do otherwise would bring jibes and disgrace upon the Irving Literary Society. They would never hear the end of it from those dudes in the Carlyle Society.

That episode set George thinking. "Looks to me," he said, "as if people like to hear something that sounds natural, the way a person would talk it off."

George had entered his junior year with "conditions" in physics and zoology, in which he had not received passing marks at the end of the previous year. In one physics test his mark was 49! He had to remove those "conditions" before the end of the first term, and he did. The explanation of his deficiencies, aside from his having found both subjects intensely uninteresting, had been a succession of good shows at the Grand Opera House. Let no reader suppose that George Ade ever permitted his class work to distract him from his studies of the drama. He was "unable to resist the theater, just as a mouse is weak in the presence of cheese." But after that night of his arrival in Lafayette when he first saw the Lake Como goat on the front curtain, he had never again gone to the theater alone. If no other student in the dormitory had George's enthusiasm for the drama, a number were glad to go with him.

Going to the theater meant a gala occasion with late supper and a little celebration. Such affairs cost money, and George took delight afterward in itemizing how much. Admission to the gallery, the *second* gallery, was twenty-five cents. "After the performance, we went to the Globe Chop House where, for fifteen cents, one might get a small steak resembling a warped ear-muff, a boiled potato, bread and butter and coffee. After we had supped at our leisure, and turned in our verdict on the play and the players, each one bought and lighted a fragrant five-cent cigar and then the jovial company went trooping across the levee asserting in song that we had been working on the railroad all the livelong day, which was far from the truth." The cost for theater, supper and cigar had totaled forty-five cents. But if the show happened to be on a Friday night with no classes the next day, the gay, carefree revelers might each buy a glass of beer, bringing the cost for the evening to half a dollar.

What a glorious variety of shows came to town. Nat C. Goodwin, the comedian, then "in his effervescent prime, could stand with his back to the audience, and, by a mere perk of his head set the house in a roar." There were Edwin Booth, Lawrence Barrett, James Thomas Keene, Madame Helena Modjeska, Mr. and Mrs. William J. Florence and the Hoyt farces, the first of which were then coming along; Hanlon's *Fantasma;* Lewis Morrison in *Faust;* the ballad singers, Chauncey Olcott, Andrew Mack and Billy Emerson; light opera stars that included Della Fox and Charles Bigelow. *La Mascotte, Olivette, Girofle-Girofla* and *Nanon* were among the light opera favorites. "In the eighties the low-comedy monarch still had a red nose and lumps on his legs, the tenor wore pink tights, and the chorus was all bundled up in superfluous clothing." Favorite pin-up "one-sheets" were of Annie Pixley, Mademoiselle Rhea, Minnie Maddern and Fay Templeton.

Besides being devoted to the "hall shows" George was enthusiastic about circuses. He never missed one. A big thrill was when he went to Barnum's circus and saw the most famous of all elephants, Jumbo.

He was certain to be in the second gallery at the Opera House when a minstrel show came to town, and he saw over and over the famous minstrel kings of laugh-makers, George Primrose, Billy Kersands, George Thatcher, Willis P. Sweatnam, "Happy

Cal" Wagner, Billy Rice, Carroll Johnson, Lew Docksteder, Frank McNish and Frank Barlow. It was an "aching regret" that he never saw Luke Schoolcraft. George Thatcher and Willis Sweatnam were the two blackface comedians that he liked best—especially Sweatnam, "a genuine and painstaking interpreter of the Negro character."

In the midwinter of his junior year George read that Willis Sweatnam was to appear in Indianapolis. Sweatnam had not played in Lafayette that season and George wanted to see him. Going to Indianapolis cost more than he could afford, and he did not like to ask his father for anything extra, as his father had recently sent money for a new winter overcoat, his first tailored garment. But the thought of seeing Sweatnam was so tempting that he decided to borrow the money. In Indianapolis he went to a twenty-five-cent restaurant for dinner, and as he was finishing his rice pudding he discovered that his new overcoat that he had hung on a rack near by had disappeared. It was plainly stated at the bottom of the menu that the management was not responsible for customer's hats, coats or umbrellas. But he reported the theft to the police.

The loss of the overcoat weighed on George's mind only until the curtain went up on the opening scene of the minstrel show, always called the "olio." Willis Sweatnam was at his best that night. He did a rambling monologue bringing in the names of an imaginary quartet and their relatives. These included George Mirth and Lee Truckmuck, son of the widow Truckmuck. The names stuck in George's memory.

A few days later he was overjoyed to get word that the police had recovered the overcoat in a pawnshop. That gave him a lasting friendly feeling toward policemen.

Of all the offerings in the theater that George ever saw, a light opera he attended in his junior year made the deepest impression.

The authors of the words and music were two Englishmen whose names he vaguely remembered, Gilbert and Sullivan. The piece was *The Mikado*. He had never dreamed that anything could be so captivating. He marveled at the wit and humor and the way the lyrics fitted into the dialogue. *The Mikado* opened new horigons and new worlds to George Ade.

The chief comedy part of "Ko-Ko" was played by Charles Drew. Since George had not yet seen a succession of others in that part, Richard Golden, Digby Bell, De Wolf Hopper and Frank Moulan, he had little means of comparison, but Charles Drew was good enough. As they walked home that night across the bridge over the Wabash, George's companions were surprised, probably George himself was surprised, at the number of verses from *The Mikado* he could repeat.

That night he lay in bed thinking of W. S. Gilbert, wondering what manner of man he could be, capable of writing such delicious nonsense. Then he dreamed about what he had just seen. He would never get over *The Mikado*.

Purdue had no glee club, no band, no dramatic club, no daily paper, no athletic association and no teams of any kinds playing intercollegiate schedules. Games of any kind played with other colleges were arranged for at the last minute. The first football team was not organized until the autumn after George Ade was graduated. George took no part in athletics beyond being an interested onlooker. Yet he found plenty to occupy him outside of classes. While a junior he had twelve unexcused absences. Not one absence from class had been on his record during the first two years. As a sophomore he joined with other youths of Republican upbringing in trying to howl down the famous orator, "the tall sycamore of the Wabash," Daniel W. Voorhees, addressing a crowd in the courthouse square in Lafayette—an attempt denounced by the Democratic press as "diabolical." And he had helped to plague Louie Bianci, the Italian who rang the bell for chapel, by climbing into the tower and muffling the clapper. But for the most part George had taken classwork seriously. In his junior year he was finding other things to do. He liked staying up late to talk. Sometimes he promoted a picnic and the crowd hired a band wagon to drive to a romantic spot on the banks of the Wabash. Riding home in the moonlight, George might lead the singing. He knew a lot of songs besides "Upidee," and the one that began with "Forty-nine Blue Bottles."

In his junior year George joined a Greek-letter fraternity. This fraternity, Sigma Chi, had gained distinction by winning a legal battle that resulted in a court order denying the right of a state university to bar fraternity members from classes. George got the impression that to be invited into such a fraternity was something like being received into the French Academy, and he at once began to wear on the lapel of his vest the largest fraternity pin that it was possible to buy. In after years when his feeling for the fraternity was still unabated, he would take out old photographs and laugh about that pin as an indication of what he called his "absolute yappiness." The fraternity had a room over a store for meetings but no dwelling house, and George continued to live in the dormitory.

Of especial importance in his junior year was the beginning of friendship with a freshman, John Tinney McCutcheon, a local boy who had grown up on what was known as the Wea Plains four miles out of Lafayette. His father, a Civil War captain, was called the most popular man in the county. Even as a youngster John showed the graciousness, warmth and charm that have characterized him through an eventful life.

Ade and McCutcheon had met before when John was in the preparatory department, but as "preps were mere children" the two had not become well acquainted.

McCutcheon has recorded his impressions of George in the autumn of '84, when he caught his first glimpse of him in chapel: "An unusual face down among the sophomores—a refined, clean-cut, delicately aquiline face—stood out among the surrounding run of rugged, freckled, corn-fed features. Several months later I learned that the possessor of this cameo-like profile was George Ade. The name appealed to me as much as the face. He had three outstanding characteristics that made him an inviting sub-ject for caricature—an unusual expanse of head behind the ears, a sweep of strongly marked eyebrows, and a striking lack of abdominal fullness, described by realists as slab belly. . . . Even my undeveloped instinct told me that here was an exceptional person."

McCutcheon had developed early a knack for drawing, and he began to do illustrations for college programs and publications. His drawing included some caricatures of George Ade. He and George became friends and George invited him to become a member of Sigma Chi. From that time on the two were in-separable.

Among other close friends of George Ade's during his later college years was a quiet lad who roomed next to him in the dormitory and was given to low gurgles of laughter, Charles Rus-sell Richards, afterward President of Lehigh University; and Paul Anderson, who became Dean of Engineering schools at the Uni-versity of Kentucky. One of McCutcheon's classmates—though not until after Ade's graduation—was a tall, slender, good-looking blond youngster named Bruce Rogers, so soft spoken and reticent that no one pegged him as a comer. But he became one of the foremost typographical artists of the world.

Though George was finding more and more to do outside of classes and prescribed studying, by no means all that he did was frivolous. He was discovering many books not necessarily required in the college courses, and he even began to use part of his modest funds to buy books when he found them at bargain rates at a secondhand dealer's over in Lafayette. He even had a bookplate made. It contained this warning: "He who borrows and returns not is a kleptomaniac." His personal library toward the end of his junior year included: Gibbon's *Decline and Fall of the Roman Empire,* Ridpath's *Popular History of the United States,* Rollin's *Ancient History,* Pollard's *Southern History of the War,* Raymond's *History of the Administration of President Lincoln,* Welsh's *Development of English Literature and Language,* Horace Mann's *Lectures on Education,* Creasy's *Decisive Battles,* Green's *Short History of the English People,* Schiller's *Thirty Years' War,* Taine's *English Literature,* John Stuart Mill's *Principles of Political Economy,* Baker's *Natural Philosophy,* Dickens' *Bleak House,* Hugh Miller's *Foot-prints of the Creator,* Swift's *Gulliver's Travels,* Emerson's essays, one volume of Goldsmith, Sheridan's plays and works of Shakespeare, Byron, Pope, Sir Walter Scott, Henry George, Sir John Mandeville, Burns and Thackeray. It was an aristocratic list, with not an item of trash, and George did not collect these books just to create a scholarly atmosphere in his room. He read them all even to the neglect sometimes of assigned work in mathematics, zoology and chemistry.

His senior year was a happy one. By that time he had completed all the required work in mathematics and was dipping into psychology, geology and political science, subjects less interesting to him than history and English literature but almost fascinating in comparison with geometry. It was a busy time for him, that year of 1886-1887. He had become the presiding officer of his fraternity and also was looked upon as a logical person to organize dances and picnics. He was losing some of his shyness.

George even saved up and bought a silk stovepipe hat in his senior year. It was a big step and he felt a little guilty over his extravagance. The first night he wore it to the Grand Opera House, he put it down beside him on a vacant seat, intending to fit it later into the little wire frame beneath his own seat. Then the curtain went up and he was too engrossed to notice that a large, richly upholstered woman was about to sit beside him. She did not see the hat and crushed it, if not as flat as a pancake at least nearly as flat as an average serving of buckwheats. The woman gasped whispered apologies, but George, interested in that first act, behaved like a perfect gentleman.

With a gesture implying that it was of no consequence he told her not to give it another thought and he added, still with one eye on the stage, "Plenty more hats where that came from."

The most noteworthy fact of all in George Ade's senior year was a meeting with a co-ed, a freshman, whose home was in Lafayette. Her name was Lillian Howard. It seemed to George that she was extraordinarily beautiful and charming, and he was right. She was a blonde with an attractive way of fixing her hair and expressive, lustrous eyes. George began to be, as the saying was in those days, "attentive to her." There was nothing coquettish about her. She was modest and quiet and a pious Methodist. But she showed a friendly interest in whatever George was doing, and at dances saved waltzes for him, knowing that he did not care so much for the schottische, the Newport or the polka. There is reason to believe that Lillian Howard was the one girl with whom George Ade would ever be in love.

With all his activities and interests beyond classrooms George got through his senior year with only two unexcused absences and a yearly average for all subjects of 89—about as well as could be expected of a young man with many irons in the fire.

At the annual Purdue commencement exercises on June 9, 1887, there were eight graduates and each delivered either an oration or an abstract of a thesis. Bennett Taylor's thesis was on Steam

Pumps. Harry T. Cory, now wearing long pants and old enough to be going with the girls, read from a thesis on the Thompson-Houston System of Electric Lighting. In contrast to subjects so technical was George Ade's oration, first on the program, "The Future of Letters in the West."

George had spent weeks on this address, "rubbing out short words and putting in longer ones." Unluckily, the full text has not been preserved, but George predicted that "the hub of the literary universe was about to shift from Cambridge, Massachusetts, to an indefinite region which included Crawfordsville, Indianapolis and Tippecanoe county, Indiana." Lew Wallace's *Ben Hur* had been published seven years previously, and other Hoosier authors, among them Edward and George Cary Eggleston and Maurice Thompson, had successful books to their credit, but it was not these that George was thinking of so much as newcomers as yet unknown who he felt sure would in a few years add to Indiana's literary glory.*

---

* Thomas L. Masson, editor of the old *Life,* once commented that Purdue probably did George Ade less harm than any other college would have done.

George Ade, the daily columnist, in 1898.

THE FABLE IN SLANG OF THE SLIM GIRL WHO TRIED TO KEEP A DATE THAT NEVER WAS MADE

Once upon a time there was a slim Girl with a Forehead which was Shiny and Protuberant, like a Bart-

THE SLIM GIRL.

lett Pear. When asked to put something into an Autograph Album she invariably wrote the following, in a tall, dislocated Back-Hand:

"Life is Real; Life is Earnest
And the Grave is not its Goal."

That's the kind of a Girl she was.

In her own town she had the Name of being a Cold Proposition, but that was because the Primitive Yokels of a One-Night Stand could not Attune Themselves to the Views of one who was troubled with Ideals. Her Soul Panted for the Higher Life.

Alas, the Reub Town in which she Hung Forth was given over to Croquet, Mush and Milk Sociables, a lodge of Elks and two married Preachers who doctored for the Tonsilitis. So what could the Poor Girl do?

In all the Country around there was not a Man who came up to her Plans and Specifications for a Husband. Neither was there any Man who had any time for Her. So she led a lonely Life, dreaming of the One—the Ideal. He was a big and strong Literary Man, wearing a Prince Albert coat, a neat Derby Hat and godlike Whiskers. When He came he would enfold Her in his Arms and whisper Emerson's Essays to her.

But the Party failed to show up.

Often enough she put on her Chip Hat and her Black Lisle Gloves and Sauntered down to look at the Bunch sitting in front of the Occidental Hotel, hoping that the Real Thing would be there. But she always saw the same old Line of Four-Flush Drummers from Chicago and St. Louis, smoking Horrid Cigars and talking about the Percentages of the League Teams.

She knew that these Gross Creatures were not prone to chase mere Intellectual Splendor, so she made no effort to Flag them.

When she was Thirty-Four years of age and was able to recite "Lucile" without looking at the Book she was married to a janitor of the name of Ernest. He had been kicked by a Mule when young and believed everything he read in the Sunday Papers. His pay was Twenty-Three a month, which was high, if you knew Ernest.

His Wife wore a red Mother Hub-

A TRAVELING MAN.

bard all during the Remainder of her Life.

This is invariably a Sign of Blasted Hopes.

Moral—Never Live in a Jay Town

5

Journalism—and Patent Medicine

GEORGE had his diploma, but what should he do next? Lacking other plans, he returned to Kentland, carrying a new suitcase that looked like leather. For the first time he did not enjoy the trip home, for he was in a low state. He loved his family and was loyal to his home town, but a day convinced him that he must start elsewhere. During his summer vacations while in college he had worked for his brother Will at farming, and even though his brother had considerately spared him the harder jobs, he still did not crave farm work, which seemed all that Kentland could offer.

It was evident that George was turning out just as the home folk had predicted. He had wasted four years by going to college they said. Instead of trying to pick up some kind of practical knowledge, he had fooled away his time on subjects that would never do him any good, and he still showed no inclination to work. They noticed that on his second day at home he got up a hayride and picnic for some of the children. George must be a worry to his father the neighbors thought. They felt sorry for his father.

John Ade did feel concerned about George. Joe and Will were able to shift for themselves, but George showed no sign of ability to make his living. It was embarrassing to have friends ask what the boy was planning to do.

At the dinner table one day George remarked that a member of a law firm in Lafayette was willing to take him into his office. George's father said he thought that might be a good plan. Sometimes men succeeded as lawyers when they seemed not to be fitted for anything more useful. Studying law would not pay George's board but maybe it would be just as well to continue sending money with the possibility that he could someday earn something himself. If he was in Lafayette studying law, at least he would not be sitting around the house reading and dreaming; and besides, the family could then answer questions about what George was going to make of himself. So it was decided that he should become a lawyer.

That was a lucky break for George, for he was homesick for Lafayette, especially for the Grand Opera House. He felt no enthusiasm for a law office and yet, with nothing better to offer, made no objection.

George gave the law a thorough trial. He kept regular hours, bending assiduously over Blackstone, trying to become interested, determined not to be swayed by first misgivings. At the end of the first day he suspected that he was not going to like it, but he stuck to it for nearly seven weeks. He then knew that the law was not for him. He was helped to this decision by an opportunity to try something else.

Republican politicians in Lafayette were starting the *Morning News*. It was to be a party organ and have a long running start toward the presidential campaign of 1888. Perhaps the publisher wished to do a favor to the lawyer in whose office George was studying. He offered George a job on the new paper. And George began his career in journalism. His weekly wage was $8, which seemed a princely honorarium. The one drawback was that he did not always receive any money at the end of the week, for there was no big demand for the new paper and the publisher was an economical person, slow to pay out more than he took in. He urged the use of old envelopes split open, for copy paper. In place of money the boss bestowed upon George a new title. He became the "assistant city editor" with no change of duties. Still the paper's only reporter, he ran behind the fire engine to fires.

In spite of the most diligent effort that George could put forth with no pay, the *Morning News* did not last. George saw the end approaching. The most alarming signal was a promise to the staff of an increase in pay. The publisher told George if he would be patient he would soon be getting $10 a week.

No one on that payroll ever got any more money. Two weeks later the paper was in its final gasps. "Payday was approaching and the funds had dribbled away, the backers had fled, the editor-in-chief had evaporated, the editorial writer had gone to Delphi to see his girl, the business manager was in retirement, the city editor had flown to Crawfordsville." Only George and the foreman of the composing room remained. They determined to get out one more issue, to have an opportunity to slip in some paragraphs expressing their feelings. Every line that went into the spaces between the "boiler-plate" matter was written by George. "We held a brief funeral service just at midnight—then we locked the dear departed in the cold forms, pooled our finances and went to an all-night beanery. Next day I went back and looked at the *Morning News*—so cold and calm, and purged of political hatreds. You could hardly believe it was dead. It seemed to be asleep."

Almost immediately George got a place on the staff of an evening paper, the *Call,* at $6 a week. In his new job he really received his wages, though sometimes partly in meal tickets at a restaurant that advertised.

The *Call* was published by a man named Septimus Vater, who believed in printing as many local names as possible, and he constantly urged George to use more names. On the rival evening paper, the *Courier,* the chief reporter was George Barr McCutcheon, brother of John. Like George Ade, George Mc-

Cutcheon was a great admirer of the minstrel-show comedian, Willis P. Sweatnam, and they often laughed together as they recalled parts of his monologue in which he talked about members of the Truckmuck family and others. One day it occurred to George Ade that he could satisfy his employer, and at the same time pay a tribute to Sweatnam, by working into the local columns mention of some of the Sweatnam characters. McCutcheon agreed that it was a good idea and said he would like to share in it. From time to time one paper or the other printed items such as:

"The widow Truckmuck is entertaining her cousin from Peru."

"Lee Truckmuck returned from Chicago yesterday and reports a neat profit on his last shipment of yearlings."

"Mrs. George Mirth will entertain the ladies of the M. E. church next Tuesday evening."

"The younger son of the widow Truckmuck is recovering from the scarlet fever."

From the time he entered Lafayette journalism, George took an interest in reporting what was going on out at Purdue, and especially the organization of that first football team in the fall of '87. "Any man who wished to play football could make the team by merely signing his name. Tall, skinny boys who wore spectacles and were bicepped like sandhill cranes put down their names because they had read about Tom Brown at Rugby and wished to get a free ride to Indianapolis. . . . Our athletes trained on pie and doughnuts." The first coach was a deaf-mute from Lafayette, who *had* to invent silent signals. One of the first games George reported was with a team from Butler University over at Indianapolis, coached by young Evans Woollen, recently out of Yale—afterward a nationally known banker and mentioned as a nominee for President.

In the fall of '88 George took part in the presidential campaign.

That is, he appeared on the rostrum with James G. Blaine, who was making a speaking tour of the Middle West, "to prove that he was not sulking over the nomination of Harrison."

George preceded Blaine on the program and stood directly in front of him. "My object in appearing on the platform was to sway the multitude. . . . I was a member of a male quartet.

"We seemed to accomplish our purpose. I am almost sure the multitude swayed while we were singing. At any rate it was restless.

"I was second tenor. A second tenor bears the same relation to vocal music that a notary public does to the execution of laws. George Barr McCutcheon was our basso profundo. He was a Democrat but he wanted to sing and we had the only male quartet in sight. We responded to a noiseless encore and then, as we left the stage, I smiled pleasantly at Mr. Blaine, who seemed pale and drawn. Next morning he was quite ill at the old Reynolds House in Lafayette, and the speaking tour had to be abandoned. I have always wondered."

George did not stay long with the *Call*. He was offered an astounding salary to enter the patent-medicine business. "Hunger and the approach of cold weather" drove him to accept the offer. He would much have preferred to stay in journalism, but his pay now would be $12 a week! Later it was even increased to $15. Harry L. Kramer, of Lafayette, owned a health resort where the customers took mud baths, and was the head of a company that manufactured and sold proprietary drug articles. The job consisted of writing advertisements, dictating correspondence and attending to the dispatch of large quantities of mail. George was called a "department manager."

"We sold to druggists at a time when a drug-store was a repository for patent medicines instead of a combination of soda-fountain, restaurant, beauty parlor, novelty shop, and radio concert.

The patent medicine business was not to be sneezed at when every prominent church worker and temperance advocate used about two large square-cornered full-quart-size bottles of 'tonic' every week. This useful remedy for whatever ailed you was compounded from No. 2 Pennsylvania rye whiskey, syrup, and a small percentage of puckery bitters. Whiskey, syrup and bitters—try to figure anything but a cocktail out of that! Yet no one ever said that the Deacon was a rum-hound or accused the druggist of being a saloon-keeper."

In that preradio era patent-medicine advertising had not yet reached the low levels of later days, but Kramer believed that everybody should take lots of laxative and he planned to market a compound containing cascara. The stuff was in tablets that tasted like candy in a handy tin box to go in a vest pocket or in a lady's purse. George coined the word Cascarets, the name under which the new product would be widely advertised, and he originated the slogan, "They work while you sleep." Another product for which Kramer had high hopes was No-Tobac, a cure for the tobacco habit. George wrote a pamphlet containing testimonials about this remedy and arranged with his friend, John T. McCutcheon, still a student at Purdue, to draw the cover design. It was a picture of a valiant Roman warrior sinking a sword into a writhing monster, part sea serpent, part alligator, labeled Nicotine. "McCutcheon drew the picture while smoking Richmond Straight Cuts and fairly earned the $5 he received." The picture was McCutcheon's first published cartoon.

Anyone who called at George Ade's office space could have detected cigarette smoke, for George used Sweet Caporals incessantly to keep his imagination stimulated. However, he had a clear conscience as he wrote his glowing copy about the cure, for he knew that the remedy would do all that was claimed, if directions were followed. The first direction read: "Immediately discontinue the use of tobacco."

During most of his later life George did not smoke. He had a three weeks' illness which left him without any desire to smoke. But he then became interested in chewing tobacco!

That $12 a week at first seemed so large to George that he was surprised when he found himself owing for board to the patient ladies, the Misses Niemansverdriet, who ran the Stockton House. He continued to see the shows at the Grand Opera House, however, and again saw *The Mikado,* this time played by the Dora Wiley Opera Company, with Richard Golden as Ko-Ko.

He even became a favorite in society. Whenever John McCutcheon could spare time from his studies as a Purdue senior, they went calling, and young women found them entertaining, for they knew an astonishing variety of songs. McCutcheon carried a little notebook in which he listed the titles of songs numbered up to 165. He would give assurance to the ladies that if any one of them picked a number, he and George could sing that song, if not all at least a part of it.

George was still reading. He went through Macaulay's essays and, by way of variety, began on the stories of Maupassant. These influenced him. "I like the way *he* writes," he said, "short simple, direct sentences, no words wasted, and how quickly he can make a scene or a person seem real."

Lafayette had plenty of amusing "characters," as well as many families of wealth and social distinction, with names "which sound like a page from the Landed Gentry Supplement to Burke's Peerage—Stuart, Reynolds, Heath, Curtis, Taylor, Pierce, Ross, Fowler, Earl, Sample, Vinton, Moore, Stockton, and Levering. Also a good scattering of staunch Irish and Scotch-Irish—the O'Ferralls, McMullens, Murdocks, and McCutcheons." George knew everybody. He even joined the local lodge of Elks. He was enjoying life, though he felt a growing urge to write something other than advertisements for patent medicine.

After October '89 he had more time than usual. His friend John McCutcheon had gone to Chicago and got a job in the art department of the *Morning News.* McCutcheon had made a trip to Chicago after graduation in June. A member of his fraternity had introduced him to Will Schmedtgen, the art editor—almost the whole art department—of the paper. Schmedtgen saw samples of John's drawing and told him that he showed talent but needed practice. He promised that if John would go back home and work for a few weeks he could have a permanent job in the fall. So it came about that George, without the companionship of McCutcheon, felt lonely and sought extra work to occupy him. Besides, he wanted to write.

One night he went over to visit with the boys of his fraternity and told them they ought to show enterprise and do something for Purdue. He suggested that they put out the next June a souvenir book to celebrate Purdue's fifteenth commencement. They could get advertising to pay for it, and he would be glad to help them write pieces to fill it.

The boys began to plan for the book. George Ade did most of the work. He wrote at least half of the material and saw to it that the printing and illustrations were done in an acceptable manner. He directed the whole job. On McCutcheon's next visit in Lafayette, George got him interested in the project, and McCutcheon obtained illustrations from one or two artists in Chicago, one of them Tom Powers, later famous for his humorous drawings in the New York *Evening World.*

George Ade's contributions to the Purdue souvenir were varied. Some were in prose, some in verse. One set of verses he entitled "The College Widow." The term was not of his invention but

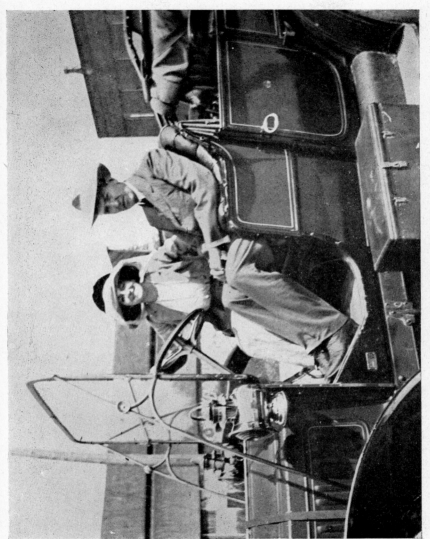

George Ade and Elsie Janis, musical comedy favorite.

Songs from Ade light operas were on the piano in up-to-date homes. (Copyright by M. Witmark & Sons. Reprinted by special permission.)

it had not yet been widely used to describe the college belle who accepts the attentions of younger admirers, as older ones move away. This particular "widow" was engaged to a professor who left for another college.

> Within a week the charmer wasn't grieving in the least,
> When I saw her with a freshman at the play.

Six years later—

> She looked a little older, but her laugh was just as gay;
> Beside her was a gallant sophomore,
> Who held her parasol aloft, and gushed the self-same way,
> That I had doubtless done in days of yore.

Another contribution was serious, an ode to John Purdue:

> No gleaming shaft nor granite block
> Nor sculptured pile of cold insensate stone,
> No chiseled epitaph of empty praise
> Marks his last resting-place.
> Himself without a home, he reared a place
> Where Science might abide, and Learning dwell;
> Where Art should flourish long and hold her court
> And grant to every worshipper his meed.
>
> He sleeps—and tow'ring here above his couch
> The products of his genius and his toil
> Speak louder far than wrought or figured stone
> Of life well lived and labor nobly done.

George evidently had read Gray's *Elegy*.

McCutcheon wrote enticing letters about the glamour and fascination of Chicago and urged George to join him. His room had a double bed so there was every reason for George to come and try his luck in the big town. He could not promise that he would find a job right off, but he would introduce George to someone in the editorial rooms of the *Morning News,* and something might come of it.

George was eager enough to get back into newspaper work, but to give up a job that now paid $15 a week seemed a big risk. He owed money to the maiden ladies who ran the Stockton House, and he doubted if any boardinghouse keeper in Chicago would be as patient as they had been. And he hoped he would not have to ask his father for more money.

Another influence that may have made him hesitate was that Lillian Howard was at Purdue, a senior. It did not seem right to leave her to be escorted by mere college boys. Some of George's friends thought they were engaged. He was in love with her but could not imagine ever having enough money to support a wife. If he should go to Chicago he might earn enough to keep himself from want, and not have to depend upon his father, but newspaper salaries were low, and how could he ever hope to be able to provide a lovely girl with food and clothing and all the luxuries she ought to have? He did not believe that he could decently forsake bachelorhood at any time within the foreseeable future.

Still he might have risked a proposal of marriage except for one reason. Lillian Howard's mother had noticed that he did not often go to church. She began to talk with him, whenever he called, about his spiritual welfare. She urged him to become a Methodist. George was having much more conversation with the mother, it seemed, than with the charming daughter. McCutcheon advised that Lillian should tell her mother not to interfere. George did not like to hear such criticism. "She has a sweet, kind nature, and wouldn't want to hurt her mother's feelings." Those talks with the mother wore him down, though, and his calls became less and less frequent. Then a handsome Baptist minister began to devote much attention to Lillian Howard. Not long afterward they were married and went to live in Minnesota. George could never forget her.

In June 1890 the patent-medicine company changed management and George suddenly found himself on the sidewalk, detached from a pay roll. He wrote to McCutcheon that, using the theatrical phrase, he was "at liberty" and would be glad to share that double bed. One wonders what would have happened if George had found a fairly profitable job in Lafayette. For many months McCutcheon had been urging him to come to Chicago, and he agreed that in the big city were greater opportunities. Yet he had been in no hurry about seeking those opportunities. Whatever may have been his reasons, probably the explanation was that his self-appraisal made him fearful of the competition of the big city.

When friends of the family heard that George had lost his job and was going to Chicago, they were *sure* he would soon be back at Kentland.

6

Chicago Was Some Laboratory

GEORGE ADE stepped from an afternoon train in Chicago around the middle of June 1890. Twenty-four years old, still a shy country boy with scant confidence in his abilities, he looked at the big town with misgivings. He had brought his trunk—that "looked like pressed paper, which it was"—and intended to stay, but he had no promise of a job. The nearest to a promise was that the city editor of the *Morning News* had said to McCutcheon he would be glad to see the newcomer.

George was happy to find McCutcheon at the station. They went at once to the hall bedroom they were to share, in a small rooming house near Michigan Avenue on Peck Court—where the Stevens Hotel now stands. McCutcheon had previously lived in a basement room at 493 Wabash Avenue. Some young women rooming there saw that he was a youngster unaccustomed to the city and were kind and sympathetic. He had liked the friendly atmosphere, but one night a shooting and police raid made it plain that the standards of the other roomers were not the highest. John had moved into the room third floor back, to which he now welcomed George Ade.

An advertisement had described it as a comfortably furnished room for refined gentlemen. After observing the thinly varnished oak bureau and washstand, McCutcheon had given his home a name. The Oaks! The room was nearly twelve feet long and wide enough for one to pass between the double bed and the lumpy sofa. Two chairs, one of them plush-covered, lurked where space permitted. A window gave upon a courtyard, a repository for empty bottles, old barrels and discarded kitchen utensils. No bathroom was nearer than the floor below, but the washstand contained a pitcher and bowl and a slop jar, the lid having a knitted cover called a husher. Behind a curtain in one corner were two or three clotheshooks—all that George and John needed. Two paintings adorned the wall, one showing cows or sheep—no one ever knew which—grazing on a mountain slope, the other, an assortment of bilious and feverish fruit.

George Ade was relieved when he learned that his half of the weekly room rent would be $2.50, less than he had been paying in Lafayette. Yet it was more than he could afford unless he could associate himself with a pay roll. With a low estimate on his prospects he knew he had one asset. He was "interested in all kinds of people and what they were doing and hoping to do."

That was not the only asset he brought to Chicago. McCutcheon, who knew him best, has listed his equipment: "A wonderful memory, an X-ray insight into motives and men, a highly developed power of keen observation and the benefit of four years of literary work in college and three years in professional fields. He had lived in the country and had retained, as on a photographic plate, the most comprehensive impressions of country life. He knew the types, the vernacular, and the point of view of the country people from the inside. He had lived in a small town and had acquired a thorough knowledge of the types and the customs of this phase of life. He had learned college life after four years of observation and had learned the life of the medium-sized town. With a memory that retained his observations of these four distinct elements of life, and an intelligence great enough to use this knowledge, he was ready to learn what a great city could teach."

The *Morning News* to which George applied was an ideal

vehicle for his talents. It was the morning edition of Victor Lawson's Chicago *Daily News* (founded by Melville E. Stone, afterward head of the *Associated Press*) and was one of the most carefully edited newspapers in the country. It appealed to the more intelligent readers rather than to those who liked hysterical headlines. Only rarely did the *Morning News* flaunt a headline of more than single column width. The paper was conservative in appearance, but the news articles showed a lively, entertaining quality of writing. The managing editor, Dr. Frank Reilly, was an unusual newspaperman, a graduate of the Rush Medical College, and a scholar, who had found, after going down the Mississippi to report a yellow-fever epidemic, that he preferred journalism to medicine. Charles H. Dennis, the city editor, also of scholarly outlook, welcomed new ideas for the paper and had high standards. He was particular about whom he hired.

George Ade favorably impressed Dennis who agreed to take him on trial. Anyone beginning in the editorial department of either of the Lawson papers received $12 a week. The pay might be more after only a few days, but $12 was always the starting point. Members of the staff said that if a newcomer could prove that he was not a college man he might be put to work in the advertising office at $40. George Ade wanted no more of the advertising business and he did not quibble about his $12 salary. Dennis told him that his only regular assignment at first would be a daily piece about the weather. If the new reporter was careless, what he wrote about the weather would not involve the paper in a libel suit nor antagonize those who advertised!

No one else could have been found who would take the interest George did in the weather. To him the weather was all-important, because it was what people most talked about. He began to write about weather with as great enthusiasm as if he had been assigned to report, say, an elopement of an archbishop with a chorus girl. After the first day his weather story was put on the first page. Chicago was having the first hot spell of the season. George interviewed people about how they were standing it. He talked to hotel clerks about how the weather affected the guests and asked headwaiters in hotel dining rooms if the heat was causing change in what people ate. He complimented Mr. Townsend, manager of the Palmer House, on never asking a guest, "Well, is it hot enough for you?" He even called up Lyman J. Gage, president of the First National Bank, to find out if the heat had slackened his energy. He asked managers of teaming companies how their horses were making out. He consulted the weather bureau and explained to readers how the bureau made its forecast and what the winds were doing to cause a possible change. When cooler weather was predicted, George's first-page story on July 1 opened: "The Chicagoan who places faith in the weather bureau put the heavy counterpane at the foot of the bed last night on the assurance that a cool wave with icicles in its hair and a claret punch in each pocket was approaching at a respectable gait . . . and would at least kiss its hand to us in passing."

When the Ade neighbors in Kentland learned that George was working for the *Morning News* they said that if he had anything to him he would be on the *Inter-Ocean,* the paper that Republican community swore by, whereas the Lawson papers were "mug-wump," independent and tried to present both sides.

George did not consider his place on the paper more than a chance, but his first letter back to Lafayette was full of cheer. It was written on Hotel Sherman stationery and addressed to his friend, Josh D. Hilderbrand, a Lafayette newspaperman, after-ward editor of a paper in Springfield, Illinois.

"As you will note by the letterhead, I am staying at the Sherman. I stopped here twenty minutes ago to get out of the rain.

"I have had a pleasant time since I got in and am anxious to locate here—have had one chance to go to work already, and am working one or two others. I am confident of catching on sooner or later and in the meantime I am not sweating blood.

"I saw O'Neill in *The Dead Heart* Wednesday evening. . . . Last evening I intended to see Dixey and get a souvenir of the 300th night but John and I . . . visited some North Side gardens, Lincoln Park, & c. Let loose your imagination on the '& c.' " (McCutcheon has given assurance that the "& c" was mild enough.)

George's chance was not long in coming. The city editor suggested that if he would stick around as much as possible there might suddenly be need of him. George spent hours in the local room reading back files to familiarize himself with what had been going on in the city and how the news was handled.

One July evening about seven o'clock, when the other reporters were either on assignments or had stepped out for a bite, a phone call gave the bare news of an explosion that had occurred on the *Tioga,* a freight steamer, in the Chicago River. The city editor was not in his office. Dr. Reilly, managing editor, looked about for a reporter. George Ade was the only one in sight. In desperation Dr. Reilly asked him to find out about the accident. George soon discovered that it was serious. The steam boiler on the freighter had exploded, killing fifteen men. George hastily telephoned to Dr. Reilly that the story was so important it would require three or four reporters. It made a hit with Reilly that this cub reporter instead of trying to spread himself too thin had shown his good judgment. Three more men were rushed to the scene, but George had most of the facts, and Reilly told the others to turn their data over to him to write the whole story. His account of the disaster the next morning, first column, first page, was considered the most dramatic, the most accurate, the best job done by any of the morning papers. The *Morning News* office had many inquiries. Who had written the piece about the explosion? From that time on George Ade no longer wrote about the weather, and weather news disappeared from the first page. His salary was boosted to $15.

A few weeks later in August George wrote again to his friend Josh Hilderbrand in Lafayette:

"I am doing as well as could be expected here, taking my assignments with charming regularity and trying to cover them to the satisfaction of the office. Last Thursday I went out to Blue Island and did the powder explosion, making a column and a half account and had the satisfaction of getting a word of commendation from Victor F. Lawson, the mogul of the paper. Just now I am taking care of the stock yards strike and I am not stuck on the job, for the strikers are pretty tough people, railroaders, and they wanted to throw me out of the yards when they found out that I was a reporter. I have had many curious experiences, pleasant and otherwise, since I put on the *News* star, [reporter's badge] but on the whole I like the job first-rate and am getting some good hard newspaper experience that will be of advantage to me *no matter what business I should ever go into*. [Italics supplied.]

"So Lafayette is quiet. Well, I don't know but I would enjoy a little Tippecanoe county quietude and rest after the daily hustle and rustle of Chicago life. This 'boom' business that Lafayette is after has been overdone here for the streets are so full of cable-cars, hansoms, drays, express wagons, chippies, policemen, and other public nuisances that a man doesn't know when he starts downtown in the morning whether he will get back at night or land up at the morgue. . . . One thing I don't like about Chicago is that I have not attended any poker seances since I came here.

My hours will not permit it. I usually go to the theater each Saturday night. . . . I am doing as well as I did in Lafayette but no better. If I have good luck I will be making my $20 per quite soon, in fact. I have already been given a chance to go on the *Times* here, but will stick to the *News* so long as they want me and show a disposition to make it worth my while."

Though one line in this letter suggests that George was not yet quite sure of staying in the newspaper business, probably nothing could have lured him from making his living by writing and by meeting all kinds of people. Human beings, "what they were doing and hoping to do," interested him more and more and Chicago offered limitless variety.

In 1890 Chicago had a little more than one million people, having doubled its population during ten years. It had more Poles, Swedes, Norwegians, Danes, Bohemians, Dutch, Croatians, Slovakians, Lithuanians and Greeks than any other American city. Indeed, it was next to Prague in the number of Bohemians, third in the world for Swedes and Norwegians, fourth for Poles and fifth for Germans.

Chicago was as wild as a hawk. Clark and State Streets and Custom House Place had many scores of so-called panel houses— houses of prostitution where a customer would be robbed by someone's reaching through a secret panel in the wall to the chair or sofa on which he laid his clothing. The "take" in these places was said to be as much as $10,000 in one night. One did not need to go far to encounter gilded vice. In the basement of the building occupied by the Chicago *Inter-Ocean* near the *News* was a café usually swarming with girls who would waive formal introduction. George came to know much about the Chicago underworld after he won the friendship of some of the police, including John Bonfield, chief of detectives. One police officer he especially liked to talk with was Detective Clifton Wooldridge, who had made thousands of arrests and caused two hundred thieves to go to the penitentiary. George was fascinated to know that Wooldridge, after arresting a thief, would sometimes compel the man to carry him on his back to the lockup.

He saw other phases of life, playing understudy to almost every man on the staff, and reporting labor, politics, city hall— sometimes even society under protest. His work took him to Clan-na-Gael picnics, *Schutzenfests,* strikes, inquests, police court trials, city council and county board meetings, charity balls, conventions and rallies. He reported sermons, too, and became a friend of Father "Ed" Kelly, so often mentioned later in the "Mr. Dooley" articles. He was in the right place to learn more about people. In after years he could truthfully say, "I knew my Chicago in the 90's and it was some laboratory."

At about the same time that George went on the staff of the *Morning News,* Amy Leslie became dramatic critic for the *Daily News,* the evening edition, a position she would hold for forty years. She was about six years older than George, and when she learned of his passion for the theater, she began to take an interest in him and shared with him the two seats on the aisle issued to her. In that way he saw many shows he otherwise would have missed.

In the autumn of 1890 George accompanied by McCutcheon made his first visit back to Lafayette. One memorable fact about this trip to both George and John was that they made a friend of a youngster from Indianapolis named Newton B. Tarkington— not yet called Booth Tarkington—who had entered Purdue to take a special course in art and had become a member of their fraternity. That Tarkington had selected Purdue for an art course seemed odd to George until he learned that the boy knew a Lafayette girl. Ade and McCutcheon both took to young Tarkington. He could twang a guitar, knew a lot of amusing songs, saw humor in nearly everything and made friends readily. He provided a football yell for Purdue. Until then the boys had just hollered: "Whee-e!"

George was sorry the Tarkington boy had his heart set on becoming an artist. "He's such a good observer, he might do well as a writer."

What made his week end most worth while to George was the account he heard of what happened to his friend Henry Vinton. At an initiation of his fraternity the members had wished to dress the candidate in a girlish shirtwaist and a garment then known as pantalets. On the Saturday evening set for the ceremony the boys had appealed to Vinton to go to the dry goods store beneath the "frat hall" and make the purchase. Being married, he could do so without embarrassment—or suspicion. The student bachelors hesitated to face the lady clerk with the request for anything so intimately feminine. Neither did Vinton like the assignment, but he consented. After his return with the bundle, his wife, shopping downtown, chanced to go to the same clerk and asked for the same article. "Your husband was just here and bought you a pair," said the clerk. When her husband got home after the initiation he had a dreadful time explaining.

After that Ade and McCutcheon contrived to get railroad passes on the Monon and make visits to Lafayette more frequently, lest they should miss hearing all the news.

7

A Boost from the Renegades' Idol

A FEW months after he had come to Chicago, George saw in the paper an announcement that stirred memories of his childhood. Colonel Robert G. Ingersoll was in the city to lecture.

While still in school at Kentland, George had read lectures by Ingersoll, whom he afterward described as "the most openly denounced and most secretively admired person in the United States, by coming out on the platform and poking fun at the Bible as a record of historical events. He was more of a rhetorician than a logician, but he was the prize orator of his day. His talk was full of scrollwork and comedy and bright colors and he became the idol of all the renegades, most of whom were afraid to speak out for themselves."

The Ingersoll lectures George had got hold of were printed in cheap pamphlet form. They "had to be bootlegged and never were read in the house—always in the haymow. We loved them. They gave us the goose pimples. Bob was defying and flaunting all the preachers and hard moralists and Sunday school tyrants and we had a terrified admiration for him because he was sassing the people who kept us locked in for so many pleasant Sabbaths and who had crushed our spirit of research when we asked *how* Jonah could have remained inside the whale so long, and *why* didn't the flames injure Shadrach, Meshach and Abednego, and were they *real* lions that walked all around Daniel without trying to bite him?

"We had been told to believe everything from 'kiver to kiver' whether we understood it or not. It was suggested that if we took a pencil and tried to figure how it would rain enough in forty days completely to cover Mt. Everest, which is 29,002 feet high, then we would recline forever on a bed of coals, like frankfurter sausages."

Such recollections came to George's mind when he saw that Ingersoll was in town. He remarked to another reporter, "I'd certainly like to meet Bob Ingersoll."

The other reporter had once tried to interview Ingersoll and been turned down. Ingersoll almost never gave interviews. He had enough trouble replying to attacks on himself without being responsible for what reporters quoted him as saying. The reporter in a spirit of mischief suggested to George, "Why don't you go and interview him? I'd want to do it myself if I weren't already loaded down."

George thought it a good suggestion. To meet Ingersoll would be a real experience. He went to the city editor, Mr. Dennis, and asked if he might have the assignment to interview Ingersoll.

Dennis was not disposed to play tricks on members of his staff, but since this young reporter wanted to try the impossible, why not let him?

A few minutes later George was on his way to the Palmer House to see Ingersoll. After getting the number from the clerk, he started to phone to Ingersoll's room. Then he changed his mind. His chances of getting in might be better if he went and rapped on the door.

It was afternoon and Ingersoll was in the room.

George found himself facing a rosy-cheeked, round-faced, slightly bald man of plump build who smilingly asked him what he wanted.

When George told him he was a reporter, Ingersoll made a deprecating gesture and said if he had come for an interview that would be quite out of the question.

"I'd like awfully well to talk with you, anyhow," George persisted. "I've read a lot of your lectures—had to read them in the haymow."

Ingersoll courteously motioned for him to sit down. "I'm sorry," he said, "but I've quit giving interviews."

"It would mean a lot to me," George confided, "if there was something on which I could quote you, even briefly."

In a fatherly way Ingersoll then asked how long he had been doing interviews.

George swallowed and said, "To be perfectly honest, you might say this is the first one—the first with anyone of consequence."

Ingersoll looked at him as if estimating his character and bade him to sit in another chair by the table.

"If you'll write out the questions you want to ask me," he proposed, "then I'll tell you what we'll do."

After George had written the questions, Ingersoll said to him, "Now, of course you don't write shorthand. Please take your pencil and write very carefully as I dictate and I will answer your questions in turn. Then you will read over what you have written and I will make sure that you have got everything right and I want you to turn in just what I have said. Don't add anything that has slipped out in my casual talk with you. If you pad out this interview by reporting some of the things I said on the side you will not get my exact words and probably you will not convey to your readers just what I meant."

For more than an hour he sat there and dictated and George took down his exact words.

Then Ingersoll said he would like to suggest two or three questions that would give him an excuse to say something that might be of interest. It was no reflection on the interviewer, he added, to have him suggest the questions, because the interviewer could not know what was in his mind.

What George turned in to his newspaper was quite different from the kind of interview too often printed. He received many compliments on it the next morning, including kind words and a frank confession of guilt from the reporter who had suggested his going to see Ingersoll. Dr. Reilly, the managing editor, patted him on the shoulder and said he had asked just the right questions.

"They seemed to me the natural questions," said George modestly.

One result of this interview was that it brought home to George the unfairness of the way men are sometimes quoted in the papers. "It is a big mistake for a busy newspaperman to grab a hurried conversation with some man who is under public appraisal, and then go back to the office about an hour later and try to repeat from memory what was said."

From then on George Ade was considered the logical reporter to talk to notables and he began to accumulate his far-reaching acquaintance with famous people.

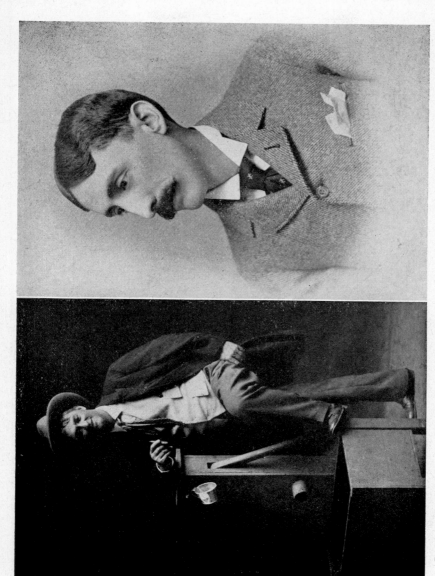

Brother Joe Ade before his return to the soil.   Brother Will in the title role of *The County Chairman* as produced at Kentland.

Thomas Meighan, stage and screen star, an Ade protege; and Booth Tarkington who, Ade thought when he first met him, should become a writer.

8

The Colorful Reporter

GEORGE ADE was soon recognized as more than a capable reporter. Within a year and a half after he came to Chicago, he was the star of his paper and had the choice assignments. This was some years before he signed anything in print, but other newspapermen in Chicago could always identify what was written by George Ade.

It became the practice in Chicago for reporters of the different papers who were covering the same event to pool the facts. The editors did not object, for this practice enabled them to do with fewer reporters. If a murder story was not too complicated, or a fire too big, one reporter could handle it, because what he did not get independently he could learn from the other reporters. This did not apply to news stories to which only one paper was "tipped off." Then a reporter could aim at a "scoop." But when reporters were gathering facts of something that all knew about, it was a breach of faith to hold out from the common pool. The superiority of one account and the reporter's ability was in the kind of writing. Here the Ade talent came into play. Certain facts trivial to others seemed to him to have more color. He could describe a fire unlike any other fire that had ever happened.

George was never too rushed to help another reporter, especially an inexperienced one. At the Washington Park Race Track an oversized youngster from another paper came up and said that holding his job depended presumably on this report, but he knew nothing about horse races. What was he to do?

"I'll tell you what to do," said Ade. "Look back in the files of your paper and find the last race meeting at this park. See how that was done. They're all the same. All you have to do is write in the names of the horses running today and their owners' names."

The young reporter, Theodore Dreiser, would never forget that meeting. "His voice was so soft, his manners and mood so kindly. He was so neat and well-dressed, in no hurry, and indicated that I need not be. He told me to do this and that and by virtue of this advice my pathetic job was saved."

At another time George Ade himself became the recipient of help graciously given. He had rushed over to the Board of Trade to get the news about an upheaval in the grain market, and wanted to interview George Stone, president of the board. Waiting in Stone's outer office, wondering if his questions would betray ignorance of the details of trading in grain, he fell to talking with a *Tribune* reporter, "a tall, rangy man with a steady eye, a comfortable suit of clothes, and an imposing mustache," who said his name was Frank A. Vanderlip. He knew the grain market and generously gave George the inside. Each took a liking to the other and a friendship began. When Vanderlip got married, George was one of his ushers. Vanderlip was from an obscure town in Illinois. He had been a machinist and then worked his way through college. Recently his paper had shifted him from the hotel beat to finance and markets. His more sensational moves in a short space of years were still ahead—from reporter to the editorship of a financial weekly; private secretary to the Secretary of the Treasury, Lyman J. Gage; Assistant Secretary of the Treasury; vice-president of the National City Bank, in New York; then president of that bank, called the biggest bank in the world.

George learned why Vanderlip had quit reporting news around hotels. He had been a failure as a hotel reporter "because the young man on the *Herald* and the young man on the *Times* had obtained interviews every day with interesting visitors whom he was never able to find. He could not find them because these interesting personages did not exist. They were created by the enterprising young men of the *Times* and *Herald,* who were working in combination against the *Tribune.* Each morning the *Herald* and the *Times* had a throbbing story told by some traveler who had shot big game in India or penetrated the frozen north, or visited the interior of Tibet, or observed the habits of the kangaroo in Australia. The visitor who told the wondrous tale invariably left on the afternoon train for New York, but his name was on the hotel register as a corroborative detail intended to give verisimilitude to an otherwise bald and unconvincing narrative. . . . The hotel clerk was a party to the conspiracy. Every day the *Tribune* reporter was rebuked because he had been scooped by the *Times* and the *Herald.* He ran from hotel to hotel frantically, but never could find the African explorer and the titled European and the South Sea adventurer who were telling breathless tales in the rival papers."

One of the designing reporters who caused Vanderlip to lose his job on the hotel beat, the *Times* man, a native of Hartford, Connecticut, afterward went to New York where he produced two hundred plays, and managed fifty stars—Charles B. Dillingham. And the *Herald* man, Finley Peter Dunne, also became well known, to all who ever read "Mr. Dooley."

The stories he was hearing about the newspaper world convinced George that he was in the right work. Sometimes, though, it was more fun in retrospect. One of his first big out-of-town assignments in the summer of 1892 was not hilarious at the time. He was sent to the Homestead steel mills near Pittsburgh the day after the strikers had shot down the Pinkerton guards.

"The town was in the hands of the strikers. Armed sentries made me prisoner when I landed from a rowboat at dusk, very much scared. They marched me to strike headquarters where I was cross-questioned and stared at suspiciously and made to feel unworthy and uncomfortable.

"Finally I was given a badge and a passport, neither one of which meant anything to the hard-breathing foreigner who brought me back to headquarters in twenty minutes, just ahead of the largest and bluest revolver I ever saw, and told the labor chiefs that I looked and acted like a detective.

"The strike, which resulted in a civil war, was, the steel workers told us, a protest against the 'tyranny' of Mr. Frick and his associates. Of course, the minute the huskies turned back the Pinkertons and found themselves in armed control of the town, the hot-heads outnumbered the conservatives and we poor correspondents who were sent there to report the situation found ourselves in the hands of a mob which had lathered itself into a most unreasoning mood.

"For nearly a week I devoted a large share of my time to being arrested and marched to headquarters. We slept in our clothes and didn't have time to shave, so after a few days I looked like a true friend of the workingman and was not molested."

While on this assignment George formed a friendship with Langdon Smith, a star writer for the New York *Herald,* who later won recognition from his poem "Evolution"—"when you were a tadpole and I was a fish." (Interest in Smith's work was revived long afterward when George, as a tribute to his friend, had "Evolution" reprinted for private distribution to lovers of "good stuff.")

Other of George's assignments in 1892 included the Republican and Democratic National Conventions. He heard Bragg, of Wisconsin, when he sent the Tammany crowd into an apoplexy of wrath and aroused the Cleveland supporters to a delirium of ecstasy with his shouted statement, still remembered, "We love him for the enemies he has made!"

Most amusing of all the happenings at the conventions, to George Ade, was the incident of the band conductor. "The Second Regiment Band under the direction of a German with spectacles, was playing a medley of patriotic airs during the inevitable dilly-dally and delay which precede every session. Most of the delegates were in their places. The German conductor with the spectacles knew his Bach and Beethoven but he didn't know American history or he wouldn't have started to play, 'Marching Through Georgia.' . . . The protest registered by the Southerners was the most maniacal, furious and frantic explosion of wrath that ever took place. All the Colonels were in their chairs and every goatee was a fork of lightning. Fortunately for Otto, the band was in the gallery."

George was present at Democratic National Headquarters on election night that year to see "real drama—with William C. Whitney smilingly complacent as Cleveland made the spectacular comeback."

But George's most interesting assignment, in that eventful 1892, was nonpolitical.

9

At the Sullivan-Corbett Fight

AT THE beginning of the nineties a golden glow surrounded the name of John L. Sullivan. The great John L., sometimes called the Boston Strong Boy, was a demigod. His idolaters insisted that he was "the most popular American ever honored in song and story." One of the catch lines in a Hoyt farce ran, "Shake the hand that shook the hand of Sullivan." The refrain of a song was: "Find me a man who can knock out John L., and my darling I'll come back to you-u." Small boys knew stories about Sullivan's lion courage and could give details of the fight of seventy-five rounds at Richbourg, Mississippi, when Sullivan knocked out Jake Kilrain in the last championship bout fought with bare knuckles! John L. met all comers, sometimes putting to sleep more men in one week than later champions would fight in a lifetime. And everyone that Sullivan had knocked out put on airs for years afterward.

Many stories were told about Sullivan's playful behavior with bartenders. He loved to invite everybody within hearing to have a drink, and then, no matter how large the bill, would give a friendly cuff on the jaw to any bartender who shoved back the change. The bartender became more than ever his worshipful admirer.

Year after year, so numerous, so spectacular had been his victories that millions of people found it hard to imagine a day when John L. Sullivan would meet his superior. They felt that, somehow, even when he was eighty, he would still be the world's heavyweight champion.

So when Sullivan's title was challenged by a former bank clerk from San Francisco named James J. Corbett, not many of Sullivan's admirers had any doubt about the result. "Gentleman Jim" wore his clothes well, was dignified and quiet-spoken, but it would take more than nice manners to handle John L. Sullivan in the ring. Yet everybody was intensely interested in the Sullivan-Corbett match, to be fought in the Olympic Club at New Orleans on September 7, 1892. Indeed, no sporting event had ever aroused so much interest. The editors of the Chicago *News-Record** knew they must send to the fight the best reporter they had, the man best qualified to get all the facts and all the drama. That meant George Ade. He was the most envied member of the staff, but none could deny that the editors had chosen wisely.

About a week before the fight George went to New Orleans and began sending news about the rival training camps. Circulation of the *News-Record,* a penny paper, began to climb.

On the morning of the fight George witnessed something that he remembered as no less dramatic than the fight itself. He had a long talk with Corbett, and Corbett was chuckling and laughing! It seemed almost incredible that a man could laugh when about to face the fabulous John L. Corbett not only laughed but was sublimely sure that he was going to "knock the daylight" out of Sullivan. What made him laugh was a report about the betting odds, ten to three against him. The odds, Corbett declared, should be reversed. He put his hand on George's shoulder in a chummy way and said: "When the fight is over, remember that Jim Corbett told you this. Sullivan cannot put a glove on me. But I can hit him at any time, whenever I want to." Billy Delaney, Corbett's trainer, was trying to be calm and confident, but he was nervous.

* The *Morning News* had become the *News-Record* and soon afterward the name was abbreviated to the *Record.*

No trace of nervousness showed in Corbett. "He was like a happy, romping schoolboy."

When the contestants entered the ring, Corbett was still smiling and confident. "Beautiful in every outline from neck to his heels, Corbett looked the ideal athlete, cut on the whitest marble in heroic proportions. The searching blue-white rays of the great electric light seemed to chill the last trace of color from his naturally white skin. It had not even the warmth of ivory white, but rather the pale tint of pure Parian marble."

Of Sullivan Ade wrote: "This was a grandly imposing shape, but no time had been wasted by nature in ornamenting it."

Writing at frantic speed in his usual legible script, George described how Sullivan drove powerful blows—into empty space! No such quick dodger as Corbett had ever been seen.

When in the twenty-first round Corbett delivered the blow that caused Sullivan to slump to the mat and stay there, George Ade rushed toward the telegraph office under the sloping seats of the wooden arena. He had already sent down a bale of copy and wondered how promptly the operators were getting it out. To his dismay he saw the long table piled high with copy paper and the operators were not at their keys. All were peeking through cracks as they had been throughout the fight, and not a line of George's copy had yet been sent. He knew that his one chance to catch the first edition of his paper was to reach the main telegraph office downtown and begin feeding in the pages.

"There was a great jam in the street but an old-fashioned two-horse cab of the ark variety was pushing through the multitude. I fought my way through the crowd and yelled at the driver that I was offering two dollars for a ride downtown. He told me to climb right up over the wheel and get on top. So I climbed up and another man broke through the crowd and came climbing up after me. The driver tried to push him back but he begged

GEORGE ADE

HAZELDEN FARM   BROOK, INDIANA

Sept. 19, 1930.

Fred C. Kelly,
The Mortgages,
Peninsula, Ohio

Dear Fred:

I have found some pages of the original College Widow
script and have picked out for you a few right in the
middle of the third act when the football game is being
played. I had an unusual experience with this play
inasmuch as I made very few changes after completing the
first draft and I don't think we made any changes after
the first performance. Usually there is a lot of tinkering and re-writing after the play has been tried out.
I hope the boy continues to get along all right at Purdue
and if I can be of any help to him at any time, have him
call on me

I am, with best wishes,

Sincerely, George Ade

In George Ade's handwriting, a page from the original manuscript of *The College Widow*, and a letter to the author.

George Ade photographed in his study by the author in 1909.

hard and so the two of us found ourselves squatted on top of the night-going vehicle as it bumped the hard cobble-stones. My companion was weeping. He was weeping real tears and moaning. Finally he grabbed me by the arm and said to me:

" 'I saw it wit' me own eyes but I can't believe it. Did Corbett really lick the big fellow?'

"I couldn't hold back the truth. Once more he wept—real choking sobs."

Then it came out that George's companion was not only a friend of Sullivan, but had gained fame of a sort in his own right by having, a few years previously, dared to leap from the Brooklyn Bridge.

"I guess you don't make me here in the dark," the man said. "I'm Steve Brodie."

George's account of the fight occupied most of the first page of the second section of the *News-Record* the next morning. Never before had the paper given so much space to a sporting event. For accuracy, color and vivid writing it was a masterpiece. The editors had made no mistake in the man they picked to report the pugilistic battle of the century.

On the first day of the next month Victor Lawson, owner of the *News-Record,* was looking over a chart showing the ups and downs of circulation during the previous four weeks. He discovered that the circulation had gone up early in September and then dropped back, but not back to the level of the previous month. It stayed about five thousand higher than the average for August. Lawson had never attended a fight, but he could understand that the general public had been more interested in John L. Sullivan and James J. Corbett than in any other two people. Why, though, had the circulation stayed up after the fight was over? He sent for the circulation manager, to ask him.

"I think," the man told him, "it's because of the way a reporter named George Ade wrote about the fight. It's my theory that subscribers believe they ought to keep on taking a paper that has such a good writer."

"Send George Ade to other prize fights," Lawson told the managing editor.

George did report other prize fights and that was how it came about that, some time after the Sullivan-Corbett encounter, he had another glimpse of Sullivan under circumstances a bit alarming.

It happened in El Paso, Texas, where George was obliged to stay for a month while efforts were being made to arrange for a fight between Bob Fitzsimmons and Peter Maher. The Texas rangers were trying to prevent any brutal glove fighting on Texas soil.

Incidentally, Fitzsimmons, who at times was clownish and loved animals, had insisted on going into the cage with a bear exhibited on the public square of a little town near the Mexican border. George loved to tell afterward of how Fitzsimmons mauled the bear and scared it half to death.

Here is what George wrote of his meeting with Sullivan: "While we were hanging around El Paso waiting for a chance to stage the battle, 'Parson' Davies came to town with his theatrical company playing 'The Wicklow Postman.' Eugene O'Rourke was the star and among the actors supporting him were John L. Sullivan and Paddy Ryan. The visiting correspondents were camped in a rooming house next to the Gem gambling establishment. John L. came and lived with us. His room was near mine. The hallway was narrow and had square turns. It was unlighted. All the conditions favored the supreme experience which came to me in El Paso.

"John L. had not counted the turns in the narrow hallway. I was awakened by a deep rumbling sound. Between me and the window I saw a vast bulk. Mr. Sullivan had entered my room and was removing some of his garments, at the same time conversing with himself on affairs in general.

"After tossing aside his coat and vest he came to bed. I rolled over just in time to avoid being his one-thousandth victim. Then I spoke to him in a very nice way, calling him 'Mr. Sullivan,' and told him that he was in the wrong room. Then he asked my name and where I came from and why and what was the idea of my being in his room.

"'This isn't your room, Mr. Sullivan,' I said. 'Come with me, Mr. Sullivan, and I will take you to your regular room. I will carry your hat and coat and vest, Mr. Sullivan, and everything will be all right, Mr. Sullivan.'

"When we arrived at his room he turned on the light and, as a special favor, showed me a wound on his head. He had taken a fall over at New Orleans, cutting quite a gash across the scalp. He wanted me to look at the stitches taken by the doctor and give him a fair, impartial opinion. I looked at the ragged cut across the top of his head and said it seemed to be all right.

"'Then you can't see straight,' said Mr. Sullivan. 'That doctor sewed me up with wire and he didn't use the right kind of wire at that. He used piano wire. How'd you like to have your head all sewed up with piano wire?'

"I told him I would prefer almost any other kind of wire and bade him a respectful good night.

"Later, when I began to estimate the supreme quality of this adventure, I was rather sorry that I had not kept quiet that night after my visitor hit the mattress, so that I could have told around, for all time, that John L. Sullivan and I once slept in the same bed. As it was, I hesitated before disturbing him, and then I made a swift guess that when he awoke in the morning and found me alongside of him he would not be in any mood to receive laughing explanations; and besides, the room was one flight up, so I may have acted wisely."

10

Specimens from All Parts

CHICAGO was "stuffed with 'entertainment values'" for a young man who had grown up in a village, where a one-ring circus was "a glimpse of paradise, 'Uncle Tom' a dramatic festival and the commercial traveler a visiting notable."

One source of entertainment for George Ade in 1892 came from his membership in the Whitechapel Club, whose rooms faced the alley at the rear of the office of the *Daily News.* George has called it "a little group of thirsty intellectuals who were opposed to everything." The more conservative favored a redistribution of property, while the radicals believed in the free use of dynamite. The club had a couple of managing editors and a few judges and a sprinkling of millionaires who were verbally scalded every time they ventured an opinion." In the list including painters, poets and architects was the most famous magician of his time, Alexander Hermann. About half of the members were newspaper toilers who were having plenty of fun in life even when complaining most vigorously about what was wrong with the world.

Sometimes the club gave a party. Rudyard Kipling was once the guest of honor. Talk at the tables near a coffin-shaped bar was a principal club activity and the most brilliant of the talkers was "Pete" Dunne, reporter on the *Herald,* not yet the famous "Mr. Dooley." He was the club's Dr. Johnson. When he talked the others listened. They were unsparing in their shots even at a distinguished guest if he uttered any banality. With equal candor they assailed any member whose newspaper story, poem or book failed to win their approval. The novelist and newspaperman,

Opie Read, couldn't "take it" and left the club. A young humorist from Michigan, Ben King, sometimes recited his verses, and one of these, "If I Should Die Tonight," supposed to have been written on a Whitechapel Club table, is still remembered. ". . . And you should come to me, and there and then, just even hint 'bout payin' me that ten, I might arise the while, but I'd drop dead again."

George Ade found among his acquaintances "specimens from all parts" and discovered that many of the most interesting were in the writing and art departments of the Chicago papers. Among the artists who afterward gained national recognition were Henry Hutt, the two Leyendecker brothers and Henry Reuterdahl, famous for his paintings of the Navy.

A young reporter on the *Herald,* a tall, quiet, good-looking boy with "a searching eye and a whimsical smile," won George's admiration because he could write humor, "bantering, fantastic, mock-serious, spoofing stuff," and also because he could draw the top salary for reporters, $35 a week. More than any other Chicago newspaperman in the early '90's, Brand Whitlock seemed likely to become famous as a humorist. But he was destined to win fame in other ways—as a writer of realistic novels, as a reform mayor of Toledo, and finally as United States Minister to Belgium during World War I, when he tried desperately, though hopelessly, to prevent the execution by the Germans of Edith Cavell.

Another youngster, Ray Stannard Baker, on the same paper with George, was the son of the Army officer who had directed the pursuit of John Wilkes Booth, the assassin of Lincoln. What "got" George was that when this lad applied for a job, he did not merely say that he had been to college, but showed the city editor his diploma. "That fellow," George said, "will get along." And he did. He soon began to win fame for his magazine articles; he charmed millions as David Grayson with his *Adventures in Con-*

tentment, and he became the biographer of Woodrow Wilson.

Then there was the solemn Eugene Field, whose "Little Boy Blue" had made him famous, but whose daily "Sharps and Flats" in the *News-Record* was unsigned. Most of his writing he did at home. When he appeared at the office it was usually to carry out some prank. One morning he brought chalk and a horseshoe and drew a horse's hoof, up the stairway and along the hall to the office door of one of the staff who talked mostly about horses. A favorite prank of Field's was to inquire at a secondhand store for an unexpurgated copy of the works of Mrs. Ann Felicia Hemans, the sentimental and highly proper poetess. One bookdealer heard about Field's search and inserted in a volume of the Hemans verses a special flyleaf with the statement that the text was complete with none of the objectionable material omitted.

Other newspaper friends of George at this time were the keen, lovable John E. Willkie of the *Herald,* afterward head of the United States Secret Service; and Kirke La Shelle, who a few years later wrote successful light operas, *The Princess Chic* and *The Ameer.* Will Payne, city editor of the *Daily News* was on his way to becoming a well-known novelist.

George was a little too late to be a contemporary of Harry B. Smith, but they became friends and George heard from him how he had got his start toward fame. When Melville Stone was editor of the *Daily News,* an actress came to see him and showed him some verses dedicated to her by a boy living on the West Side. Stone liked the verses and offered the boy a job. With that encouragement, the boy wrote more verses and it wasn't long until he had written *Robin Hood,* the first of the light operas and musical comedies that made his name familiar on billboards.

In the art department of the *News-Record* was a newcomer from Kentucky, a tall, dressy fellow by the name of Carl Emil Schultze. He had "the manners and whisker adornments of an

Austrian nobleman." Afterward he created the comic series, "Foxy Grandpa." To the young men on the paper his greatest achievement was a scheme to dress elegantly on a small salary by inducing a tailor to sell clothes for $2.50 a week. That was a help to Ade and McCutcheon who were having financial difficulties.

The "hall-bedroom twins," as George and John were known to their friends, regularly faced the problem of providing themselves with food. Toward the end of each week they found themselves short, even though each now "commanded" $20 a week. George operated on a narrow margin, for he was still sending money to those ladies at Lafayette who had trusted him for board at the Stockton House.

Payday was on Tuesday morning. With $40 it seemed that both could eat well for a week. Invariably they *dined* on Tuesdays, and Wednesdays and Thursdays they ate first-class. The Italian restaurants on Van Buren Street and the French on Monroe Street—they knew them all. Fridays they went to the Boston Oyster House with apple sauce and pickles free. On Saturday they often called on Mr. Heyman, who ran a little establishment with a safety-deposit vault and private rooms in the *Inter-Ocean* building. This was their only banking connection. Alternately, in return for $5, they left with him George's watch or John's ring. On Tuesday they paid $5.50 and took back the watch or ring.

"When Mr. Heyman saw us coming across Madison street, he would begin making out the certificate of deposit and ten minutes later two rising young journalists would be seen partaking of food at a select place kept by Burcky & Milan."

Skipping a call on Mr. Heyman now and then, they tried to avoid every extravagance, and felt guilty for wearing 35-cent chrysanthemums when Purdue played Chicago at football. Each week they had some unexpected expense, as when their house guest, a Purdue friend, wore all their clean shirts and collars.

One Saturday soon after George came back from the Sullivan-Corbett fight, they sat in their room wondering if they could do with beans over the week end. There was a rap on the door. Who could the caller be? None of their friends had ever been here. Rooming houses were sometimes raided. Was it the police?

A tall, well-dressed man gave his name, Charles T. Atkinson. He was a businessman (afterward president of the Board of Trade). Atkinson had heard from someone on the paper that McCutcheon could draw. McCutcheon had never signed his sketches in the paper and was surprised that anyone knew about him. What Atkinson sought was ten little humorous drawings as place cards for a dinner he was giving to pay for a bet on Sullivan. He wanted to show scenes of the fight. Would McCutcheon make them? How much would he charge? To make cards for a dinner at the Hotel Richelieu seemed overwhelming. McCutcheon hesitated, but a glance from George made him decide. He said he would try to draw something by four o'clock.

George Ade waited for the steps to reach the end of the hall.

"That man looks well-to-do. I'd soak him. I'd charge him five dollars."

"Now, George," said McCutcheon, "I couldn't do *that*. I'll ask him a decent price, but it wouldn't be right to charge him five dollars."

"It's a lot of money," George conceded, "but you'll probably never see him again."

When Atkinson came back and saw the drawings, he was delighted. "I never dreamed they would be so good! And now how much do I owe you?"

John, bracing himself to soak the rich, faltered, "Would five dollars be all right?"

Atkinson paid it like a man and even looked pleased. George

wondered if they could not just as well have got six or maybe eight dollars.

"And now," said Atkinson, "I want to ask one more favor. I'm on my way to a little party out at Mr. and Mrs. Shaw's, my brother-in-law and sister. They'll have good food and some interesting people. Won't you boys come along?"

They went to a cheerful home on the North Side where they had a lively evening and were invited to come again. As guests of the Shaws about two years after the first meeting, they were asked to give their frank opinion of a newly arrived baby girl named Evelyn. For bachelors they expressed themselves with well-feigned enthusiasm. They continued to drop in and one night when little Evelyn was about two years old, her uncle suggested that maybe McCutcheon would draw some pictures for her. He did so, and each time after that when he came she climbed on his knee and wanted more pictures.

"Everybody takes to Mac, even children," remarked George Ade. "I'll bet that little girl saves those drawings the nice man made."

George was right. She has the drawings yet, and others, for she became Mrs. John T. McCutcheon.

11

Daily Columnist

"THE WORLD's greatest achievement of the departing century," wrote Ade, "was pulled off in Chicago. The Columbian Exposition was the most stupendous, interesting and significant show ever spread out for the public. As a demonstration of civic pride, community enterprise and nation-wide cooperation—revealing the progress and culture and creative impulses of the whole world—it has not been matched."

Chicago was " 'wide open' by preference and deliberately attempting to outdo Sodom and Gomorrah, while incidentally determined to acquire all the graces and merits and garnishments of New York, London and Paris. It talked loud and boastingly and then made good on the bragging."

Even before the World's Fair opened in May 1893, Charles H. Dennis, managing editor of the paper, set apart the last two columns of the editorial page under the heading, "All Roads Lead to the World's Fair." Other reporters contributed to these columns, but most of the stories were Ade's. His one assignment was to tell of what he saw at the World's Fair. What he wrote was not intended to have news value but to touch off characteristic incidents at Jackson Park. Here was the greatest show on earth and George could wander as he pleased behind the scenes. His enthusiasm for that "city of gigantic white buildings, fluttering myriad flags, that bloomed in splendor on the shores of Lake Michigan," was based on intimate knowledge. He never lost his sense of wonder. He was "like a farm hand on a circus lot" afraid of missing something.

A thing that never ceased to amuse him was the kind of straw
hats in style for men that summer, with the widest brims ever
seen, as if designed especially to be blown off in "the windy city";
and the hats were usually equipped with a form of wind insurance,
a black cord fastened to a little button on the brim, the other end
looped into one's coat lapel.

On the opening day the President of the United States was the
star. Grover Cleveland had come from Washington for the dedication and to review a parade. He and Daniel S. Lamont, the Secretary of War, stood on the platform. It was a cold and blustery
May day with an icy wind. A member of the local committee
walked out on the platform, followed by a waiter who carried a
tray with two glasses "containing some kind of compact bever-
age." "I thought," said the committeeman, "possibly you might
want something to warm you up." The President replied, "Lamont
doesn't use this stuff"—and poured the two into one!

George found stories along the Midway Plaisance, that "jumble
of colors and medley of noises," on the Ferris Wheel—365 feet
high—at Buffalo Bill's Wild West Show, in the great buildings or
while he listened to Sousa's band. He studied the "acres and acres
of visitors"—716,000 on Chicago Day! The trip to Chicago was
for many thousands the first away from home. Never had so many
Americans gone traveling, and George reveled in observing all the
varieties of behavior.

The town had other attractions aplenty. *Ali Baba* was at the
Chicago Opera House, with Eddie Foy, and in the chorus Frankie
Bailey, the girl whose legs were the shapeliest ever reported.

The Exposition closed in October and George returned to the
reporting staff of the *Record,* as the paper was now called. To
his regular assignments he added little stories of everyday people
along the highways and byways. The interest of these lay not only
in the subject but in the style—the stamp of George Ade.

"You can imagine what happened to my placid little yarns about shopgirls and stray dogs and cable-car conductors. . . . I would turn in a third of a column about a cooperative attempt to start a balky horse in Wabash avenue. Usually it got past the copy readers. They were under instructions to keep every story down to the essentials, but they were helpless when they tackled something which had no essentials, being unalloyed 'guff.' So the matter would get into type and ride past the proofreaders and get to the make-up slab and be all ready to sneak into a favored position on the front page. Then an alien on the West Side, with a name something like Cryzmyzysk, would come home in a peevish mood and hit his wife on the head with a hatchet. . . . The man on the night city desk would hot-foot down the hallway to carry the glad news to the night editor. 'Goody! Goody!' he would exclaim. 'The copy's been running awful tame, but this will help some.' . . . The whole crew would go on a run to the make-up corner. . . . 'What's that?' asks the night editor, pointing to a rectangle of white type metal. . . .

"The foreman, reading backward from the wrong-way-to type resting in the galley, replies, 'It's something about trying to start a balky horse on Wabash avenue. A man with a brown derby built a fire under him.'

" 'My Lord!' exclaims the efficient night editor. 'What are we running here, anyway? Hold it over—forever.' "

Sometimes George's human nature stories were grievously mutilated by the bright young men on the copy desk who seemed to delight in making hash of good writing. The managing editor shared George's exasperation, for he knew that "whatever he wrote was amply good enough to appear in print exactly as it came from his hand." So Dennis gave George and McCutcheon the columns formerly taken by the World's Fair feature to use as they liked. What they turned in would be protected by HANDS

OFF! signs. George could "go ahead and revel in the inconsequential."

"Stories of the Streets and of the Town" was the two-column line for the new department which appeared first on November 20, 1893. This feature, along with "Sharps and Flats" of Eugene Field, did much to put the Chicago *Record* in the topmost rank as a paper of quality. A historian of today, reading the "Stories of the Streets and of the Town," glimpses a golden age of journalism. McCutcheon did illustrations of striking excellence and Ade wrote not merely clever newspaper stuff but *literature!* What he wrote was not signed. Not until some years later did George's name or his initials identify the author. He did not write, as do columnists today, in the first person. "No newspaper man of that day ever dreamed of such a thing as a daily contributor featuring himself. . . . Never, by hint or suggestion, was it made known to our subscribers that behind the story department there might be hiding a human being with thoughts and emotions worth recording. I peered through the camera for seven years and never stood in front of it once."

Even the smells of the big city interested George Ade. They were still in his memory long afterward when he wrote: "Starting from a zone that was one hundred per cent ozone, our long walk to the editorial dungeons led us through many city odors, some of which were curdled to the dignity of smells.

"If we had been blindfolded and led along on familiar city trails, we could have called the corners and the landmarks because of the aromatic variations.

"For instance, there was a German place just on the border of the residence district. A sweet-sour exhalation of a happy flavor used to come through swinging doors and permeate the street until overcome by the smoky fumes of pitch from the new asphalt.

"Further along, a suggestion of soap works, plowing by invisible current through an alley, was pleasantly modified by the sharp, tangy odor spilled from a huge red building in which leaf tobacco was ground into a smoking mixture.

"A mist of gentle decay hung over the sluggish river, but the first diagonal street to the south brought a quick assortment of most agreeable scents, all suggestive of the sunny tropics. Every doorway breathed of spices or coffee turning in a roaster. At the corner where the wagons were heaped full of bananas and the sidewalks were stacked to the awning with varieties of citrus, the redolence was heavy and almost cloying in its sweetness.

"The neglected down-town pavements gave out a flat malarial vapor in the morning sun and a cold gust of rancid mud and mildew arose from the LaSalle street tunnel.

"Even the city hall had a character of its own. From the apertures we could get whiffs of dead tobacco smoke and a convincing proof that the crowd huddled inside should have been hung out for a thorough airing."

George's ambition was "to be known as a realist with a compact style and a clean Anglo-Saxon vocabulary and the courage to observe human virtues and frailties as they showed on the lens." He aimed to report people as he knew them, he did not caricature, exaggerate, or "embroider fancy situations." He told episodes in their lives through the medium of their own talk. His ear became infallible at catching the talk of everyday folk on the street, their use of words, their vernacular.

Sometimes he used a paragraph of verbatim conversation. "A Dearborn street lawyer met a LaSalle street lawyer. They are high in legal circles, have a fine standing in court and are cultivated gentlemen."

Hello, old man.
Why hello. How are you?

First class. How's your corporosity?
Haven't a word to say. Business good?
Some coming in; nothing to brag of. How's the world using
   you?
Can't complain. Don't see much of you. What s new with
   you?
Nothing. Same as usual. How's it coming with you?
So so; getting a living. Well, so long, old man, I'll see you
   later.
So long. Take care of yourself.
Sure.

George's first story for the department carried the heading, "A Young Man in Upper Life." Young Mr. Ponsby could not keep his mind on his work as he stared from his sixteenth-story office window at the men on the steel skeleton of a new building, and tilted back to wait in vain to see one of them fall. It was just a vivid flash of city life.

Ade and McCutcheon went about together. Instead of taking his subjects for illustrations from manuscript, the artist knew his character, his scene at first hand; he sketched many of the pictures on the spot. It was exceptional teamwork and never did two old friends have the privilege of working together in a manner that provided more daily fun and adventure. It was not work, it was so fascinating. Yet George was turning out from 1,200 to 1,800 words each day—"all hand-made stuff, too," for it was done with a pencil. He never used a typewriter. If some of his material did not suit him, George discarded it at the last minute and McCutcheon obligingly made his pictures to take up more space!

A few of his subjects show the range of his stories. Problems of a streetcar conductor, small shops of the city, a young man's search for a good boardinghouse, story-book detective and real detective, the junk shops of Canal Street, a stenographer's new job, at the French table d'hote, vehicles out of the ordinary, sidewalk merchants and their wares, restaurant sign language, life at a museum of freaks, a Pullman porter's story, Sophie's Sunday afternoon, the glory of being a coachman, whisker designers, Clark Street Chinamen, what goes on at the coroner's office, all about going to a fire, queer ways of making a living. George could do interesting paragraphs about so trifling an episode as the return of a customer to complain that the hat he had bought did not fit. (The clerk said: "Neither do your clothes.") One story was about the man who took on airs while showing his brother from the country the sights of the big city. Another told of the Chicago man from a small town who kept running into his boyhood acquaintance, Monty Hannibal, who had a habit of changing jobs. Monty was a streetcar conductor, then an elevator operator, driver of a wagon that carried a big advertising sign and later a waiter. His present job was always what he wanted. The story ended with a quotation from the village weekly: "Monty Hannibal is back from the Windy City and has accepted a job with Fred Murphy husking corn."

A story told to this day originated in 1895 in "Stories of the Streets and of the Town," "Mr. Benson's Experiences With a Maniac." A Chicago citizen visiting the violent ward of an insane asylum was pursued by one of the inmates. The visitor ran for his life but was overtaken. "He felt a hand on his back and a voice close to his ear. 'You're it! You're it! Now see if you can catch me.'"

So popular the stories became that selections from them were issued by the *Record* in a series of paperback books and sold at twenty-five cents each. First published in April 1894 the series continued, once or twice a year, until there were eight books. The *Record* did not exaggerate in advertising the stories, when it said that they were "commonly conceded to be the best things of their kind printed." Few copies have survived, but when one does turn up, the owner may be astounded at the price it will bring. A selection of the "Stories of the Streets and of the Town" was printed in a limited edition by the Caxton Club of Chicago in 1941, and copies are said to have brought as high as $150.

In January 1894 Ade and McCutcheon were invited, along with about ten other Chicago newspapermen, to be guests of a civic organization in California, to attend the Midwinter Fair in San Francisco with all expenses paid. Ade and McCutcheon set out carefree, modestly unaware of leaving gaps hard to fill at the *Record*. They traveled in Mr. Pullman's private car, the Monadnock, a gleeful, congenial group. The only one not from Chicago was an undersized reporter from the Cleveland *Press,* Elmer Bates. He had accompanied a friend to the train and was persuaded to join the party, though he carried not even a toothbrush.

To enliven the long cold journey George Ade suggested a dramatic entertainment. They rigged a stage at one end of the Pullman. McCutcheon drew little handbills which he distributed in other cars. Those crowded into the space were the first to witness an act by George Ade. George had written a skit in two scenes about two prize fighters who had quarreled over a girl. Cast for the part of the more aggressive fighter, who got licked, was the smallish Elmer Bates. Then Ade and McCutcheon came on in "A Sidewalk Conversation." They passed jokes back and forth and wound up with a song. One verse went something like this:

> Romeo and his soubrette
> Often in the café met,
> Ordered solid food and "wet"
> And Romeo and Juli-et.

While in San Francisco on this trip George had a strange experience. He went for a stroll up Market Street, and when he observed a crowd in front of a newspaper office gazing at the latest bulletins, he joined the throng. The crowd so filled the sidewalk that he was forced into the street. Of a sudden he was seized with dizziness. He could hardly keep his feet, and the buildings seemed to be moving. He hurried back to his hotel and called a doctor. The doctor after an examination could find no reason for the dizzy spell and asked George to tell exactly what he was doing when the spell came on. As George explained, the doctor began to smile. "Ah," he said, "you evidently were standing on the turntable for the streetcars."

Their trip to California did something to both Ade and McCutcheon. Neither had ever been so far from Indiana and so many sights surprised and fascinated them that they began to thirst for travel to distant places. Somehow they would go to Europe. By good fortune each received about then a raise of $10 a week to $35. George suggested, "Let's just pretend we never got the raise and each save the extra ten toward a trip to Europe." They went to Miss Harriet M. Dewey, cashier at the *Record* who handled the pay envelopes, and asked her to withhold $10 a week from each until further notice.

George was busier than ever. Besides his daily two columns of "Stories," he had become assistant to the dramatic editor and was writing criticisms. This extra work gave him free entree to the theaters and the privilege of interviewing stage folk. He helped to organize a little supper club, called The Green Room, which had a distinguished guest at each get-together. The guests included Henry Irving, Joseph Jefferson, William H. Crane, E. H. Sothern and Otis Skinner, all of whom became George's close friends.

One of the actresses with whom he formed a friendship was Minnie Maddern Fiske and he had the satisfaction of telling her of his joy in seeing her performance at the Grand Opera House in Lafayette just after his arrival there to enter Purdue.

Of all the stage women he met, he thought Madame Helena Modjeska was "the most queenly and femininely captivating. She was mistress of all the arts of her profession and played somber roles, but between performances she was as gay, unaffected and mischievous as a school girl."

After he came to know Lillian Russell, the famous beauty, he said he thought she retained her good looks because she was "so saturated with pleasant intentions that the years had no chance to sour or wrinkle her."

"I was no good as a dramatic critic," George said long afterward, "because I was sympathizing with the actors all the time and pulling for them when I should have been shooting poisoned arrows into them. I never could get enjoyment from a play so bad that it was supposed to be amusing. All I could see was a group of conscientious, willing and hard-working performers trying to get results from impossible material and meager talents." He sometimes defended stage "hokum," too. When some of his sophisticated friends made fun of Bartley Campbell's famous line, "Rags are royal raiment when worn for virtue's sake," he would smile and say, "But it's true, isn't it?"

Backstage at the Olympic theater—the "Olymp" he called it—then in its heyday for high-class vaudeville, was his favorite place. Vaudeville people, he found, were often "characters" off stage. He listened eagerly to their talk about tricks of stagecraft—about how to put an act *over*. What he wrote sometimes "made" a vaudeville performer. That was particularly true when he wrote his enthusiastic tribute to Charlie Case, then a newcomer in vaudeville. No one who ever heard Charlie Case's monologue will forget his stories about his father. "One day mother said to my brother and me, 'Boys, I think your father has had a little too much to drink.' We never would have known father had been drinking, but mother knew. When we looked at him *we* thought he was *dead*." Charlie Case all the rest of his life felt that George had given him his real start toward "top billing," and George always insisted that the Case monologue was one of the best acts ever in vaudeville.

George continued his quest for odd or amusing characters and he liked best those whose talk was individual and colorful. One mine of material was a girl behind the cigar counter at the Palmer House. When he wanted to entertain Booth Tarkington on his visits to Chicago, George invited him to listen to that girl's vocabulary. He sought conversation with everyone. One cold night he found some newsboys hovering over an iron grating in an alley at the rear of Boyle's chophouse, and he stopped to ask them questions. He did not talk down to them but was so friendly that they began to talk freely. One of them who had a captivating grin and used astonishing slang told about himself in a way that gave material for a "story." He had run away from home in Galveston, Texas, and had worked for a while at an engraving plant in Omaha. He loved to draw pictures and wished he had a chance to work where he could learn to draw better.

"Drop around and see me tomorrow," suggested George and handed the boy his card. When he saw Chicago *Record* on the card, the boy said, "I'll bet you're the fellow that writes those stories in the paper."

The next day the boy showed up at the *Record* office. George knew that a youngster from Dundee, Scotland, named Stanley Adamson, who had been helping the men in the art department, was about to quit. Through McCutcheon he got the job for his new acquaintance. The boy's name was Charlie Williams. He developed rapidly under the kindly guidance of McCutcheon and the other artists. So began the career of a famous illustrator in New York, who did the etchinglike illustrations in the early editions of *Monsieur Beaucaire*. The boy he replaced was also to be

nationally known as an artist, under the name of Penrhyn Stan-
laws.

After three years in the hall bedroom on Peck Court, George
and John moved. They would have gone sooner, for after John
was stopped one night by a holdup man, they had felt it prudent
to walk home in the middle of the street; but they knew that their
landlady had a tubercular daughter and needed the weekly $5.
With two or three congenial newspaper workers, one of them
James O'Donnell Bennett, afterward famous as a dramatic critic
and war correspondent, they established themselves in an apartment which they called the Commune, at 188 Chestnut Street.
Within a short walk was Tom Moran's saloon, on Chestnut and
Clark, a hangout for many "characters" among them Old Zig, a
colored man whom readers of the "Stories" were soon to know.
Near by was the Doussang all-night restaurant and bar, with private rooms above, and George was likely to drop in there around
midnight when homeward bound, for a bite of Brie cheese. Among
the regulars were some well-born, well-mannered failures with
mysterious pasts, remittance-man types, soon to figure in one of
George's most popular series of sketches.

George and John estimated that by April 1895 they would have
accumulated $520 apiece, from a year of weekly savings, and they
planned to start then on their trip to Europe. It seemed unlikely
that they could obtain a leave of absence for the several weeks they
hoped their money would last. They intended to resign and take
their chances on finding places on one of the Chicago papers when
they returned. George assumed that readers might be tired of the
"Stories." This trip would provide a good excuse to terminate
them. To their surprise the managing editor told them they must
not think of resigning. He proposed that they send in two illustrated travel articles each week. Their salaries would continue.

They might even draw their money in advance. That settled everything. Their friend, Frank Vanderlip, by virtue of being a financial and business reporter, had a pull with steamship lines and got them a special rate of $110 apiece for the round trip. In their absence "Stories of the Streets and of the Town" would be written by Ray Stannard Baker and illustrated by Ade's protegé, Charlie Williams.

Accompanied by Carroll Kent, son of the founder of George's home town, they crossed on the old Cunarder *Etruria*. It was an exciting adventure from the time the *Etruria* steamed out of New York harbor. George became interested in his fellow passengers, among them James J. Hill, the railroad man, restlessly pacing the deck; Lord Curzon, just married to a Chicago heiress, Mary Leiter; several grand opera singers; and a couple of international crooks.

In one of the first letters to his paper George made a near prophecy: "Some day, perhaps, there will be invented a device by which ocean steamers may tap the Atlantic cable for news bulletins and stock quotations, or else receive them by special transmission through the water, and then the last refuge will be denied the business slave who is attempting to get away from his work."

The young tourists had the thrill of their lives as they rode to the old Victoria Hotel in Northumberland Avenue. "London!" George murmured, as he tried to take in the strange sights and sounds. "London, England!" To their surprise they were instantly recognized as Americans. McCutcheon's fedora hat excited curiosity. George had a letter of introduction from his friend "Billy" Pinkerton, of the famous detective agency, to a man at Scotland Yard, who invited them to the morning hearings at the Bow Street police station. The first case was a large blonde woman whom they recognized as one of their recent fellow passengers. She had been brought in from a street fight with another lady. The man with her on the boat was a well-known American crook, Tim Oates. "Don't show that you know him," their Scotland Yard acquaintance cautioned them. "Anyone seen with him is being shadowed."

The twice-a-week articles under a heading, "What a Man Sees Who Goes Away from Home," were eagerly read. For the most part they were breezy, straight reporting of what interests a man seeing Europe for the first time. George avoided the guidebook kind of descriptions. He told what the food cost in restaurants, and he took the trouble to find out the weekly salaries of performers in London variety shows. His humor, not frequent, was of the subdued variety, as his report of a conversation with an Englishman on a train:

" 'Is it true that in some of your public houses over there a man who refuses to drink with another is liable to be shot?'

" 'Perhaps it is true of two or three mining camps.'

" 'And you have a song in America that is very popular, I believe. It is something about Way Down on the Old—some sort of river, is it not?'

" 'Way Down Upon the Suwanee River.'

" 'Ah, yes.'

"Having satisfied himself on those points regarding America, he asked no further questions."

Only occasionally he introduced exaggeration in the Mark Twain vein, as in Italy, "the energy of the people is expended on trifles. In Naples a man carrying two fish, each five inches long, will devote more time, more muscular exertion, more lung power and more nervous energy to the sale of those two minnows than would be needed to run a department store for half a day. A man with four oranges in a basket will develop more fervid eloquence in the praise of his goods than would be necessary to effect the sale of a dozen corner lots."

Ade and McCutcheon covered Ireland, England, Holland, Belgium, Germany, Switzerland, Italy and France for $800 apiece.

They came back on the *Lucania* feeling convinced that the cost of that European tour was the best investment they had ever made. "We felt that we had been much broadened by travel because we were absolutely flat." His provincialism was "sandpapered away," George said, and he "began to see things from a new angle." From then on travel was one of his chief enthusiasms. "The planet you are now visiting may be the only one you'll ever see. Even if you get a transfer, the next one may not have any Grand Canyon or Niagara Falls."

George resumed his daily columns and what he wrote was better than before.

12

Literary Experiments

GEORGE ADE was not content to do an acceptable job. He kept making his "Stories" better, in quality and variety. As his characters and settings mirrored every phase of city life, his columns were social history. He experimented with every literary form: narrative, dialogue, light verse, the short story, the fable, sometimes the dramatic form. His department was a testing ground for all that he did afterward. He was getting practice in dialogue and in compression. Not a waste word slipped in. "Everything was condensed on our papers, even the salaries."

At the Whitechapel Club, at the Newspaper Club, in barber-shops—especially in barbershops—George picked up stories. Men on rival newspapers gave him suggestions. One came from a lively, sandy-haired youngster on the *Inter-Ocean,* Victor Murdock from Wichita, Kansas, later prominent in Congress.

In the sporting department of the *Record* was a boy whom George found extraordinarily helpful. Devoted to horse racing, he often guided George to hangouts of jockeys, touts, and race-track gamblers. It was Johnny Hertz who afterward made enough money to fill a woodshed by founding the Yellow Cab industry.

Though George did not encourage contributions from readers, as later columnists have done, he sometimes received useful suggestions from a student at the Armour Scientific Academy, "a solemn boy with an itch to write," by the name of Adams, to become famous for his columns signed F.P.A.

Bicycling was at its height and George was proud of his blue Napoleon that cost $80. The bicycle craze gave him material for many of his sketches. One was about the boy who captured the girl by first becoming thick with her father after it was discovered that they rode the same make of bike!

The merit of the "Stories" was being recognized not only by the general reader, but by persons of literary attainment. Hamlin Garland, the novelist, wrote to George as early as 1895 and urged him to do a novel.* A letter came from Henry B. Fuller, whose novels with a Chicago background had won him a high place, saying that "when you feel the disposition to write the 'Chicago novel' that people are beginning to expect of you, I don't know of anybody who wouldn't be glad to pull off to one side and give you all the room you need!" Fuller praised the story of cousin Walter Miller, "the urban pinhead who passes for a 'wise city mug' —one of the most obvious and perennial of the types, but you are about the first to capture him. I don't know why the thing that lies right in the way should be the thing that everybody passes by." One of the city's foreign language papers, the *Danish Pioneer,* said editorially, "We do not hesitate to compare George Ade with Dickens; indeed, he generally surpasses his great predecessor in his almost incredible power to give the most trivial things of life a new and fresh human interest."

Charlie Williams, the boy in the art department, did his sponsor a favor. He was a master of the street-corner slang of the "wise kids," and George used some of his talk. Then George got an idea that readers might like his "Stories" better if they found familiar characters recurring. These began in December 1895 with a brash, goodhearted young man, "Artie" Blanchard. Artie was an office employee, not in a newspaper art department, but the char-

---

* Garland, a native of Wisconsin, had moved to Chicago from the East because he believed Chicago would become the American literary center. At the time he first wrote to Ade he had been reading him with enthusiasm but had never met him. Soon afterward he met both Ade and McCutcheon at the home of Eugene Field. As he recorded in his memoirs, he found Ade "singularly laconic, and McCutcheon almost entirely wordless."

acter and colorful talk were those of Charlie Williams. Charlie
had told of being persuaded to buy a ticket to a church entertainment. "I didn't do a thing but push my face in there about eight
o'clock last night and I was 'it' from the start. Say, I like that
church and if they'll put in a punchin' bag and a plunge they can
have my game, I'll tell you those." That went into a "Story."
Charlie soon had a girl and his courtship gave George rich material. He depicted the courtship scenes with refinement and tender-
ness, notwithstanding the slang. "Artie" was a young man of
sound morality, decent manners and little flashes of wisdom.

Early in '96 George received a flattering offer of $25 to write a
book. A Chicago publisher wanted to put out some stories for
children, six little books, each two inches square, to be sold as a
set for a dollar. Over a week end George did one of these called
Circus Day and it bore his name. It was illustrated by McCutcheon.
Then George did one more of the six, *Stories From History,* about
Columbus, Washington, Lincoln and Israel Putnam. The publisher did not wish to have more than one book in the set signed
by the same author, and George used the name "John Hazelden,"
from Hazleton, in his family background. Few people ever suspected the identity of "John Hazelden," but *Circus Day* even in
later reprints became a much-sought collectors' item.

Then in May of the same year George received another publishing proposal. The firm of Herbert S. Stone & Co. (two sons
of Melville E. Stone), who had introduced H. G. Wells and
Bernard Shaw to American readers, wanted to make a book of
the "Artie" sketches. Hamlin Garland heard of the offer and
wrote to George suggesting that he be rigid in the exclusion of
all hastily written matter. George linked together the best of the
stories, and *Artie, a Story of the Streets and Town* appeared in the
latter part of '96.

The book received enthusiastic reviews. One paper said editorially: "No one can read it and fail to have greater respect for the American boy . . ." It was through *Artie* that George Ade was "discovered" by William Dean Howells, dean of American literary critics, who observed Ade's work with admiration from then on. Indeed, Ade became his favorite author. Of *Artie* Howells wrote: "On the level which it consciously seeks I do not believe there is a better study of American town life in the West."

A cigar was named for *Artie!*

After *Artie* appeared, George was invited to join the Forty Club, whose dinners were a happy meeting place for a local "cluster of immortals," and he became its president. Incidentally, the Forty Club had a chaplain, the Reverend Ernest Stires, who later went to the fashionable St. Thomas church on Fifth Avenue, New York, and became a Bishop. George said of him: "To be with him was almost enough to induce a man to attend church and try to lead a better life."

Today under Ade's photograph in the Forty Club's Golden Book is this toast:

> If every joy that he has given
> To make our laughter crowd out tears
> Would add one tittle to his span
> George Ade would live a million years.

The *Artie* series in the *Record* was followed by "Doc' Horne," a gentlemanly liar and his satellites who lived at the "Alfalfa European Hotel"—suggested by some of the remittance-man types at the Doussang restaurant. Doc' Horne "was bald on the top of his head. His face had the fulness of youth, but it was wrinkled. The chin beard was white. When it is said, further, that he wore clothes such as might be worn by any old gentleman who had ceased to be fastidious on the point of personal adornment, the reader knows as much as anyone would know in taking a first glance . . ." With his sure touch George gave the key to Doc's character in a sentence: "If they had built the Mississippi levees as I told them to, long before the war, they wouldn't be washed away every year."

Toward the end of '96 George began the stories of "Pink Marsh," a colored bootblack in a basement barbershop. In these he was the first to catch the talk and character of the sophisticated northern Negro. The stories were told by Pink in conversations with the Morning Customer who stirs Pink's envy by the way he can "swing the language," using big words, "wahm words." Pink's ethical sense was not too high. He overcame the educational superiority of a rival in a love affair by promising his girl a bicycle that he had no intention of buying, and then got out of buying her candy by saying that he was 'conomizin' for the bicycle. When he lost the affections of that Dearborn Street belle to a Pullman porter, he accepted the inevitable. "Dat lady jus' 'e same to me as day befo' yesterday." He also announced his intention to find one of those that "if you give 'em a few peppermints and stan' faw cahfaih (car-fare) 'ey think they're bein' used good."

The "Pink Marsh" sketches ran until around the end of May 1897, and the "Doc' Horne" continued through most of that year. In '97 Stone & Co. published *Pink Marsh,* and in '99 they brought out *Doc' Horne.* Both impressed the critics. Long afterward Mark Twain wrote to William Dean Howells: "Thank you once more for introducing me to the incomparable Pink Marsh. I have been reading him again after this long interval, & my admiration of the book has overflowed all limits, all frontiers. I have personally known each of the characters in the book & can testify that they are all true to the facts, & as exact as if they had been drawn to scale. And how effortless is the limning! It is as if the work did itself, without help of the master's hand.

"And for once—just this once—the illustrator [McCutcheon] is the peer of the writer. The writer flashes a character onto his page in a dozen words, you turn the leaf and there he stands, alive & breathing . . .

"Pink—oh, the shiftless, worthless, lovable black darling. Howells, he deserves to live forever."

In one of his discussions of the "Chicago School of Fiction" Howells wrote in the *North American Review** of Ade's lack of literary pose, "his perfect control in dealing with the American as he knows himself. The level struck is low: the level of the street, which seems not depressed in the basement barber shop where Pink Marsh polishes shoes, or lifted in the office where Artie talks to his friends and evolves himself and his simple love story. It is the same level in the entrance floor of the Alfalfa, where Doc' Horne sits with his fortuitous companions and harmlessly romances. You are not asked to be interested in anyone because he is in any way out of the common, but because he is every way in the common. Mr. Ade would not think of explaining or apologizing or at all accounting for the company he invites you to keep. He knows too well how good it is, and he cheerfully takes the chance of your not yourself being better.

"But our life, our good, kind, droll, ridiculous American life, is really inexhaustible, and Mr. Ade, who knows its breadths and depths as few others have known them, drops his net into it anywhere, and pulls it up full of the queer fish which abound in it."

Along with the sketches in series that he was writing in '96, George was also doing in his columns short stories of the quality of those for which he would later receive a dollar a word. When the critic, H. L. Mencken, read a collection of them some years later, he declared that there were "two or three of the best short stories ever written in this republic."

---

* May 1903.

One of these preserved today in Howells' anthology, *Great Modern American Stories,* was "Effie Whittlesy." It told what happened one day at the home of a Chicago man who had been brought up in a small town. He heard the good news from his city-bred wife that she had just obtained a jewel of a new house-maid. At dinner that night a strange thing happened.

"Mr. Wallace turned to look at the new girl and his eyes enlarged. He gazed at her as if fascinated either by cap or freckles. An expression of wonderment came to his face and he said: 'Well, by George!'

"The girl had come very near the table when she took the first overt glance at him. Why did the tureen sway in her hands? She smiled in a frightened way and hurriedly set the tureen on the table.

"Mr. Wallace was not long undecided, but during that moment of hesitancy he remembered many things. He had been reared in the democracy of a small community and the democratic spirit came uppermost.

" 'This isn't Effie Whittlesy?' said he.

" 'For the land's sake!' she exclaimed, backing away, and this was a virtual confession.

" 'You don't know me.'

" 'Well, if it ain't Ed Wallace!'

"Would that words were ample to tell how Mrs. Wallace settled back in her chair, gaping first at her husband and then at the new girl, stunned with surprise and trying vainly to understand what it all meant.

"She saw Mr. Wallace reach awkwardly across the table and shake hands with the new girl and then she found voice to gasp: 'Of all things!'

"Mr. Wallace was painfully embarrassed. He was wavering between his formal duty as an employer and his natural regard for an old friend. Anyway, it occurred to him that an explanation would be timely.

" 'This is Effie Whittlesy from Brainard,' said he. 'I used to go to school with her. She's been at our house often. I haven't seen her for—I didn't know you were in Chicago.'

" 'Well, Ed Wallace, you could knock me down with a feather,' said Effie . . ."

Then there was conversation as at an old settlers' reunion until Mrs. Wallace said, "That will be all for the present, Effie."

Mrs. Wallace could not quite catch the democratic spirit of a small town, and Effie had to go, but George Ade saw to it that the situation was handled sympathetically and gracefully.

Howells called the story "a contribution to American fiction of a value far beyond most American novels; . . ." and added that "no American worthy of his birthright can fail to feel a thrill of pride in the higher citizenship which it divines."

About two weeks after "Effie Whittlesy" appeared in his columns, George wrote a burlesque on grand opera, "Il Janitoro."

Mr. and Mrs. Taylor in their fifth floor apartment discover that the building is on fire.

"Mrs. Taylor: I think I smell smoke.

"Mr. Taylor: She thinks she smells smoke.

"Mrs. Taylor: We must escape!

"Mr. Taylor: Yes, yes, we must escape!

"Mrs. Taylor: We have no time to lose.

"Mr. Taylor: Ah, bitter truth, Ah, bitter truth,

we have no time to lose.

"Mr. and Mrs. Taylor: Sad is our, sad is our lot,

To perish in the flames so hot.

(enter the Janitor)

"Janitor: Hold, I am here.

"Mr. Taylor: Ah, it is the Janitoro.

Ade and McCutcheon, the onetime "hall bedroom twins," in 1910.

The house that George built.

Living room at Hazelden.

"Mrs. Taylor: Can I believe my senses
            Or am I going mad?
            It is indeed the Janitoro.
"Janitor: I come to inform you that you must quickly fly
            The fearful blaze is spreading, to tarry is to die."
And so on, for more than a column.*

A story a year or so later that many critics rank with "Effie Whittlesy" was that of "Willie Curtin," who in helpless shame saw his sister insulted, then secretly took boxing lessons and avenged the dishonor, only to be scolded by his family, including his sister, for getting into a saloon brawl.

Such was the variety of "Stories of the Streets and of the Town."

Though some of what he wrote for his columns in '96 alone was enough to give George Ade permanent recognition in American literature, he was still a reporter, covering shows and going out of town on special assignments.

He reported the Republican and Democratic National Conventions. "Just behind me sits an eagle-faced correspondent from Omaha, unhonored and unnoticed. His name is Bryan. Shift to Chicago and a bedlam known as the Democratic National Convention. The Omaha correspondent is now swathed in glory and leader of an enchanted host. I didn't believe one word of that 'Cross of Gold' oratorical paroxysm, but it gave me the goose-pimples just the same."

His observation at national conventions led him afterward to have a fictional character thus describe a rich man in politics: "Here's a man with a ninety dollar suit an' a pleated shirt, his whiskers trimmed, nails polished—and yet anybody walkin' up street with him is under suspicion."

---

* Years later "Il Janitoro" was used for a skit at the Lambs Club in New York. Someone who saw it there liked it so well he took the idea to London and under a different title it ran for a season at the Empire Theater. George Ade got no credit— nor royalty.

As soon as characters seemed to George to grow stale he developed new ones. He brought in "Min Sargent" an office girl of self-assurance, a counterpart of "Artie," and "Edward Worthington Swinger" who could win the interest of girls but yet had his troubles. We shall meet Swinger again. Then there was "The Frisbee Club," and a series about "Ollie and Freddie," well-bred young men who were particular about stylish clothes and avoided slang. A series about "Mac, Jim and Barney" came out of talks between Ade and McCutcheon and a Purdue friend who tarried with them for a time as house guest. Many of the talks were about the borrowing habits of the guest. "Jim" said that "Barney" was what a banker would call "good but slow." Another character was a slangy gamin, "the Hickey boy."

A series begun in '97 and continued into '98 was of burlesque detective stories, the nickel library variety, suggested by George's haymow reading in boyhood. The first bore the title, "Handsome Cyril, or the Messenger Boy with the Warm Feet." It was preceded by an announcement: "It is the intention to present occasionally in this column stories which will appeal to the younger members of the family. These stories will deal, in a realistic style, with life in Chicago, and will be more or less permeated by adventure."

One "nursery tale" had a title, "Clarence Allen, the Hypnotic Boy Journalist, or the Mysterious Disappearance of the United States Government Bonds." A chapter from it gives a hint of the series.

"The Daily Beacon, like all great newspapers, had a pack of genuine Siberian bloodhounds, to be used for tracking criminals.

"Our hero, after making out an expense account, selected two of the largest and fiercest bloodhounds and showed them the plaster cast of the footprint which he had taken at the Hare residence.

"The intelligent animals knew at a glance what was expected of them, and in a few moments they were on the scene, followed by our alert young hero, Clarence Allen, the hypnotic boy journalist, who carried a revolver tightly clenched in his right hand.

"For nearly an hour no one spoke.

"Then the dogs stopped in front of an old stone house with tall elms surrounding it.

" 'This is the place,' said Clarence Allen, concealing himself in a thicket to await developments.

"After a few moments he chanced to look around, and his blood froze in his veins.

"Some one had stolen the dogs!"

A few of the stories in this series were afterward published in colorful pamphlets, and later many of them as a book with the title, *Bang! Bang!*

George Ade was probably the first newspaper writer to recognize the growing appeal of golf to the general reader. As early as the autumn of 1897 he was doing skits about golf. One of these, on October 1, was in the form of a three-act comedy. "The hero, Mr. Arbuckle, and the heroine, Miss Meadows, are discovered in a vast wilderness playing golf. They have been out two days and are dying of hunger, but they are still playing. The caddie weeps bitterly and asks to be taken home. They see a man crawling out of a sand pit (called a hazard) and they hail him."

The collaboration of Ade and McCutcheon ended late in '97, never to be resumed as staff members of the *Record*. Their friend, Frank A. Vanderlip, then Assistant Secretary of the Treasury, offered them and Edward M. Harden of the *Tribune,* an opportunity to go around the world, from Newport News to California, via Suez, on the new revenue cutter *McCulloch*. George declined. "Too many days at sea and too few ports," he said.

McCutcheon and Harden went, and the *McCullough* chanced to

arrive at the Philippines in time to join Admiral Dewey's fleet and take part in the Battle of Manila Bay. Harden's report to his paper of the Battle of Manila was one of the great scoops of newspaper history. Admiral Dewey's own cable to Washington suffered a delay in transit but Harden's got through and President McKinley first learned what had happened when a newspaper editor telephoned, getting him out of bed, to read to him Harden's story.

McCutcheon stayed in the Philippines to become a war correspondent and showed that he could use his pencil for writing as ably as for drawing. His *Stories of Filipino Warfare,* as well as his *Notes from Foreign Lands* and the *Chicago Record War Stories* made him famous in a new field. Before he got back to Chicago in 1900 he had gone to South Africa for a look at the Boer War.

Meanwhile, George Ade, too, went traveling again in '98, "rummaging through southern and eastern Europe for nearly three months, appointing correspondents for Victor Lawson's newspapers and trying to convince them that a king heading a parade is not important news for Chicago readers. He was in France, Switzerland, Italy, Austria, Hungary, Roumania, Servia, Bulgaria, Turkey, Syria, Greece and Corfu.

He was in Venice when the German Kaiser was there on board the imperial yacht, and he went by gondola to have a look at the yacht. "As we moved alongside we saw a distinguished looking member of the royal family standing by the rail, looking out toward the Lido. Then we saw the Kaiser himself come up from a companionway and approach his friend on tiptoe and give him a swinging blow in the back which almost knocked him overboard. When the assaulted party turned around and looked at Wilhelm, the latter roared with laughter and the Baron, or whatever he was, had to join in. It was apparent, even in 1898, that anyone who had that kind of sense of humor might eventually hit the wrong man on the back."

George's European trip in '98 gave him material for a series of travel articles that appeared in his regular space every few days, from September '98 until toward the end of June '99, first under the title, "What a man Sees Who Goes Away from Home," and then headed "Quiet Adventures of a Journey in Europe."

While the Spanish-American War was on, Victor Lawson sent George a message asking him to go to Spain. George replied that he did not believe Spain would be a desirable place for an American. "Pass yourself off as an Englishman," came a message from Lawson.

"I couldn't fool even a Spaniard into thinking I'm an Englishman," said George. "They would know I'm from Indiana."

During George's absence abroad his "Stories of the Street and of the Town" were written by Trumbull White, afterward editor of *Everybody's Magazine*, "Billy" Inglehart, later publisher of a newspaper in Salt Lake City, Kennett Harris and Ray Stannard Baker.

There was still no lack of talent on the *Record*. A newcomer on the staff was a young cub reporter, just out of Chicago University, who seemed handicapped by his extreme diffidence. He never uttered a word unless spoken to and looked frightened when anyone said so much as good morning to him. Gradually he got over his shyness and in later years, when Secretary of the Interior, became competent at expressing himself—Harold L. Ickes.

George was permitted to sign his columns beginning in 1898. An increasing number of people in Chicago were becoming aware that a man of rare talent was in their midst. Albert Nicholas Hosking, editor and publisher of a short-lived magazine, *Pickwick, The Town Crier*, devoted a special issue to Ade.

A year or two later a Chicago publishing firm brought out

Short Story Masterpieces "by the Best American Authors" containing two stories from George's department in the *Record*. This was the first anthology to include Ade material.

Not many knew that George was doing another department of stories once a week. Friends of his had started a weekly paper, the *Evening Lamp,* that appeared on Saturday, and to help them he wrote for each issue during several months, a column of stories similar to those he did for the *Record,* under the signature that he had used once before, "John Hazelden." Many told George that he had a clever imitator.

Busy as he was, George was frequently lending a hand in the work or careers of others. He helped "Alf" Ringling, the circus man, compile the circus yearbook, a record of one season on the road, and he referred to the elephants as "a ponderous pyramid of primitive pachyderms." In ecstasies Ringling exclaimed, "You have struck the keynote of circus advertising."

Not long afterward George was invited by Will J. Davis, theater manager (whose wife, Jessie Bartlett Davis, was a famous light opera singer), to accompany him to a summer theater to hear a young woman from Milwaukee, named Nora Bayes, said to have a good voice and stage presence. Davis wanted advice about engaging her. "She was as dignified as a church soprano up in a choir loft. The jury met her later in the evening and she had a ready sense of humor and a quick wit, a most amusing vocabulary, and a practical, sensible view of things in general." George said it would be wonderful if she were more the comedienne. She promised to try and discovered that she could be a comedienne as well as a singer. It was the beginning of a long friendship, and after she became famous in vaudeville and revues, Nora Bayes always said George had done most to give her a start.

As early as '95 George had helped to reshape the career of his friend McCutcheon. The managing editor thought that with a presidential campaign in the offing the *Record* should have daily cartoons, and he wanted McCutcheon to do them. McCutcheon did not think his talents suited to cartooning; but George urged him and promised to supply the ideas. Every afternoon during the McKinley-Bryan campaign George sat down with the managing editor to determine "what Mac ought to draw." George provided the subject as well as the title above the cartoon and the legend below. Later he suggested that John do a series on life in a small town. "Call the town Bird Center," he proposed. That series became one of McCutcheon's great successes in a career that made him the dean of American cartoonists.

13

The First Ade Fable

"ONE MORNING," wrote George Ade, "I sat at the desk and gazed at the empty soft paper, and realized the necessity of concocting something different. The changes had been wrung through weary months and years on blank verse, catechism, rhyme, broken prose, the drama form of dialogue, and staccato paragraphs.

"Why not a fable for a change? And instead of slavishly copying Aesop and LaFontaine, why not retain the archaic form and the stilted manner of composition and, for purposes of novelty, permit the language to be 'fly,' modern, undignified, quite up to the moment?

"Now, up to this time I had gone fairly straight. . . . I had written slang, but always in the third person. People in my stories had talked slang, but only when they had to do so in order to be plausible and probable. If I used a word or a phrase which was reasonably under suspicion, I would hang up the quotation marks so that the reader might know that I was not approving the language, but merely utilizing it for picturesque effect.

"Of course I had been tempted a million times to use the new idioms and the current catch phrases, because they were the salt needed for the proper savoring. But I didn't want to fly-speck my compositions with quotation marks, and I had a real fear of the law against dealing in contraband."

Long afterward George wrote of his first fable that it seemed advisable for the thing to be called a "Fable in Slang," ". . . so that no one might accept the article under a misapprehension, and further, lest the critical-minded might suspect that the colloquial-isms were used through a vulgar ignorance of proper speech and not in a mere cut-up spirit . . ." But "after affixing the 'Poison' label," he could put in anything.

The first fable, September 17, 1897, carried no such label; but George made it plain that he was just cutting up. The long words had the syllables hyphenated as in *Swiss Family Robinson* and other tales for children.

"Once there were two Sis-ters. They lived in Chi-ca-go. One was a Plain Girl, but she had a Good Heart. She was stu-di-ous and took first Hon-ors at the Gram-mar School.

"She cared more for the Graces of Mind than she did for mere Out-ward Show. Her Sis-ter was a Friv-o-lous Girl. . . .

"The Friv-o-lous Girl who had naught to com-mend her except a Beauty which fad-eth, became Cashier in a Quick Lunch Es-tab-lish-ment and the Pat-ron-age increased largely. She chewed **Gum** and said 'Ain't,' but she be-came pop-u-lar just the same. . . ."

When George rewrote the little story, he called it "The Fable of Sister Mae Who Did As Well As Could Be Expected." He dropped the hyphens and made other changes but kept the plot. Luella was a good girl, but her features did not seem to know the value of Team Work. Her clothes were an intermittent Fit. She was a lumpy Dresser. She worked in a factory, and every Saturday Evening when Work was called on account of Darkness, the Boss met her as she went out and crowded Three Dollars on her. Sister Mae was different. She was short on Intellect but Long on Shape. She became Cashier in a Lunch Room and was a Strong Card. Her Date Book had to be kept on the Double Entry System. She married a Bucket-Shop Man who was not Handsome but was awful Generous. Mae bought a Thumb Ring and a Pug Dog and the Smell of Cooking made her Faint. But did she forget Luella? No indeed. She took her away from the Factory and gave her a

Position as assistant cook at Five a week. The moral was: Industry and Perseverance bring a sure Reward.

The revised version George liked better, but the original form had pleased the customers. "Next day the score-keepers told me I had knocked a home run. The young women on the staff told me the piece was 'just killing.'"

George had no intention of doing other fables in slang. "It was simply a little experiment in outlawry. . . . It went into the grist as a thousand other items had gone before . . ." A month later another fable appeared, about two boys, Bill and Dan, who lived on adjoining farms, but it was not in slang. Then he did a fable, also free from slang, about a Chicago traveler who was always finding fault with his home town. For eight months he wrote no more fables and evidently was trying to live down what he feared was a youthful indiscretion. Events however were shaping his plans.

"The publishers kept dinging at me to stop trifling with the fragmentary sketches, and to write a regular full-book story, a novel—possibly the great American novel.

"A virtual promise was made to the publisher—that as soon as the bank account could stand alone George would retire from the newspaper shop and get off in a quiet corner somewhere and write one story large enough to fill a book. . . .

"The subject matter and even the title were settled upon—also the binding. One day I saw a beautiful 'dummy' of my book-to-be, full size, in gray and green, with the title, 'The College Widow,' stamped on the back.

"How proud I was of that book—that 'dummy!' Of course, the pages were still blank, but the whole was outlined in the back of my head, and all I had to do was to sit down, some time or other, and transfer it from the caput to the yellow paper. Which I never did. . . . I learned that somehow I couldn't jump off the journalistic treadmill. The old weekly pay envelope was a certainty which I hesitated to exchange for an uncertain payment of royalties somewhere in the glimmering future.

"The publisher camped on my trail. He had been promised a book. The salesman had gone on the road and exhibited beautiful 'dummy' copies of 'The College Widow,' and had taken orders and made indefinite promises of shipment.

"I couldn't keep a department going and write a novel on the side. I had rashly promised something which could not be delivered."

George had joined the Chicago Athletic Club. Some of his friends there, especially John Jenks, kept quoting so enthusiastically from his one fable in slang, and urging him to do others, that one July day, ten months after the publication of the first one, he devoted his space in the *Record* to two more, plainly labeled "Fables in Slang." One was about the girl whose soul panted for the higher life and who dreamed of the ideal husband who would be wearing "a Prince Albert coat, a neat Derby Hat and godlike Whiskers." But she finally was married to a janitor named Ernest. "He had been kicked in the Head by a Mule when young and believed everything he read in the Sunday papers."

George found that "it was a great lark to write in slang—just like gorging on forbidden fruit. The bridle was off and all rules abolished."

Then his book publishers took notice. Despairing of ever seeing that Ade novel advance beyond the "dummy" stage, Stone & Co. urged him to do enough of the fables to make a book and they would substitute it for *The College Widow*. They would call the book *Fables in Slang*.

"Closed in upon by frantic advisers, the harried young author began to write fables in slang with both hands.

"In vain did he protest that he was not a specialist in the easygoing vernacular, and that he wanted to deal with life as it is instead of verbal buck dancing and a bizarre costuming of capital letters.

"The friends told him to take the gifts that were falling into his lap, and not crave the golden persimmons that grow on the hill tops.

"So the crazy fables became a glaring feature of our newspaper department."

After the fables got to appearing about once a week, the managing editor asked George if he would turn them in a few days in advance. Some papers in other cities had been reprinting the fables and now had offered to pay for them if they could use them on the same day as the *Record*.

Nothing was said about more money for George, but he began to wonder.

In June '99 he wrote to Victor Lawson that he had "passed the limit of usefulness in the 'streets' department" and would like to be "at liberty for an indefinite period." He suggested that he might turn in material for his department only twice a week.

Lawson's reply made George hesitate. Regarding the notation that he had passed the "limit of usefulness," Lawson wrote, "It is a pleasure to say to you that you are probably the sole and exclusive owner of that information." He added that he and the managing editor would not divulge that secret. "If we can't get six stories," said Lawson, "we are just one-third as satisfied to get two."

George decided to stay with the *Record* and do his daily department a little longer, but he promised himself that he would become a free-lance writer not later than the end of his tenth year with the paper, around July 1, 1900. Meanwhile, Stone & Co. were making plans to bring out *Fables in Slang* in December '99. Perhaps the book would provide him with enough money for a little holiday. He was now receiving $65 a week, a top salary on the paper, and it would take courage to cut loose from the pay roll, but he believed that he could somehow contrive to make a living. At any rate, he would see if he could write something beyond the scope of his newspaper department. Possibly he might at last do that novel, *The College Widow*.

In October he had a "memorable meeting" with his great admirer, William D. Howells, who stopped in Chicago on a trip to Iowa. Howells, while complimenting him on some of the Fables he had seen, urged him to do a series or a book of straight realism about real people—something of the *Doc' Horne* variety. Why, suggested Howells, wouldn't it be a good idea for him to travel for two or three weeks with a circus?

George liked that idea and proposed to his friend Alf Ringling that he join the Ringling show when it began its tour the next spring. Ringling told him he ought to make the tour not in the spring but immediately, as the show was in the South and there would be more local color in the black belt. George accepted Ringling's advice, arranged with the managing editor to substitute a circus series for the street stories and set out to join the Ringling show at Union City, Tennessee. His observations on circus life, about a dozen articles, which occupied his space off and on for several weeks, were headed "With the Elephant and the Clown in Dixie."

By way of repaying the circus hospitality George offered to help in the press relations department. In doing this he discovered how easy it is to commit a grievous error. When a newspaperman asked him how many elephants the show had, he said fifteen, the number he had seen in the ring, and the paper referred to that number. Then the manager of the circus came to George almost in tears to remind him that there were nineteen elephants. Sadly he said, "I know you meant all right, but, my boy, no circus man should ever underestimate the number of elephants."

One thing George found out—but which he did not then publish—was that the Eskimo man and wife in the side show, "hailing from beyond the Arctic circle and subsisting on tallow candles and whale blubber," owned a neat little bungalow in Kendallville, Indiana, and went south every winter because they disliked cold weather.

He spent much time in the side show, listening to the comments of the spectators regarding the freaks, and vice versa. He heard a colored woman exclaim over the tattooed Venus: "Look at all the pictures on huh tights!" Her companion said: "Them pictures ain't on no tights, chile. That's the lady huhself."

The three-legged boy started some banter with another colored woman, but she got mad and said she wouldn't stand for no insults, "no mattah how many legs he's got."

When a powerful six-foot yokel tried to get funny with the midget woman, she told him: "Run along, little boy."

George took pity on two little colored boys looking wistfully at the entrance to the side show and asked permission to pass them in. But when he bade them to enter, they ran away in alarm. Somebody had told them the show was looking for some boys to wash the snakes!

One day George noticed an unusually big crowd on the circus grounds and remarked to the ticket seller that they should have a packed tent. But the ticket seller shook his head and declared that the crowd inside would be thin. How did he know? "They haven't any money. They're not eating. If they had money they'd be eating bananas, bologna, and popcorn."

George warmed up to the man in charge of the elephants, who got tired of being asked if they fed the elephants raw meat or cooked meat, and always replied out of the corner of his mouth: "Roast quail."

A story George heard, thenceforth one of his favorites, was

about a song-and-dance team who worked in the concert that followed the regular circus acts. One of the team fell in love with
the tattooed lady in the side show and married her. His partner
was indignant. "You're breakin' up our act," he said. "How'd
you happen to fall for that dame?"

"I'll tell you," replied the bridegroom. "She's a nice woman and
awful good company, and besides, I just love to look at pictures."

14

He Shows Us Ourselves

FABLES IN SLANG was announced for publication on December 9, 1899, but not many copies reached the bookstores until January. Immediately it caught the public favor. It was called the book of the year. By the end of 1900 the publisher advertised that it was "nearing its one hundred thousandth copy sold." Actually, 69,000 copies were sold during 1900. Its success followed closely that of *The Gentleman from Indiana,* the first novel by George's young friend Booth Tarkington.

George Ade became suddenly famous. People of every kind of reading taste were talking about the Fables. They were quoted by high school boys, college boys, college professors, plain people, millionaires, writers, everybody. William Allen White, Kansas editor and novelist, told George in a letter: "I would rather have written *Fables in Slang* than be President."

Apologetic for taking so many liberties with the language, Ade expected attacks from the higher critics. But they, too, praised *Fables in Slang.* Brander Matthews, of Columbia University, told the publisher that it was one of the best things he had ever read. William Dean Howells said: "His portrayal of life is almost absolute in its perfection—you experience something of the bliss of looking at your own photograph. . . ."*

Fables in Slang owed part of its success to its variety. One Fable

---

* Howells' approval of the Fables meant much to Ade, for he knew that even Mark Twain had leaned on Howells for advice. Years afterward when he came upon some pages of the "Editor's Easy Chair" in *Harper's* containing Howells' comments on the Fables he wrote on the margin for his secretary: "Don't lose this. I am more proud of this article . . . than of anything else written about me."

was about the lady with the lorgnette who had nothing else to do, and no children to look after, so she thought she would be benevolent. Another was about the preacher whose pew-holders began to think he was common, because they could understand everything he said, until he started in to "hand out a little Guff." A memorable one dealt with the amazing Mr. Byrd and his manner of entertaining the Country Customer. Still another told of what happened the night the men came to the women's club. Ade seemed to have observed every kind of human foible. Anyone who read the Fables learned more about the neighbors.

Here is a sample Fable, "The Two Mandolin Players and the Willing Performer," always a favorite with Ade himself:

A very attractive Debutante knew two Young Men who called on her every Thursday Evening, and brought their Mandolins along.

They were Conventional Young Men, of the Kind that you see wearing Spring Overcoats in the Clothing Advertisements. One was named Fred, and the other was Eustace.

The Mothers of the Neighborhood often remarked, "What Perfect Manners Fred and Eustace have!" Merely as an aside it may be added that Fred and Eustace were more Popular with the Mothers than they were with the Younger Set, although no one could say a Word against either of them. Only it was rumored in Keen Society that they didn't Belong. The Fact that they went Calling in a Crowd, and took their Mandolins along, may give the Acute Reader some Idea of the Life that Fred and Eustace held out to the Young Women of their Acquaintance.

The Debutante's name was Myrtle. Her Parents were very Watchful, and did not encourage her to receive Callers, except such as were known to be Exemplary Young Men. Fred and Eustace were a few of those who escaped the Black List. Myrtle always appeared to be glad to see them, and they regarded her as a Darned Swell Girl.

Fred's Cousin came from St. Paul on a Visit; and one Day,

in the Street, he saw Myrtle, and noticed that Fred tipped his Hat, and gave her a Stage Smile.

"Oh, Queen of Sheba!" exclaimed the Cousin from St. Paul, whose name was Gus, as he stood stock still, and watched Myrtle's Reversible Plaid disappear around a Corner. "She's a Bird. Do you know her well?"

"I Know her Quite Well," replied Fred coldly. "She is a Charming Girl."

"She is all of that. You're a great Describer. And now what Night are you going to take me around to Call on her?"

Fred very naturally Hemmed and Hawed. It must be remembered that Myrtle was a member of an Excellent Family, and had been schooled in the Proprieties, and it was not to be supposed that she would crave the Society of slangy old Gus, who had an abounding Nerve, and furthermore was as Fresh as the Mountain Air.

He was the Kind of Fellow who would see a Girl twice, and then, upon meeting her the Third Time, he would go up and straighten her Cravat for her, and call her by her First Name.

Put him into a Strange Company—en route to a Picnic—and by the time the Baskets were unpacked he would have a Blonde all to himself, and she would have traded her Fan for his College Pin.

If a Fair-Looker on the Street happened to glance at him Hard he would run up and seize her by the Hand, and convince her that they had Met. And he always Got Away with it, too.

In a Department Store, while waiting for the Cash Boy to come back with the Change, he would find out the Girl's Name, her Favorite Flower, and where a Letter would reach her.

Upon entering a Parlor Car at St. Paul he would select a Chair next to the Most Promising One in Sight, and ask her if she cared to have the Shade lowered. Before the Train cleared the Yards he would have the Porter bringing a Foot-Stool for the Lady.

At Hastings he would be asking her if she wanted Something to Read.

At Red Wing he would be telling her that she resembled

Maxine Elliott, and showing her his Watch, left to him by his Grandfather, a Prominent Virginian.

At La Crosse he would be reading the Menu Card to her, and telling her how different it is when you have Some One to join you in a Bite.

At Milwaukee he would go out and buy a Bouquet for her, and when they rode into Chicago they would be looking out of the same Window, and he would be arranging for her Baggage with the Transfer Man. After that they would be Old Friends.

Now, Fred and Eustace had been at School with Gus, and they had seen his Work, and they were not disposed to Introduce him into One of the most Exclusive Homes in the City.

They had known Myrtle for many Years; but they did not dare to Address her by her First Name, and they were Positive that if Gus attempted any of his usual Tactics with her she would be Offended; and, naturally enough, they would be Blamed for bringing him to the House.

But Gus insisted. He said he had seen Myrtle, and she Suited him from the Ground up, and he proposed to have Friendly Doings with her. At last they told him they would take him if he promised to Behave. Fred warned him that Myrtle would frown down any Attempt to be Familiar on Short Acquaintance, and Eustace said that as long as he had known Myrtle he had never Presumed to be Free and Forward with her. He had simply played the Mandolin. That was as Far Along as he had ever got.

Gus told them not to Worry about him. All he asked was a Start. He said he was a Willing Performer, but as yet he never had been Disqualified for Crowding. Fred and Eustace took this to mean that he would not Overplay his Attentions, so they escorted him to the House.

As soon as he had been Presented, Gus showed her where to sit on the Sofa, then he placed himself about Six Inches away and began to Buzz, looking her straight in the Eye. He said that when he first saw her he Mistook her for Miss Prentice, who was said to be the Most Beautiful Girl in St. Paul, only, when he came closer, he saw that it couldn't be Miss Prentice, because Miss Prentice didn't have such Lovely Hair. Then he asked her the Month of her Birth and told her

Fortune, thereby coming nearer to Holding her Hand within Eight Minutes than Eustace had come in a Lifetime.

"Play something, Boys," he Ordered, just as if he had paid them Money to come along and make Music for him.

They unlimbered their Mandolins and began to play a Sousa March. He asked Myrtle if she had seen the New Moon. She replied that she had not, so they went Outside.

When Fred and Eustace finished the first Piece, Gus appeared at the open Window, and asked them to play "The Georgia Camp-Meeting," which had always been one of his Favorites.

So they played that, and when they had Concluded there came a Voice from the Outer Darkness, and it was the Voice of Myrtle. She said: "I'll tell you what to Play; play the Intermezzo."

Fred and Eustace exchanged Glances. They began to Perceive that they had been backed into a Siding. With a few Potted Palms in front of them, and two Cards from the Union, they would have been just the same as a Hired Orchestra.

But they played the Intermezzo and felt Peevish. Then they went to the Window and looked out. Gus and Myrtle were sitting in the Hammock, which had quite a Pitch toward the Center. Gus had braced himself by Holding to the back of the Hammock. He did not have his Arm around Myrtle, but he had it Extended in a Line parallel with her Back. What he had done wouldn't Justify a Girl in saying, "Sir!" but it started a Real Scandal with Fred and Eustace. They saw that the only Way to Get Even with her was to go Home without saying "Good Night." So they slipped out the Side Door, shivering with Indignation.

After that, for several Weeks, Gus kept Myrtle so Busy that she had no Time to think of considering other Candidates. He sent Books to her Mother, and allowed the Old Gentleman to take Chips away from him at Poker.

They were Married in the Autumn, and Father-in-Law took Gus into the Firm, saying that he had needed a good Pusher for a Long Time.

At the Wedding the two Mandolin Players were permitted to act as Ushers.

MORAL: *To get a fair Trial of Speed, use a Pace-Maker.*

The country-wide popularity of the Fables did not come from a public thirst for new slang, for the Fables assayed a surprisingly small amount of slang, little coined by Ade. It was not slang so much as the vernacular. H. L. Mencken wrote, "Those phrases of his sometimes wear the external vestments of a passing slang, but they were no more commonplace or vulgar at bottom than Gray's 'mute, inglorious Milton,' or the 'somewhere east of Suez' of Kipling. They light up a whole scene in a flash. They are the running evidences of an eye that sees clearly and of a mind that thinks shrewdly. . . . How easy it was to imitate Ade's manner—and how impossible to imitate his matter."

One reason for the success of the Fables was their indigenous American quality; and they were American because George Ade, brought up in an American way, in a typically American region, had liked the people about him. As Carl Van Doren says, Ade was "intimately kin to the folk and yet detached from it by genius."

Readers not only gave the Fables the praise of the merriest laughter; they loved the author. He was their friend. He seemed sure that the characters he wrote about would appreciate the joke. He never sneered. He taught us to laugh at ourselves. When he rapped affectations and hypocrisy, it was not because they annoyed him; they made him happy. He liked people to be harmlessly or unconsciously funny. As Booth Tarkington observed, "Ade did not say, 'See this fellow, how ridiculous he is'—but rather, 'How priceless he is. Pray heaven he be left untouched!'" No one ever saw George Ade angry, or even confused, and no one ever got angry at him, but angry people tickled him.

Ade himself said the idea "was to tell the truth about what is going on and get a little fun out of the foibles and weaknesses and vanities of a lot of our neighbors without being brutal or insulting."

Only occasionally did he let his needle sink deep enough to draw blood, as in the Fable (in a later series) about the Honest Money-Maker whose overworked wife gave out. "Next afternoon he was out Dickering for a Bull, and his Woman, lying on the cheap Bedstead, up under the hot roof, folded her lean Hands and slipped away to the only Rest she had ever known since she tied up with a Prosperous and Respected Farmer." The moral was: "Be Honest and Respected and it Goes."

While *Fables in Slang* was gaining hilarious readers, George Ade received a proposal from a New York publisher, R. H. Russell, for a series of Fables once a week to newspapers. Russell had been successful in syndicating the "Mr. Dooley" articles, and George was willing to let him try selling the Fables. It was agreed that Russell should offer to the newspapers a series of ten, the first of them to be released for publication on September 30, 1900.

George assumed in the beginning that at the most there would be only one more short series to follow the first. He had already delivered to his publishers, enough new material for another book to be called *More Fables*. He did not expect ever to write anything else that was labeled slang, and he was so sure that line was about played out that, soon after leaving the *Record*, around July 1, 1900, he felt warranted in setting out for a vacation trip to China and Japan, and a visit with John McCutcheon, who was still in the Philippines.

Russell, too, expected only a modest success from that series of ten Fables, and, when he began to call upon managing editors, his hopes sank lower. Today successful columnists take in money by the bale and number their papers by the hundreds; but at the turn of the century syndicating was only beginning. The day when a paper would pay $100 for each Ade Fable was in the future. Managing editors thought Russell was asking too high a price. Only two papers, the *Record* in Chicago, and the New York *Herald* paid as much as $30 a week at first. Victor Lawson, owner of the *Record,* was upset when Russell quoted the price. He remembered only that he had been paying George Ade $65 a week. The thought of paying $30 for a single item shocked him. But when Russell made a motion as if to put the contract back into his pocket, remarking that another paper wanted the Fables, and that Ade had insisted upon the *Record* having the first chance, Lawson reached for his pen.

Only thirty-nine papers had bought the Fables. The *Commercial-Appeal,* at Memphis, Tennessee, dropped the series rather than pay $2.50 a week; and the Detroit *Free Press* complained that $6 a week was too much unless the paper could have exclusive rights for the entire state of Michigan. However, a rival Detroit paper took them at $8. Managing editors had underestimated the extraordinary pull the Fables would have with readers, but before long they began to find it out. Sales of the Fables began to increase.

When George Ade returned from the Orient in the autumn of 1900, the reports from the syndicate and from his publisher did not make him feel poverty-stricken. He had left Chicago with what he had not been quite able to believe was a literary success; now it began to look as if he had also a bonanza. Soon he joined Room Number Six, an inner circle that occupied one floor at the Chicago Athletic Club, and he no longer stinted himself on living expenses. His "share of the conspiracy" was nearly $200 a week, and soon it had doubled. *Fables in Slang* was still selling, about one thousand·copies a month. In December *More Fables* appeared and it sold almost as well as the earlier volume. It was advertised on Broadway, in New York, by men carrying sandwich signboards, a form of advertising prohibited in Chicago.

Reader interest in the Fables kept increasing. It became an important asset to a newspaper to have a contract for them. Mem-

bers of a family were on the front porch waiting for the boy with
the Sunday paper, each one eager for first chance at the Fable. For
a while each issue of *Collier's Weekly* carried a syndicated Fable
even though it had already appeared in newspapers. Magazines
of the highest literary quality besieged George for Fables, and
Robert Underwood Johnson of the *Century* persisted until he got
one or two which he published with no apology for the slang.
Harper's Weekly also wanted them. The Fables were to be a
newspaper syndicate feature off and on for thirty years.

Each week George found himself with $500 to $1,000 for which
he had no immediate need. Instead of depositing the spare funds
in one of the Chicago banks, he sent his checks to his father for
deposit in the little bank in which the father was still cashier, at
Kentland. "I sent him all my checks," said George, "so that he
could show them to the loyal townspeople, well-wishers, and
members of the Helping Hand who had told him in 1883 that
it was a mistake to send me to college." George suspected that
his father feared he was concealing some of his sources of income,
whereas in truth he could have had even more money, for Arthur
Brisbane, top editor of the Hearst papers, went to Chicago to invite
him to become a Hearst writer, and name his own salary, but this
offer did not tempt him.

Some of the subjects and phrases from those early Fables and
later ones stick in the memory: The Lady who invariably was
first over the Fence in the Mad Pursuit of Culture; the Boarder
who belonged to a Social Purity Club that had a Yell; the parents
who knew all about the unbridled Deviltry of the City, having
seen the large colored Illustrations in the Sunday papers; two
Maidens who had their Traps set and baited; the Goddess who
took her Mocha in the Feathers; the Music Teacher who came
twice each week to bridge the awful gap between Dorothy and
Chopin; the Nice Man who said Whom and wore Nose Glasses;

the man who had heard that one is permitted a certain latitude with widows, and went in for the whole 180 degrees; the woman who told the man it was terrible to hear such things as he told her and to please go ahead; the Banker whose Side Whiskers were a Tower of Strength in the Community.

And some of the Morals: It is proper to enjoy the Cheaper Grades of Art, but they should not be formally Indorsed; life is a series of Relapses and Recoveries; a Friend who is very Near and Dear may in Time become as useless as a Relative; to insure Peace of Mind, Ignore the Rules and Regulations; for Parlor Use the Vague Generality is a Life-Saver; those who Marry to Escape Something usually find Something Else; don't try to Marry an entire Family or it may work out that Way.

One day George jotted down several pages of figures of speech for use in his Fables, and the pages have been preserved. Here one finds such expressions as: destiny put a tag on him; land of the deadly lap-supper; gold-plated trap baited with orchids; kept hurling bouquets until he lost control; staggered and threw a shoe; got elbowed into background; blew up in the stretch; played his long-stemmed rose on a dead one; put the casters under him; homicide wagon; held on like a summer cold; town trifler; excess baggage; damp firecracker; social fizzle; couldn't be seen with binoculars; chinless Percy wearing a lady's watch chain; fellow with all goods hung out in front; bigger than a church debt; like superintendent of a morgue.

He was particular about names for his characters. One man he named Mordecai F. Quinsy, and a plump woman he called Azalea. He liked the names Otis and Herbert for men and Flora or Myrtle for women. (Once when he introduced Otis Skinner, the actor, at a dinner, George said he thought one reason he was loved was for the name Otis, when it might have been Rupert or Algernon.) In his desk he had a list of names fairly common in Indiana, but "not much used anywhere else." Among these were Orvie, Baz, Melvy, Jethro, Eck, Cad, Harve, Zimri, Lutie, Sep, Clute and Elmer.

Even as to the slang George stuck to certain niceties of distinction. "I never referred to a policeman as a 'bull,' because that word belongs in the criminal vocabulary, and mother and the girls are not supposed to be familiar with the cryptic terms of yeggmen. I never referred to a young girl as a 'chicken.' The word originated in the deepest pits of white slavery. . . . A young girl may be a flapper, a bud, a peach, a pippin, a lollypaloozer, a nectarine, a cutie, a queen, the one best bet, a daisy, or even a baby doll, without being insulted; but never a 'chicken.'. . . . There are words of popular circulation which don't sound well in the mouth or look pretty in type. 'Slob' has always been in the *Index Expurgatorius*. Our fellow citizen may be a dub or even a lobster, and possibly a mutt, but let us draw the line on 'slob.'"

He usually wrote a Fable at one sitting. And some of the early manuscripts, still preserved, show that he seldom changed a word.

While contributing to Indiana's literary fame, George helped to start another Hoosier author on the road to success. His old friend, George Barr McCutcheon, still city editor of the *Courier* in Lafayette at a modest salary, showed up in Chicago and said he wanted some sound advice. He confided that he had been writing novels. Indeed, he had completed six, and he felt sure they were better than many being published, but though he had spent plenty of money on postage to send them to various publishers, he had received almost no encouragement. Finally, for one of them, *Graustark,* he had an offer of a paltry $500 with no royalties. He thought the offer an insult and was not inclined to accept.

"Out of the wealth of my wisdom," George has written, "I spared him the following advice: 'Go ahead and accept. If the publisher gets your book for a small figure he will advertise it extensively, for the profits of the sales will accrue to him. If the book is a success, you can get more money for your next ones. The important thing is to break into print at once, get your name on a good book issued by a first-class publisher and make yourself known to the public, but—don't sign up for any future books. Keep yourself free and get your important returns on books that come later."

McCutcheon acted on the advice and turned over the manuscript for $500. *Graustark* was an astounding success and brought the publisher so much money that he was enough conscience-stricken to give the author $2,000 more. The book was followed by *Brewster's Millions* and a long list of others that made the author famous and a millionaire.

Perhaps we may properly pause to wonder what it was about Indiana that caused it to continue to produce successful authors. To what extent has the Hoosier background been responsible for the literary achievements of Edward Eggleston, Lew Wallace, Riley, Ade, Tarkington, the McCutcheons, Meredith Nicholson, David Graham Phillips, Theodore Dreiser and others? For one thing, Indiana in its beginning was a happy combination of pioneer spirit with a surprisingly high degree of culture. Anyone who visits those old Ohio river towns of Vevay and Madison, as quaint and charming as any in New England, is likely to conclude that the early settlers were cultivated. As long ago as 1872 Indiana ranked sixth of all the states in the number of colleges, and seventh as to number of college students. It was not so much that the colleges turned out authors. The point is that the colleges helped to create an atmosphere of culture in which it was respectable to be an author. As George Ade himself has expressed it, the

Hoosier "is a student by choice, a poet by sneaking inclination and a story-teller by reason of his nativity."

George thought in 1900 that after a few more months he would break away from Fables. "The idea was to grab a lot of careless money before the reading public recovered its equilibrium, and then, later on, with bags of gold piled in the doorway to keep the wolf out, return to the consecrated job of writing long and photographic reports of life in the Middle West."

He knew that humor is dangerous, that anything really funny sets a precedent hard to keep up. "The successful humorist is often an adventurous person who goes up in a balloon without previously making any arrangements for alighting. He sails skyward in a gust of public favor and then drifts until a merciful twilight hides his slow collapse and descent to earth."

To his great admirer, Howells, he wrote, "Four times I have given my ultimatum, 'no more of this sickening slang,' and on each occasion Mr. Russell has shown me the balance-sheet and painted for me a picture of the mortgages being lifted from the old homestead in Indiana, and my resistance has become more feeble."

Howells had written to him: "I read you morning and night—the first thing and the last thing." He added that he wished George would write another *Doc' Horne*.

In his reply George also said: "It cheers me exceedingly to read your kind words, especially since you choose to remember that picked-up and pitched-together little volume of 'Doc' Horne.' I believe that the sale of 'Doc' Horne' has been, approximately, eight copies—the Fables, four million (publisher's statement). Don't cease to hope for me, as I shall get around to the work I like and swear off on Capital Letters sooner or later."

So sudden had been George's national fame that thousands of Ade enthusiasts did not even know how to pronounce his name.

About half of his readers called it Addie. Once when he registered at a hotel the clerk inquired, "Is that a name or a laundry mark?"

Though George spoke exceptionally good and simple English, he had to pay a penalty for his fame as an expert in the vernacular when he made trips to other cities. Reporters thought it clever to quote him as if his conversation were like that of a Bowery character. "I hit your burg last night and, say, this hotel is a swell joint." He formed the habit of trying to forestall this sort of thing by saying to the interviewers, "Don't expect me to use slang. I put all the slang I know into my Fables and have none left for private consumption." Or in mock indignation he would say, "I have never used slang except when compelled to, to make a living."

Yet he sometimes defended slang. Once he said: "I have learned that certain small-town school teachers and normal school professors have been horrified because I took liberties with our well-known language; but I never met a professor of English in a great university who was not thoroughly interested in the enlargement of our vocabulary by the introduction of new words and new and interesting combinations of the old ones."

Another penalty for his fame came from having current quips attributed to him. One of these, hung on him with the best of intentions by his friend "Biff" Hall, nearly ruined him. Hall sent a weekly letter from Chicago to the *Dramatic Mirror* in New York, and he often put in anecdotes that he had picked up or invented. To round out one letter he wrote that George Ade had been talking with an emotional lady who gushed: "Isn't it wonderful how many bright people come from Indiana!" And George was supposed to have replied: "Yes, and the brighter they are the faster they come."

Indiana papers frothed with indignation. An editorial in a South Bend paper was headed, "Fouls His Own Nest," and among other things it said: "The names of Benjamin Harrison, Thomas

A. Hendricks, Gen. Lew Wallace, and James Whitcomb Riley will be remembered and honored long after the puny reputation of the whippersnapper who slandered our grand old commonwealth is buried in hopeless oblivion."

Knowing that Hall had meant to do him a kindness, George did not embarrass his friend by denying the story, but it took some time to live it down.

To live down the slang was more difficult. *More Fables* he believed and hoped would be the last of his slang books. But as series after series of Fables was syndicated to newspapers, they went into more books until there were about a dozen collections in book form, including *Forty Modern Fables, The Girl Proposition,* and *People You Know,* published by R. H. Russell.

All that material has had its influence on the American language. Gelett Burgess, himself a coiner of words now in the dictionaries, says: "As Slang is the illegitimate sister of Poetry, his work made a high and enlivening contribution to American literature. But he did more than that. He was one of the iconoclastic precursors of the present freedom in literary narrative. He dealt a heavy blow at the old sacrosanct 'literary style.'"

Those books of Fables are now out of print, but they are widely treasured and avidly read. Carl Sandburg, the poet and biographer of Lincoln, always keeps them within reach. He says, "About half of the Fables I go on reading and find their flavor does not stale."

In a letter written forty years after they first appeared, Ade himself said of his Fables, "The backgrounds have changed a little but people and their foibles and tomfooleries are about the same and will continue to be about the same. . . . When I read them over I have a feeling that . . . I have a very little to 'take back' or materially change."

Sometimes the discovery of the Fables by those too young to have known them when they first appeared is startling. John Abbot

Clark, a teacher of English at Michigan State College, found several of the Ade books left behind by a former student—a young man who, as it happens, was on his way to Columbia University to take his Master's degree in English. After reading them for the first time, Clark began to wonder what that student could possibly pick up in graduate school half so precious as the Fables he had left behind!

15

The Playwright

WHILE doing his daily stories for the *Record*, George Ade tried his hand at writing for the stage. His friend Ed Stair—afterward owner of the Detroit *Free Press*—was manager of the comedy team, Hap Ward and Harry Vokes, then playing a long engagement at the Great Northern Theater. Well aware that George was alert to what was going on in Chicago, Stair asked him to write an act dealing with local events. A legislative committee was then investigating reports of dark and dreadful doings in Chicago, and that suggested to George a "satirical take-off on the attempt to discover wickedness in our beloved city." When he saw his skit, *The Back-Stair Investigation*, on the stage, he said he realized that he had "committed either a misdemeanor or a crime." Stair agreed with him that it was not a masterpiece, and long kept hanging over him a threat to dig up and publish the scene.

Only once before had George written anything for the regular theater. In Lafayette he and John McCutcheon had collaborated on some verses containing local allusions for Vernona Jarbeau, a well-known comedienne in a musical play at the Grand Opera House. The verses had drawn a few giggles from the home folk and George had felt flattered, but now he doubted if he would try anything else for the stage.

Then one night in 1898 Amy Leslie gave a little supper party and seated George next to the buxom May Irwin, famous as a comedienne in farce and vaudeville. Miss Leslie had told Miss Irwin she had heard George mention an idea for a one-act play

Ade and his friend, Kenesaw M. Landis.

As John T. McCutcheon saw a picnic at Hazelden. Ade himself, James Whitcomb Riley, Booth Tarkington, Judge Landis and others appear.

or vaudeville sketch about a woman temperance reformer. She faints while in her husband's office, is revived by two drinks from a bottle sent to him by a friend in Kentucky and acquires a harmless jag without knowing that she has taken anything to drink. Miss Irwin needed a one-act play and urged George to dramatize the temperance lady for her. When George demurred, Miss Irwin offered to pay $200 and take the risk. That settled it. In a few days he said he had "slapped off" the playet, *Mrs. Peckham's Carouse.*

Miss Irwin had paid for the sketch but nothing more was heard of it, and George supposed she had found it worthless. "Every time I saw her I began to apologize for taking all that money.... I couldn't hand the money back to her because I didn't have it, but I felt very guilty and remorseful."

Eight years later May Irwin was in Boston trying out a George V. Hobart farce, *Mrs. Black Is Back.* "The players kept speeding it up until they had the running time down so that the comedy would not fill out the evening, even after they held back the overture and strung out the intermissions. May Irwin dug my play out of her trunk and used it as a certain raiser, and it must have got over pretty well because after the first performance she put the little play at the end of the bill, after the regular comedy was over. ... Later on a great many plays introduced the innocent 'bun' as a sure-fire producer of laughs, but I think 'Mrs. Peckham' was the first perfect lady who became lit up without scandalizing herself."

George had contrived a scene lasting only a few minutes in which the temperance lady never leaves her chair. She had a few gestures only and not many lines, but May Irwin made the most of the scene, acting as a fussy, meddling woman might behave when relaxed into good humor by intoxicants she did not know she had taken. The husband, pretending to be shocked by his wife's behavior, assures her that the bottle from Lexington has been destroyed; that she had the only two drinks. "And," says she, in blurred satisfaction, "the strange part of it is that they never had the slightest effect on me!"

Mrs. Peckham's Carouse became May Irwin's trade-mark in vaudeville. After many years she released it to her sister Flo, who used it for a long time. At the moderate royalty of $50 a week George would have made at least $10,000 from the little sketch. But he did not suspect how good it was at a time when he needed encouragement.

Once more he was sought by Dunne & Ryley, who had produced the musical comedy success, *Floradora*. But he had so little confidence in what he wrote that he insisted his name must not be used.

"I found myself concocting something meant to be a farce comedy, to be called *The Night of the Fourth*. John Dunne and Tom Ryley were managing Matthews and Bulger, a most popular team of patter comedians and parody singers. The opus was really written for these two stars. It had enough dialogue and connective tissue to hold it together and make it a framework on which to hang songs and dances. Dunne and Ryley took the script out west with them and produced the play in San Francisco before I knew they had accepted it. A telegram brought word that the piece had scored a resounding hit. Then came the newspaper clippings— most complimentary.

"The company worked eastward and I went to St. Paul to look at a performance and bolster up some of the weak spots. . . . It seemed a most sickly and unreal mixture of nothing much. . . . But the house was crowded and many of the lines seemed to score and the producers told me it was really a 'vehicle.'

"Well, it was a success on the road and a fizzle when done at Hammerstein's Victoria in New York with new scenery, beautiful costumes and a large company. My name was not printed on the bill and I escaped the lambasting which was accorded the play, but I suffered intensely just the same. One critic said *The Night of the Fourth* made him feel like the morning of the Fifth."

Matthews, whose health had failed, was replaced by Joseph Coyne, soon to become a musical comedy favorite, and the piece continued on the road. But George Ade still refused to let his name be used and finally sold all rights in the comedy for less than $500. Few ever learned that he was the author, even when, many years later, there was talk of making a motion picture of *The Night of the Fourth*.

George's next request to write a play came in a surprising way around July 1, 1900, a day or two before he left the *Record*. He received a call from a nineteen-year-old boy, English-born, named Alfred Wathall, who was playing first fiddle over at the Great Northern Theater and was also an amateur composer. The boy confided that he had written some tunes which he believed might be suitable for light opera. He had been a reader of "Stories of the Streets and of the Town" and thought George was the man to supply the verses. He wanted George to prepare a "book" for a light opera to be produced by some amateur organization in Chicago. George thanked him but said he did not know when he would ever find time for such an enterprise.

Then George set out for his trip to the Far East. He stayed a while in Manila with McCutcheon, and the Philippines interested him. One series in his columns had been "Stories of Benevolent Assimilation," spoofing our new imperialistic policies. He was housed with a group of correspondents who were reporting the Aguinaldo insurrection, among them, besides McCutcheon, Oliver King Davis and Frederick Palmer. From these correspondents he heard strange and amusing tales regarding the American negotiations with Hadji Jamalol Ki-Ram, the Sultan of Jolo, the chief island of the Sulu archipelago, "an untamed Moro chieftain who was trying to adapt himself to Uncle Sam's rules and by-laws without giving up any of his beloved native customs. The Americans were trying to 'assimilate' him without incurring his opposition and it was a real problem because Sulu was committed to polygamy and slavery. . . . The situation in Sulu had all the ingredients of comic opera and I believed that a good satirical musical play could be built around the efforts of our American civilizers to play ball with the little brown brother. After I came home I tried to give the idea to Frank Pixley, the librettist, and also to Lew Dockstader, thinking that Lew might work up the story I gave him into an after-piece for his minstrel show." But those to whom George offered the idea failed to share his enthusiasm. That might have been the end of the idea if something else had not happened.

Soon after John McCutcheon's return to Chicago around the end of 1900, it developed that he had picked up a variety of germs in his travels and had a serious lung infection. His physician told George that the only chance to save John's life was to send him at once to Asheville, North Carolina. John's condition was too critical for him to be moved on a stretcher or cot into a Pullman car except through a window, and there would be one or two changes of trains. It would be necessary to have a special car and nurses. That meant more immediate outlay of cash than George had on hand. He went to Victor Lawson to suggest that he, as John's employer, bear most of the expense.

A special car from Chicago to Asheville, said Lawson, would cost an astonishing sum.

"But," asked George, "won't it seem a mere trifle if it saves John's life?"

There was no denying that, and before George left his office Lawson was telephoning to railroad offices about arrangements to send John to Asheville in a private Pullman. George went ahead to obtain a house. John, whose love of travel had become a passion, began to show improvement almost from the moment he was on the train. George's prompt action had saved his life.

For three months George stayed in Asheville to make sure John had good care. As he could write his weekly syndicated Fable in a few hours, he had time to spare. Then he recalled young Alfred G. Wathall, who had asked him to write words to go with his tunes. Why not try an *opéra bouffe* story of that bewildered Sultan, Hadji Jamalol Ki-Ram, with his eight wives and genial spear throwers? He knew a dramatic and musical club on Chicago's North Side that might be willing to produce it. He thought of Gilbert & Sullivan, and of that night in 1885 at Lafayette when he first saw *The Mikado*. Without imitating any of Gilbert's work, he would follow his formula to the extent of having a story of cumulative interest, musical numbers to fit the situations and be an integral part of the dramatic construction, the lyrics dovetailing into the dialogue. The dialogue should be free from current "gags" and local allusions. He set to work on his first light opera.

16

The Sultan of Sulu and Peggy

AFTER George Ade had returned to Chicago from Asheville, he worked with the young musician, Wathall, to fit together verses and tunes. From then on, as Wathall wrote long afterward, he looked upon George as a "kindly, patient, long-suffering older brother." George did not need to grope for a title for their piece. When the time came to copyright *The Sultan of Sulu,* though, he was surprised to discover that, many years before, someone had given the title to a play with a totally different plot. As that play had never been produced, George could keep his title. George did not attempt to follow what had happened on the island of Sulu but to show "what might have happened." For the Sultan, however, he used the actual name, Ki-Ram. An early scene is the morning roundup and roll call of the Sultan's wives. The Sultan becomes the governor at a fixed salary and is provided with a high silk hat as the insigne of his new office. With polygamy no longer permitted under the American occupation, the Sultan is beset with problems of alimony for the "charter members of his harem," who become American grass widows. When he finds himself limited by monogamy, he coaxes to be allowed two little wives instead of one big one.

Ade and Wathall were having fun all to themselves with nothing more alarming than an amateur production to worry about. Then George showed an incomplete script to his friend Harry G. Sommers, treasurer of McVicker's Theater. Sommers—soon afterward a theater manager in New York—liked what he read and he told Henry W. Savage about it. Savage, the head of a stock company in Boston, was just beginning to be a producing manager. He had a show at the Studebaker Theater in Chicago. When he learned that Ade and Wathall were getting up something, he invited them to his office. After hearing the story of the *Sultan* and the tunes, he offered to give the piece a professional tryout at the Studebaker. Young Wathall showed his delight, but George Ade was alarmed.

"Having attended several first nights by Chicago authors in Chicago, and knowing that the proposed risk was what any insurance man would classify as 'extra hazardous,' I screamed with fright and ran up the street, with Colonel Savage in close pursuit. This may have been the only case on record in which the incipient playwright did not pursue the manager.

"Colonel Savage had Yankee persistence and vast persuasiveness. He wanted new plays by new authors, and he nagged us until we completed *The Sultan of Sulu.*"

It was produced at the Studebaker Theater on March 11, 1902. The Chicago critics praised it, but Savage was a hard taskmaster and suggested all kinds of doctoring and rewriting. George wrote verses for more than fifty songs before he got twenty-two that were finally retained. He had hoped to avoid slang. "Could I get away from my unholy reputation by running into a theater? Not at all. I was advised to speed up every slow spot in the 'book' by putting in more of my 'characteristic stuff.' If I submitted a new scene or a new set of verses, the jury in the manager's room would say, 'It isn't bad; but people expect from you more of that real, snappy, up-to-date slang.'"

The piece ran for eleven weeks in Chicago. When it took to the road in the fall, there was much further revising and tinkering. It reached Boston on December 1, and Wallack's Theater at Broadway and Thirtieth Street in New York on December 29. By that time even the cast had been revised. About the only member remaining from the original Chicago cast was Gertrude Quinlan—

later in another Ade success. Frank Moulan was in the role of Ki-Ram at the New York opening, and his friends said he was a most suitable Sultan as he had long enjoyed a reputation as a charmer. The biggest salary in the company, $125 a week, went to Maude Lillian Berri, one of the best known of light opera singers.

George Ade was in a state of mind bordering on terror the night of that New York opening. Still a country boy at heart, he could not think of himself as a playwright capable of taking all the hurdles on Broadway. "It was believed, and for good reasons, that no play written by a Chicago author and first produced in Chicago would succeed in New York. It was assumed that the critics would travel as far as Hoboken or even Newark with their cleavers sharpened to welcome the play to a massacre."

When George spread in front of him all the fervent newspaper comments and realized that the piece was a hit and would stay in the big town for months he had probably the most relieved and the happiest hour of his life.

. . *The Sultan of Sulu* remained in New York for 192 performances, nearly a whole season—a good record for those days—and had a long run on the road. It made theatrical history. Mark Sullivan in *Our Times* calls it "one of the best of American musical comedies of any time." The text of the play, published by R. H. Russell and sold in the lobby at Wallack's is today a sought-after and prized item.

(A few years after the production of the *Sultan*, George Ade made another trip to the Philippines and he and the real Ki-Ram were in Manila at the same time. Some of the newspaper correspondents offered to arrange a meeting of George and the former Sultan, but George thought it would be imprudent. He feared that Ki-Ram might have learned of the liberties taken with his name.)

Some of the lines in the *Sultan* have become part of the language
—especially "the Constitution and the cocktail follow the flag,"
and "the cold gray dawn of the morning after." Playgoers still
remember the song, "R-E-M-O-R-S-E," sung by Ki-Ram:

> The cocktail is a pleasant drink;
> It's mild and harmless—I don't think.
> When you've had one, you call for two;
> And then you don't care what you do.
> Last night I hoisted twenty-three
> Of those arrangements into me;
> My wealth increased, I swelled with pride.
> I was pickled, primed, and ossified;
>   But R-E-M-O-R-S-E!
>
> The water wagon is the place for me.
> Last night at twelve I felt immense;
>   Today I feel like thirty cents.
> My eyes are bleared, my coppers hot
>   I'd like to eat but I cannot!
> It is no time for mirth and laughter—
> The cold, gray dawn of the morning after.

When someone complimented him on the song, saying it was a
good lyric, George said: "It was not a lyric; it was autobiography."

Another hit song much whistled over the country was "Since I
First Met You." The verses with such lines as "Each flower has a
new perfume," George considered shamefully banal; but the song
usually got ten encores.

Since both Ade and Wathall were unknown in the theater, each
was paid only two percent of the gross box-office receipts, probably
the minimum royalty allowed the author and composer of a
musical play. At that time no manager had dared to charge the
astonishing prices that later prevailed. The best seats sold for $2
each. During most of its run in New York *The Sultan of Sulu*
took in about $10,000 a week. Today a big musical show must do

$30,000 a week or go to the warehouse! George's weekly royalty was about $200. He was not yet in the big money, but still, as he said, it was a living.

George had joined the theatrical club, the Lambs, to which he was introduced by R. H. Russell, and began to feel at home in New York. At the Lambs he found "more laughs and more good cheer than in all the other clubs put together." He once described it as a club "in which you do not find frigid gentlemen with fishy eyes looking about apprehensively for fear they will be entrapped into social recognition of some one who doesn't quite belong."

One night at the Lambs he met James J. Corbett whom he had not seen since he reported the great Sullivan-Corbett fight at New Orleans. Something was said about the flight of time, and Corbett mentioned his age. It seemed to George that Corbett had understated. After a little figuring with his pencil, he said, "Well, Jim, considering that you were only fourteen years old that night in New Orleans in September, '92, you put up an awful good fight against Sullivan."

While in the East before *The Sultan of Sulu* arrived for its New York opening, George had his first meeting with Mark Twain, which he considered one of the events of his life.

"Dr. Clarence C. Rice, a long-time friend and traveling-companion of Mark Twain's, came to me at my hotel—and invited me to accompany him on a pilgrimage to the One and Only. Of course I accepted the invitation. Probably no person, then alive and gifted with a pair of movable legs, would have done otherwise. And especially so myself. For a good many years I had been waiting and hoping to meet Mark Twain."

They spent the afternoon with Clemens at Riverdale, on the Hudson.

"Although, at that time, I was regarded in some quarters as being a bit of humorist myself, I do definitely recall that I had no thought of conferring with Mark Twain as a fellow fun-maker.

"Courteously, Mark Twain asked about my trip to New York. He remarked that he and I would have been born in adjacent states if the damned geographers had not maliciously thrust Illinois between Indiana and Missouri. . . . Our host was happy, expansive. He began his discourses by warning me that I was soon to be made the victim of a fantastic plan, evolved by a woman of family acquaintance, to translate some of my 'Fables in Slang' into French.

" 'She cannot possibly find any French equivalents for your specimens of American vernacular,' said Mr. Clemens, 'but she is determined to make the effort and I am waiting until it is done so that I can watch some Frenchmen go crazy trying to read it.' " The translation was never made.

George hoped to see Mark Twain again and have the next visit "take the form of a newspaperman's interview." But though they met again, at a formal dinner, the interview was not to be.

Soon after the *Sultan* opened in New York, George's name appeared in a new book, *In Babel,* that was free from slang. John S. Phillips, of the publishing firm of McClure-Phillips & Co., had persuaded him to make this compilation of some of his stories from "Stories of the Streets and of the Town." (The title George first proposed was "Here In Chicago.") This was the collection that H. L. Mencken said contained two or three of the best short stories ever written in this republic. Some of the reviewers, un-familiar with his earlier work, gave high praise to what they thought was George Ade's first slangless writing. George had hoped to have his next piece for the stage also unseasoned by slang.

But since he had written a play that was a money-maker, he was still "on a sidetrack trying to get back to the main line." Savage, wanting another musical play, urged George to let himself go, to put in plenty of his "characteristic stuff." George worked on "a literary souffle," *Peggy from Paris,* while still tinkering with *The Sultan of Sulu,* and in the newer piece he abandoned all effort to stick to the Gilbert & Sullivan formula, but yielded to his "most evil impulses" and did "the most dreadful things to the English language."

After a tryout in South Bend *Peggy from Paris* opened in Chicago on January 26, 1903. The plot had to do with the career of a girl from Hickory Creek, Illinois, who for several years had been studying singing in Paris and has just returned to America to fill an operatic engagement in Chicago. All the scenes are in Chicago except a prologue laid in the parlor of an Illinois village hotel. The girl's "hayseed" father, Captain Alonzo Plummer, who "speaks Illinois and a little English," hears of her return and goes to Chicago to bring her back to the old home town. But she is receiving an enormous salary and cannot afford to have it known that she hails from Hickory Creek. She has passed herself off in Chicago as Mademoiselle Flourette Caramelle, a Parisian opera singer. She is determined to keep her new character and tries to convince her father, when he appears backstage, that her maid is his daughter, naturally somewhat changed in appearance after her long absence in Paris.

Ade had introduced material not vitally connected with the plot. One of the jokes was about a girl who walked in her sleep and whose mother always gave her carfare before she went to bed.

On the opening night in Chicago Savage made a little speech before the curtain and said that more than the plot was of Illinois as all members of the chorus had been selected in Chicago and were from there or from near-by towns. At least one of the chorus girls had never been far from her native village and when the show reached New York and she was asked if she would have some broiled lobster she said, yes, she was hungry enough to eat a whole can of lobster.

The show got good reviews in Chicago, but when it reached New York for its opening on September 10, 1903, after a stay in Boston, the critics said, and George agreed with them, that it was not so good as *The Sultan of Sulu;* and the music by William Loraine seemed less tuneful than that of the earlier piece. It ran in New York less than half as long as the *Sultan* had, but still it stayed for 85 performances, and it prospered for several seasons on the road. At least two members of the New York company are worth mentioning, Helen Hale, just out of an eastern college, and William Hodge; and a few years afterward they were married. Thus George was the indirect cause of bringing two interesting people together, and later he influenced Hodge's career in another way.

For *Peggy from Paris* the royalty rate was three percent instead of two. As the *Sultan* was still on tour, George Ade was doing well as a writer of musical plays. Meanwhile, he had done something else. A few days before *Peggy from Paris* reached New York, he had a new show opening in Chicago. It was a huge success, and it was slangless.

17

The County Chairman

In his first play "for talking actors instead of singing dancers," George Ade broke away from what he called his literary outlawry. "I resolved to make a stand against the forces that were trying to transfer me from Olympus to the Bowery. I had, in the incubator, a play of country-town life in the Middle West called 'The County Chairman.' It was all about the home people, and I didn't propose to have them straining over verbal gymnastics." He deliberately laid the scenes in the early eighties to avoid the kind of speech which adorned the Fables. If asked to do so in rehearsal he could assume a horrified air and explain that it would be an anachronism to use in a play of 1880 a phrase invented many years later.

Henry W. Savage was alarmed when George said he wanted to do a straight comedy-drama of village life and politics. His experience had been with musical shows, and since the two by Ade had been successful, why change the formula? But he gave his doubtful assent.

"While I was incubating the play I had been the guest, in Vicksburg, Mississippi, of Harris Dickson, author of the 'Old Reliable' yarns and many other entertaining stories of Southern atmosphere. He showed me around his home town and, among other points of interest connected with the famous siege directed by General Grant, we visited the old Court House where some of the shells, sent over by the Union gunners, were still imbedded in the walls. In the lobby of the Court House was a bulletin-board bearing the names of citizens who were delinquent in their taxes. Perhaps because I have always been interested in names I read the list as posted on the board and found that it was a grand roster of good old Anglo-Saxon names. I secured a copy and, later, when I was ready to devise names for all of the undiluted American 'types' to be found in Antioch, scene of *The County Chairman,* I brought out the names of the tax delinquents and found all of the Hacklers, Rigbys, Wheelers, Tollivers, Watsons and others needed for a cast which would seem authentic and home-grown."

"*The County Chairman* contains no mystery, sex, crime, or triangular complications," said Ade. "It deals with neighborhood factions and local political feuds in a decidedly one-horse town. It is homely and it is largely an attempt to go back to the queer eighties which preceded the gay nineties and reproduce something of the temper and atmosphere and crudities as they cropped up in a settlement of corn-fed natives, far from the allurements and distracting influences of any big city."

The story was of a county political campaign in which young Tilford Wheeler is a candidate for State's Attorney, opposing the father of the girl he wants to marry. "The idea was to work into the story a goodly number of 'types' and give them a chance to score with comedy lines or in situations which were directly connected with the development of the plot." Ade succeeded. It seemed that all the principal "types" in small towns appeared in the opening scene in front of the general store and post office on Main street, among them the store-box orator whose wife kept the boardinghouse, the old settler, the manager of the fife and drum corps, the flirtatious milliner and the self-confident visiting drummer.

Savage provided actors of talent. Maclyn Arbuckle was a "natural" for Jim Hackler, the County Chairman. Best of all, the piece was directed by a master of stagecraft, George Marion. He had directed the earlier Ade pieces, and he and Ade worked together in harmony. As the time came for the first rehearsal something happened which helped to make the play succeed. George Marion had been with minstrel shows in his early days and George Ade liked to reminisce about some of the old-timers he had seen in Lafayette.

"Too bad the old minstrel shows are no more," remarked George Marion. "There's not much outlet for talents such as Willis Sweatnam's. He's in need of a job right now and can't get one."

Then Marion went on to problems of staging *The County Chairman*, but George Ade was not listening. His thoughts were back in the days when Willis Sweatnam and George Thatcher and other minstrel performers were among his heroes. Finally he interrupted Marion to say: "You know there's a ne'er-do-well white-trash character in this play. Why couldn't I re-write that part and make him a black-face character? Then we could give Sweatnam a job."

That night he wrote in the part of "Sassafras" Livingstone, the colored loafer who was always begging or borrowing.

"It was easy to write dialogue for Sweatnam. All I had to do after I wrote a speech for him was to close my eyes and listen to him repeating it and if it sounded like Sweatnam I left it in."

George's generous thought was well repaid, for Sweatnam's playing of the part was one of the hits of the show. As George said: "The little crust of bread tossed upon the water came back as frosted coconut cake!"

George had noticed that in plays produced by that master of stage trickery, David Belasco, the heroine was likely to be picking up various articles and laying them down again, and that each of these movements, whether a glance into a hand mirror or the fixing of a flower in the hair, helped the continuity of the story. He knew that the actors needed something to do with their hands. Why not have everybody in *The County Chairman* come in carrying something? The stage director liked the suggestion. "So I had the colored man bring in a basket of eggs, the hired man come in riding a bicycle, the girl from the boarding-house with a wringer to be repaired, the traveling man with the model of a patent windmill, the politician a poll-book that needed verifying, the boy a fish-pole and a string of fish, the sweet young heroine a basket of wild-flowers, the station agent the mail bag, and so on throughout the whole play."

The County Chairman had its first performance at the Auditorium Theater in South Bend, Indiana, toward the end of August 1903. As the audience seemed to like it, George Ade felt fairly serene and comfortable about the outlook.

"Strangely enough, Henry W. Savage did not share my confidence in the fate of our production. In every previous play which he had engineered the public response and appreciation had been made evident by encores. He was now up against a new kind of game and he was baffled and puzzled. In the two musical plays for which I had written the talk and the verses we had been compelled to do a lot of revising and substituting of numbers in search of hits. He felt that our small-town political play, with the assorted characters and realistic incidents and not very exciting plot, was a sort of fizzle because there were no encores or hoop-la finales."

On the way from South Bend to Chicago to open at the Studebaker Theater Savage tried to cheer up the author. He said: "This play will have to be fixed up a lot but don't be discouraged. We'll get right to work and make something out of it."

"Colonel," George Ade replied, "we have a lot of characters and a lot of episodes and a story. If the stuff goes over with the public, well and good. If it doesn't, we are sunk. We can't tinker with this as we have with our musical shows. You can't tear it to pieces unless you throw the whole thing out the window."

At the opening night in Chicago there were shouts for the author, and in a brief curtain speech Ade explained that his intention had been "to depict the Middle West with a minimum of gold bricks and chin whiskers." The *Chairman* played to packed houses in Chicago for several weeks before it succeeded *Peggy from Paris* at Wallack's in New York. Critics called it the best of all the rural dramas. The New York *Tribune* said it "represented the Mr. Ade of the best of his Fables without the slang." After playing 237 nights in New York, it closed on June 4, but reopened in September for a few weeks more, and it lasted on the road for three or four years. For a time there were two companies on the road and in the second company the part of "Sassafras" Livingstone was taken, at George Ade's request, by another old-time minstrel performer he had admired, George Thatcher. The play became a favorite for amateurs and was put on in the Ade home town of Kentland with George's brother Will in the title role. Thirty-three years after its first appearance in New York it was revived there with a professional production by the Players with Charles Coburn as the Chairman. It became a motion picture for Will Rogers.

After the success of *The County Chairman* George Ade hoped he was all through with plays having song-and-dance numbers. As he later observed, "A good musical comedy consists largely of disorderly conduct occasionally interrupted by talk. The man who provides the interruptions is called the librettist." One night at the Lambs seated at a table with a fellow librettist, Henry Blossom, George wrote this expression of his feelings:

I'd rather be a burglar than the man who writes the book,
For the burglar is anonymous—a self-effacing crook;
When they catch *him* with the goods he merely does a term in
   jail,
While the author has to stand and take a roast from Alan Dale.

Nevertheless, besieged by Savage, who found musical plays profitable and librettists too few, George set to work on a comic opera with music by Gustav Luders. "We called it *'The Sho-Gun,'* a bad title, but I didn't seem to know it at the time." (Savage thought the title should have been "The Great Promoter.") As in *The Sultan of Sulu,* once again the setting was the Far East. *The Sho-Gun* was a satire on commercial expansion, and the story revolved around William Henry Spangle, born in Grand Rapids, educated in Chicago "and polished off at the old Waldorf." He lands on an island near Korea and starts in to spread the most advanced ideas, especially in trying to revolutionize the commercial life. Some of the characters he meets, besides the Sho-Gun of Ka-Choo, are the dowager Hi-Faloot, Omee-Omi, Kee-Zi, Tah-tah, Yung-Fun, Hanki-Panki, and the Princess Hunni-Bun. One character was a dispenser of proverbs, and at least one of the proverbs is still remembered: "Early to bed and early to rise, and you'll meet very few prominent people." Henry Savage called for more and more new verses for songs to replace those he thought less likely to be hits, and George determined to write a set of verses that would end the demand for more. He would fill them with words that the ladies of the chorus could not memorize. The result was "The Microbe's Serenade." Though never used on the stage, George recited it so often at friends' requests that it became well known, and was once attributed to an anonymous author in the London *Lancet.* Here is the opening verse:

> A love-lorn microbe met by chance
> At a swagger bacteroidal dance
> A proud bacillian belle, and she
> Was first of the animalculae.
> Of organisms saccharine,
> She was the protoplasmic queen;
> The microscopical pride and pet

Of the biological smartest set.
And so this infinitesimal swain
Evolved a pleading low refrain:
"O lovely metamorphic germ!
What futile scientific term,
Can well describe your many charms?
Come to these embryonic arms!
Then hie away to my cellular home
And be my little diatom!"

Savage gave *The Sho-Gun* an excellent company. In the cast at one time or another were Fritz Williams, John Henshaw and Trixie Friganza, famous laugh-producers in their day. After a run of a few weeks in Chicago the piece opened in New York on October 10, 1904, following *The County Chairman* at Wallack's, and it stayed for 125 performances. New York critics showed restraint in their enthusiasm, but it lasted on the road and won its highest acclaim on the Pacific coast. George had spent more time on it than on any other play he ever wrote. He always considered it the best of his musical shows and better, as a piece of writing, than anything else he did for the stage.

Charles Frohman, the famous theatrical producer, had said that if a recognized playwright averaged one big success in five he was doing well. George Ade had just had four successes in four attempts, all within two years, and before *The Sho-Gun* had even arrived from Chicago, New York theatergoers were flocking to still another.

18

The Native Returns

In 1898 after *Artie* and *Pink Marsh* George Ade found himself with a modest bank account. His brother William, when he learned that George had $5,000, began to worry. He was afraid some slick salesman for gold-mining stock or for lots in a city subdivision might take the money. George had been lucky, and could not count on saving so much again. He should put it in a safe place. To Will Ade the safest investment was farm land in the corn belt. He was a good judge of land values in his own locality, and he understood farming. George accepted his brother's advice to invest that $5,000 in 108 acres of unimproved land on a main highway three miles from Kentland.

A year later brother Bill advised George to sell the place, because he knew a man who would pay $50 an acre, which meant a profit of $500 and one season's crops. George conceded that a profit of $400 was not to be despised, but he had adopted his brother's theory that land was a good investment, and now what should he do? Brother Bill said to wait patiently for another bargain.

When George started on his trip to China and the Philippines in 1900 after quitting his job on the *Record,* he left with his brother legal authority to sign checks for him in his absence. As he was about to leave San Francisco, he got a long telegram from brother Bill telling him of the purchase in his name of 160 acres at $65 an acre with a mortgage for $5,000. Never before had George owed so much. *Fables In Slang* was selling well, and he might receive a little return from the series of Fables to be syndicated but, still, a $5,000 debt upset him. He was tempted to wire brother Bill that his trip was now spoiled.

For the next few years George invested in farms. "If I seemed to be writing a good many plays—it was not because I had a flaming ambition to enrich dramatic literature. I was simply trying to keep up with brother Bill."

As he traveled over the world, he came more than ever to accept his brother's advice. "Travel taught me that there was a . . . limit to the amount of productive lands within easy reach of the principal markets. The corn belt had been widened, but it could not expand much farther. The demand for grains would continue to grow. . . . All good land would increase sharply in value when new tracts could not be opened up for development. These self-evident truths helped to make it clear that black prairie loam with a clay sub-soil, near a railroad leading direct to Chicago, was bound to be a safe investment."

Thus George Ade became a farmer. "I could not break a colt, or show the tile-ditcher where to put the laterals, or ring a shoat, or guide a self-binder. Questions asked by visitors at the farm often confuse me and compel me to look down into the abysmal depths of my own ignorance as a practical agriculturist. Of course, if the visitors are from the city and come with their minds open and blank, I can talk fluently. I am an honest-to-goodness farmer . . . because I invested in farmlands all the money I made in the cities . . ."

Under his brother Bill's guidance George bought and traded farms until he had in his native Newton county nearly 2,400 acres. It was a profitable investment. But none of his farms had for him the sentimental importance that he came to attach to the one of 417 acres he acquired in 1902 near the town of Brook. It could be had for $100 an acre.

"Just to show you that I think this farm is worth buying," said brother Bill, "I'd be willing to do it in partnership with you, each of us to own half."

While his brother was explaining about the excellent quality of the soil, George was looking at a grove of century-old oaks at one corner of the farm clipped by the Iroquois river.

"Right at the far edge of that grove," said George, "would be a nice spot to put a little cottage. Then if I wanted to get away from Chicago to work where it's quiet, I could come here. I think I'd like to buy the whole farm myself."

Then George called up a Chicago architect, his old friend "Billy" Mann, a Purdue graduate, and asked him to prepare plans for a bungalow to go into that oak grove. Just a little shack, he told the architect, to cost not more than $2,500.

The architect began making little suggestions. Since George had many friends in Chicago and elsewhere, some of whom he might like to have with him over a week end, should there not be a few guest rooms and also space for housekeeper, cook and other employees to look after the guests?

George nodded acquiescence to most of the suggestions and the house cost nearer $25,000 than the $2,500 he had intended. It was of Elizabethan design "about the size of a girls' school, with added wing for the managers, otherwise known as employees." Nothing like it had been seen in that part of Indiana, and neighbors were puzzled, especially by one reversal of custom, more plaster on the outside walls than on the inside. One neighbor, noticing a mantelpiece of brick, said it seemed strange that George didn't pay a little more and have bird's-eye maple.

Another item in the original order was a dog-house-shaped garage to hold the tiny one-cylinder, curve-dash, rudder-steering roadster which John McCutcheon had christened the Rolling Peanut. But the architect reminded George that the road to the railway station at Brook was often a sea of mud and he would be obliged to keep a team of horses and carriage to meet trains from Chicago. The garage and stable was of a design to match the house, with sleeping rooms overhead for coachman and gardener. For a year or two the team and carriage did prove to be of more practical use than the Rolling Peanut; but George tried to go about by automobile when he could, and one time when Booth Tarkington came over to see him, he proposed driving all the way to Chicago. A shower came up, "just a gentle, pretty shower, but soon the mud was hub deep." They left the car in the corner of a rail fence and set out on foot across the fields to the nearest railway station.

The Rolling Peanut became famous, for its maker, the Oldsmobile company, got George to write a testimonial which the company published in a little brochure—now a collectors' item. "The 'Peanut,'" he wrote, "is beginning to look like a machine with a past. . . . Once I tried to make it climb a tree in order to avoid killing a dog. Another time I closed my eyes to keep out the flying dust and when I opened them again I was locked in the close embrace of a coal wagon. . . . The 'Peanut' has never required the attentions of a hired man in a leather suit. All I have to do is to pour a little gasoline into a hole under the back seat, speak a few kind words to it and it behaves itself like an instructed delegate."

The architect had continued to suggest that while they were at it they might as well do this or that, and presently his plans included: a swimming pool; three-room house adjoining the pool, for dressing rooms and shower; greenhouse, "afterward used for storing garden tools and equipment and articles which should not have been purchased"; English-type cow barn, with storeroom above; caretaker's cottage, only twice as large as that originally planned for owner; fuel supply house and storeroom; forty-foot tower for water tank. Hazelden, as George had named the place, was beginning to be an impressive estate.

George sent for landscape experts who laid out elaborate gardens with grape arbors and rose arbors. He tried to interest himself in getting effects from mass planting of flowers, but that, he said, proved to be a rash attempt, for he was color-blind. Decorators came from Chicago to plan the interior of his house and the furnishings. Here George asserted himself. He hung colorful tapestries bought as souvenirs in his travels and put out pieces of Oriental bronze, ivory carvings, and Chinese porcelain, and the living rooms took on an exotic quality. The upstairs was mostly early American with some four-poster beds. But in numerous ways his own personality showed itself. After one look at the master bedroom he removed one layer of curtains, too fussy, and sent for a village paperhanger to replace what the decorator had ordered with a design much simpler. He noticed a bowl of shining artificial fruit on the dining-room table and promptly took it away. "It might be all right in the city," he said, "but here in the country the fruit is supposed to be genuine."

Every man has his feminine side and George showed his in his fondness for the choicest kinds of table china and for good linen including linen sheets for the guest rooms.

Hazelden was homelike, and George was soon as deeply attached to it as if he had been there since childhood. At first he kept his room at the Chicago Athletic Club, but he stayed there less and less. At the farm he was well isolated from city atmosphere, for there was not a town of 20,000 people within fifty miles. He referred to himself as a blanket Indian who had returned to the reservation.

The little shack, the hideaway, that he had first planned had become a country estate, but his idea that it was to be a quiet place to work was unchanged. His office at one end of the house on the ground floor with its immense flat-topped desk and bookcases was his favorite room from the first. When he settled down at Hazelden early in the summer of 1904, his first thought was that now he could write without too much interruption something that had been in the back of his head for a long time. He would put his new house to practical use. And what a profitable use it turned out to be!

He still had a copy of that "dummy" of a novel to be called *The College Widow,* but he decided now to write it not as a novel but as a play. During the six years he had kept the story "in one of the pigeon-holes of the cerebellum" he had made no notes, but when he sat down now to outline the scenario he knew pretty well what was going to happen. "The scenario was a thing of three or four pages and was merely a condensed guide for getting .the characters on and off the stage and into the necessary combinations.

"The play was then practically completed, although not one line of dialogue or directions had been written, and I had nothing to show the anxious manager except a mass of notations which meant little to him. The dialogue and directions for 'business' were written in less than three weeks."

Perhaps the quiet of the country had something to do with it. What George wrote in less than three weeks was so clear in his mind that scarcely a word of it would ever have to be changed.

19

The College Widow

WHEN George Ade wrote *The College Widow,* a play about college life and football was something new. "Wise people" in the theater did not believe the playgoing public was much interested in undergraduates or college athletics; but George thought they might be if the students were human and the play a comedy rather than a melodrama. "The best way to write comedy is also the simplest way. Give the people natural types that they can recognize and have them say things that people can understand. Be careful not to hurt anyone's feelings. Try to amuse the public and not offend good taste." For the setting of his play he did not pick a big school, Harvard or Yale, or even Purdue; the college was Wabash, at Crawfordsville, "a town small enough to have its local characters and provincial coloring."

After completing the four acts in less than three weeks, he went to New York to read the play to Mr. Savage. Savage was about to go to Boston, so George went with him. The stage director, George Marion, went too. As Ade read *The College Widow* on the train Savage never smiled. The lines were clever, he said, but he wished the play was about something other than college athletics. It would interest only those who had been to college. Marion was less discouraging. He thought it might succeed if it moved so swiftly the audience could catch the excitement. Savage was willing to take the risk and proposed to start rehearsals in August.

Ade's friends, newspaper and theatrical, showed little enthusiasm at the final rehearsal and he felt sure they thought it would fail. The tryout was at the Columbia theater in Washington early in September 1904. Everybody was apprehensive, George most of all. The dialogue, spoken over and over again to empty benches, seemed to have lost all sense and flavor. George was having dinner at the home of his sister, Mrs. John W. Randall, the night of the opening. He ate only a little ice cream. All felt sorry for him. Members of his fraternity at George Washington University wanted to attend in a body and give a reception afterward, but he begged off, because, he said, he might be hiding under a bed or perhaps his body would be floating down the Potomac. "No other terror," he explained, "is so extreme as that surrounding a first night."

The weather was hot and Washington seemed deserted. Congress was not in session. It was a campaign year with Alton B. Parker running against Theodore Roosevelt for President. About two-thirds of the seats at the theater were occupied. George expected the worst. The opening act was intended to introduce the characters and start the story but was not supposed to contain much comedy. To George's happy astonishment the audience began to laugh and applaud. The second act went with a bang, and the third, about the thrills of a big football game, put the audience in an uproar. The scene showed a section of the grandstand with plenty of action and cheering and people rushing in and out of the main entrance—all in a fine frenzy. As staged by George Marion it was hard to believe that a great football contest was not actually going on. At the end of that third act George Ade was compelled to make a speech. As he was pushed in front of the curtain and stood blinking before the footlights, he found himself standing at the edge of the stage above a box at his right in which were Admiral George Dewey, hero of the Battle of Manila Bay, accompanied by his wife and General and Mrs. Fred Grant. George thanked the audience, and said he hoped their applause was sincere. Then Admiral Dewey stood up in his box and said, "George, it's wonderful!" It was the first time George had ever seen Admiral Dewey. He saluted and said, "Admiral, God bless you for them kind words."

The plot of the piece, slight enough, revolved about the football rivalry between fresh-water colleges, Atwater and Bingham. Bingham is a Baptist institution and Atwater dyed-in-the-wool Presbyterian. Bingham has quadrangles and chapels and "endowed furbelows" provided by Hiram Bolton, a railroad president, in gratitude to the college for having expelled him in his freshman year and given him his chance to enter profitable business. His son Billy, a famous halfback, is about to enter Bingham, but stops off at Atwater with his father who is an old friend of Dr. Witherspoon, Atwater's president. Bolton leaves his son there and starts for London to put through a big deal. Atwater's football team is in desperate need of a halfback, and the boys persuade Jane Witherspoon, the belle of the town, known as the college widow, to use her fascination to induce young Bolton to enter Atwater and play on the team instead of going on to Bingham. He does so, and makes the winning play for Atwater. While the game is on, his father returns from London and bitterly upbraids his son, saying, "You're a hell of a Baptist!"—a phrase still quoted. Billy has fallen in love with the "widow" and is disconsolate when he discovers the reason for her interest in him. But it all turns out happily.

The story, however, was only a detail. It was the bits of character that made the piece. No one could forget Gertrude Quinlan's playing of Flora Wiggins, the sarcastic daughter of a boarding-house keeper, trying during the four acts to collect $18 from a student. "I've met so many of you college comedians I haven't a laugh left in me." Nor would one soon forget "Silent" Murphy, the Jim Jeffries type, who had been snatched from a foundry to take a course in art, that he might play center rush, and who suffered all evening in a borrowed dress suit and too tight shoes. "It gets me right across the instep." Another memorable character was "Bub" Hicks, from Squantamville, the gawky youth who at first "would ruther be at home," but who in a later act has become a sport, wearing the most extreme collegiate clothes, and "knows a lot of things the faculty can't find out." Most of all would everyone remember that football scene, "the wildest, craziest, most pandemonic scene ever staged."

The play was a success all week in Washington, but George was apprehensive about what might happen in New York. It opened on September 20 at the Madison Square Garden Theater, on E. Twenty-seventh Street, some distance from the Broadway theater section. On the night of the opening he and Booth Tarkington had dinner together at the old Holland House, and George went over the list of characters, telling which students in his memories of Purdue had suggested some of them. A huge fellow named Teter, who played football around 1890, was the original of "Silent" Murphy. Tarkington long remembered how worried George was.

George did not need to worry. The piece was a hit from the rise of the curtain. Not content with applause, the audience began to cheer. At the end of the second act the applause kept up until George made a speech. "You will have perceived that this is not a problem play," he began; and then he went on to explain that he had not tried to caricature college boys but just to treat them as human, "though they may not deserve it."

At the end of the third act, containing the big football scene, an extraordinary thing happened. The applause never ceased during the twelve minutes of the intermission until the curtain rose for the final act!

The next day the critics without one dissenting vote tried to outdo each other in praise. Alan Dale, never easily pleased, said that George Ade had hit the town hard with his "unerring aim." Irving Lewis in the *Telegraph,* the theatrical daily, called it the best American comedy in a decade. One reviewer noticed that there was not a cocktail or barroom joke in it. George had stuck to his rule that everything he wrote must be fit for mother and the girls.

The old saying that plays are not written but re-written was not true of *The College Widow.* Scarcely a line was ever revised, even in rehearsal; it remained as George first put it on paper. It had about ten good parts, and, as George said, "when you have ten good parts in one play, you have accidentally put over a miracle."

Letters of congratulation came to Ade from all the better-known American playwrights, from William Vaughn Moody, Paul Potter, Charles Klein, George Broadhurst, Clyde Fitch and Augustus Thomas. These were men he had always wanted to know. Now they were seeking opportunity to meet him. Nor was this feeling limited to this side of the Atlantic. James M. Barrie, the British playwright, told a newspaperman Ade was the American he would most like to know. Later they became friends.

An unusual thing was the flood of letters from theatergoers who wished to express their gratitude for the pleasure the comedy had given them. Members of a theater audience are seldom conscious of a debt to the author, no matter how well they like the play, but George Ade's human warmth seemed to make devoted friends of those who never expected to meet him. One letter that George treasured came from Dr. James H. Canfield, the librarian at Columbia, former president of Ohio State University. He asked George to bear with an old man who couldn't resist telling how he and his wife and daughter after seeing the comedy had sat up until 2:00 A.M., talking and laughing over some of the lines, enjoying them all again. (The daughter referred to became the well-known novelist, Dorothy Canfield Fisher.)

A joking letter came from the humorist, Charles Battell Loomis, who warned that he was thinking of becoming a playwright and asked if the country wasn't big enough for them both. It had occurred to him, he wrote, that while Ade was making a hit with clean plays, there might be money in unwholesome plays, full of lust and evil. He was sure that he could pack all the disreputable theaters!

Those were happy days in New York for George Ade, meeting old friends, making new ones and enjoying in his modest way his triumphs. He was now called the most successful American playwright. It was hard to dodge his plays on Broadway. When *The College Widow* arrived, *The County Chairman* was still running at Wallack's, and it stayed for a while before being succeeded by *The Sho-Gun*. Thanks to the competition of Charles Frohman, who was generously raising royalty rates, Savage gave George a sliding scale of royalties that increased with the amount of the box-office receipts, and it was evident that the *Widow* would give him a comfortable fortune, though small in comparison with what an equal success would give a playwright today.

George seemed to have everything. He was an exceptionally handsome young man, still in his thirties, six feet tall, well-proportioned, weighing around 170 pounds and dressed in excellent taste. His face, shrewd yet kindly, would have made him recognized in any group as a cultivated person. His hair, beginning to gray, added to his appearance. He was rich and famous and sought after. With his humor and charm and pleasing voice he was one of the most companionable of men and he knew interesting people everywhere. If he cared to interest himself in women, he could meet the most beautiful. "A good many people I met

The two responsible for the Ross-Ade Stadium, from the paintings by Robert Grafton in the Purdue University Memorial Union.

Ross-Ade Stadium with Purdue University in background.

seemed to take it for granted," he said, "that inasmuch as I was a foot-loose and fancy-free bachelor who was writing plays and could go back-stage any time, I was probably cutting up many a dido. . . . I met a lot of nice girls in the various companies, but it always seemed to me that they regarded the author as a viper who might have improved all their parts and given them twice as many fat lines. . . ."

At the time of *The College Widow* success George even had a town in Indiana named for him. The railroad that established the station and town wanted to call it Georgeade, but George asked them to name it Ade for his father, an Indiana pioneer. They did so, but the name was accepted as a tribute to George, and one may remark that no neighbor or anyone in Indiana ever wondered why.

The College Widow continued in New York for nearly a year. For a time three companies were playing it in different parts of the country. Before it went on the shelf, the gross returns were more than two million dollars.

When the second company was being formed, George asked Savage to select for the part of the "widow" charming young Frances Ring, who had been in *The County Chairman*. He also told Savage of an actor he wanted to see play the part of Billy Bolton, the halfback. This actor was not well-known. Savage had never heard of him. George had seen him only in summer stock companies but thought so well of him that he induced Savage to give him a trial. The little-known actor was Thomas Meighan, who afterward made his fortune in motion pictures. That part of Billy Bolton at a salary of $80 a week was his first real chance. George introduced him to Frances Ring and they promptly fell in love. It was a happy marriage. "Most of the marriages I have arranged seemed to turn out well," George would say. Tommy Meighan naturally became one of George's most devoted friends. He always said that to George he owed most of his success. He was one of the many that George helped to "make."

Another man who got his start in one of the *Widow* companies, in the part of the football coach, was Robert Kelly, who later played the preacher missionary in *Rain,* one of the most interesting and most detestable parts ever seen on the stage.

With three *Widow* companies playing and his earlier plays continuing on the road, George Ade's royalties were sometimes as much as $5,000 a week. It was not too difficult now for him to keep up with brother Bill in paying for more farm land in the Indiana corn belt.

The College Widow has been called "one of the theater's indestructibles." During the more than forty years since it was first produced, there has never been a year when amateurs or a stock company, somewhere, have not played it.

20

London Sinks with a Cry

MR. SAVAGE, who had feared that New York would not be interested in a comedy about football, came to believe that *The College Widow* should have a strong appeal anywhere. After it had finished its run in the United States, he took it to London for an opening at the Adelphi theater April 20, 1908. In the company were Gertrude Quinlan, from the original cast, Thomas Meighan and Frances Ring. The London production was presented over the protests of both Ade and Marion, the stage director, who thought the English theatergoers could scarcely be expected to understand either the situations or the vernacular.

The manager of the theater foresaw the audiences' need for translations of some of the unfamiliar American terms and phrases, and had a glossary distributed with the program at each performance:

Act I

put up a holler	indignantly protested
pinkest collection of farm hands	dullest lot of creatures
a couple of husky ones	couple of enormous men
prexy	nickname for college president
a corker	a champion
burning a student's lamp	smoking a cigarette
trying to get new	trying to be impudent
the campus	the college lawn
Kappa Delt-Sigma Theta	college secret societies
the way she strings them	the way she leads them on
the rush line	the forwards in football
a jerk-water railroad	a little branch line

the Rockefeller stunt	endowing colleges
a squab	a bobby
cutting up didos	playing pranks
old side-partner	old crony or "pal"

Act II

angel food	a kind of cake
foundered	overfed
bucking the line	football slang, meaning breaking through the line

Act III

quitters	men who give up in a fight, cowards
rattled	confused
a dead-head telegram	one that is sent free, franked
to rub dope on	to rub linament on

Act IV

a web-footed Rube	an uncouth countryman
a jim-crow school	an inferior school
the tall grass	the country, the far west
pin-head	a man of inferior capacity
easy money	money found or obtained easily
a gasoline runabout	a motor-car
a tintype	a photograph taken on tin
sicked the widow on him	urged the widow to flirt with and fascinate him

Besides the glossary the theater distributed a little book of pictures and explanations of the "Indiana types." In this one learns that Atwater College and Squantamville are fictitious names; and that having a "trainer" for a football team is simply one of Mr. Ade's fanciful creations! George had listed Flora Wiggins as a "prominent waitress," but the booklet explained that Mr. Ade was simply being humorous in describing her as prominent.

Now, this was not the first time that Ade humor had needed translation in England. Andrew Lang, famous critic of the London *Daily News,* had done a review of *Fables in Slang* in which he confessed his puzzlement over "staking a person to a meal ticket," to "make a horrible beef," "is the graft played out?" a "one night stand," a "jay town"; and what, he asked, could be the nature of "niftiness"?

Lang naturally did not quite know what to make of this one: "She could get away with any topic that was batted up to her, and then slam it over to second in time to head off the runner." He decided that "there seems to be a combination here of cricket and rugby football."

"Does 'spaghetti joint,'" asked Lang, "refer to an Italian surgeon of renown who has made a certain joint his peculiar study, or does he keep a restaurant where the joints are excellent?" All these expressions so perplexed Lang that according to George "he sank with a bubbling cry and did not come up for three days!"*

Yet Lang's bewilderment was mild compared with that of the London theater critics at *The College Widow.* It nearly drove them crazy! They were hard put to it, trying to determine how much of the piece was a true picture of American college life. The critic on *The Pall Mall Gazette* was of the opinion that the incident of the undergraduate thrusting his fingers into the mouth of a newly arrived freshman to examine his teeth and judge his fitness was probably only satire. All the critics agreed that the piece was somehow good entertainment. One of them said of the football scene, "We were bruised and numb with the fury of it and sat back gasping."

---

* A little later at least a few Londoners became familiar with some of the Fables. The Savage Club for a number of years followed a plan of having one of the actor members recite a Fable from memory when a visiting American was a guest of honor. A favorite, often recited by Walter Churcher, well known in his day, was the one about the Country Customer.

The humor was too American for successful export in 1908, and the London run was short—only thirty performances.

Today, after meeting American soldiers during two world wars, England knows more about the American vernacular and kind of humor. *The College Widow* in London today might go.

21

An Ade Decade

ADE'S NEXT success, a year after *The College Widow,* was *Just Out of College.* It had a good run in New York, was on tour for two or three years and was made into a motion picture. The principal character was one that had figured in "Stories of the Streets and of the Town," Edward Worthington Swinger. He falls in love with the daughter of a wealthy "pickle king" who agrees to give him a check for $20,000 if he will stay away from his daughter for three months and try to demonstrate during that time that he has any business sense. He uses the money to back a rival pickle concern which the "pickle king" has to buy. Swinger assuages the old man's anger and takes charge of everything, including the daughter. This was the first Ade play produced by Charles Frohman, for whom George came to have great admiration.

A few months previously George had suffered his first setback. He had gone on a ramble to Japan and perhaps did not allow enough time for the finishing touches to a play about the folly of promiscuous almsgiving, *The Bad Samaritan.* "It was written for Richard Golden and it was all wrong. It had a bad title, and the people wouldn't come out to see it even the first night." Though *The Bad Samaritan* survived for only fifteen performances in New York, George Marion who, besides staging it played a small part, always insisted that it could have been saved.

A version of *The Bad Samaritan* was used on the road by Ezra Kendall, famous for his vaudeville monologue and for his books of humor. But, never a success, it was one of George Ade's painful experiences.

Since Ade's success had been record-breaking, his first failure made his fellow playwrights wonder how he was taking it. At a dramatists' dinner Bronson Howard asked him, "How does it feel, George, to be one of us?" Referring to the habit successful playwrights had of strolling on Broadway, George replied: "I have discovered the beauties of Sixth avenue."

George tried in 1907 a play based on "Artie" of his Chicago newspaper days. In the cast were two young players who later became well-known, William Harrigan and Frank Craven. It had a short run in New York and was on tour for part of a season. But it was "one of our children," as George said, "that didn't live."

George was downhearted after *Artie,* but the next year, 1908, Mr. Frohman produced his *Father and the Boys* for the popular William H. Crane, and the New York critics pronounced it the best comedy in town. Crane played it for three years. It was all about how the "old man" gets the better of the young folk, instead of the other way round. The piece had plenty of the Ade kind of slang, provided by "Matty" McGowan, boxing instructor.

Under Mr. Frohman's sliding scale of royalties—5 percent on the first $4,000 for each week, 10 percent on the next $2,000, and 15 percent on everything over $6,000—*Father and the Boys* was one of George Ade's highly profitable plays. But dreading the first night ordeal as he always did, he was not present at the New York opening. He had escaped to Bermuda.

Later on George gave William H. Crane a play not so good, called *U. S. Minister Bedloe,* about a man from "Springfield, U.S.A.," who becomes U. S. Minister to San Quito, in the Central American republic of Caribay, and has just landed there when a revolution breaks out. It opened the new Blackstone theater in

Chicago but was never in New York. "I knew it was a goner," said George, "ten minutes after the curtain went up, but I had to stay there all evening while the blood slowly froze in my veins."

In this play George paid tribute to one of his friends. Bedloe says to his wife, "Mother, here's a book that came down from the states. It's called Abe Martin." And he reads some of the inimitable Abe Martin sayings.

As Bedloe and his wife sit chuckling, she asks, "Who wrote that book, Jackson?"

"Kin Hubbard," he tells her.

"Anyhow," George used to say, *"that* part of the play got applause."

George wrote for the Harlequin Club at Purdue "a kind of happy-go-lucky musical play called *The Fair Co-Ed."* His old friend of Chicago days, Charles B. Dillingham, insisted upon taking it over and it opened in New York in February 1909. Elsie Janis was the star, a co-ed who masquerades in a boy's clothes. She played it for three seasons. Then she was in another musical success, based on an Ade magazine story, *The Slim Princess.*

"From the very start of my dealings with the managers," George Ade wrote, "I wanted to get away from the musical plays, but these same managers have stars under contract, and musical plays, which look so trivial and easy-to-write, are hard to get. The first thing I knew, Mr. Dillingham had me talked into fixing up a play for Fred Stone and Dave Montgomery." Once again George's musical collaborator was Gustav Luders. *The Old Town* opened in New York on January 10, 1910, and was there for 171 performances. Fred Stone's acrobatic dancing was a feature of the show. When asked by friends how his play was going, George replied, "It will do well enough so long as Fred Stone's legs hold out."

The Old Town marked the end of Ade's ten-year career as an active playwright. While turning out full-length plays, he had done his share of shorter ones. "I had good luck with the one-act plays after May Irwin . . . started me on a life of shame. *Marse Covington, The Mayor and the Manicure, Nettie,* and *Speaking to Father* managed to get by and hang on for the usual span of life." *The Mayor and the Manicure* was played in vaudeville by William H. Crane. All those short plays were comedies except *Marse Covington.* It was about a proud but seedy, old-fashioned southern gentleman, saved from embarrassment at a gambling house by a former colored retainer.

Since he had been extraordinarily successful—with only three plays out of twelve that could be called failures—George's friends wondered why he did not continue.

He explained, "If a man writes a book that does not arouse public interest, the book dies a quiet death. But if he writes a play that fails to score, he is pilloried in public. He is scalped to slow music, on a high pedestal with an amber light turned on the scene of his humiliation and thousands of people apparently enjoying the fun. If he succeeds, he has simply laid another pole across the hurdle, and at his next effort he must make a higher jump.

"It seems to me that my experience resembled the list of symptoms on a large bottle of bitters—the kind that good church members used to take before the government began checking percentages of alcohol. I had dizziness, fainting spells, nausea, lassitude, shooting pains, periods of depression, dimness of vision and suffocation.

"Even when the final ring-down leaves the play-house tingling with the electrical knowledge of a sure success, the playwright feels so much like a wet towel that he cannot find any joy."

The one recompense for all the suffering, he said, "aside from the vulgar details of royalties," was to meet and know the players. "I think that all of them are still my friends . . ."

Looking back upon his years of theatergoing and playwriting,

George made this comment: "Talk to any manager for whom you are compounding a sure-fire drama and he will tell you that your play will fail unless you saturate it with love interest and have a closely woven plot with suspended interest. He will tell you this despite the fact that many of the most successful plays ever done on the American stage were absolutely devoid of love interest and had faltering plots. . . . Three successes depended largely on the characterization: *"Lightnin', The Old Homestead* and *Rip Van Winkle.* Plays of every type succeed if they can arouse in the audience a friendly, sympathetic and brotherly interest or an admiration of the way in which the scenes are enacted or an active curiosity as to how the whole thing will turn out."

During that decade beginning in 1900 when he was writing plays, George was also producing short stories, many of them of life in a country town. A memorable tale that he did for the *Saturday Evening Post* (in 1903) was "Getting Sister Laura Married Off." An old man had provided in his will that none of his estate could go to any of his heirs, three sons and a daughter, until all are married. The sons manage to find wives, but there is still sister Laura. The reader felt sure that only George Ade could have found what to do about her.

He did a newspaper syndicate series of "Old Stories Revised" in which he modernized *Rip Van Winkle, Enoch Arden, Vicar of Wakefield, Gulliver* and others. His version of the McGuffey Reader story of "The Boy Who Cried Wolf" said: "If a Famishing Hobo broke into a Summer Kitchen and stole a Ham, he would begin shrieking about a Carnival of Crime and shake up the Police Department. If the Second Alto of the Church Choir at Lonesomehurst eloped with a Piano-Tuner he would announce a Scandal in High Life."

Another Ade story, "To Make a Hoosier Holiday," that first appeared in *Collier's Weekly* in December 1904, is preserved in an anthology, *The World's One Hundred Best Short Stories*. Surely this is one of the most hilarious of all short stories. It is about the rivalry between the Campbellites and the Methodists for a church entertainment that would fetch the crowd, and just how Doc' Silverton puts over a wedding at the church between two local characters, Baz Leonard and Miss Beula Wheatley. They hardly know each other, but Doc' starts a rumor, and then gets everybody to offer congratulations until the two can't wriggle out of going through with it. George contrived to make it all plausible.

An important decade in American literary history was that first one of the new century, and George Ade had helped to make it so.

22

Exploring His Adopted Planet

ADE, LIKE McCutcheon, never lost his enthusiasm for foreign travel. "Twice I went all the way around the planet of my adoption." About ten times he roamed over Europe. He made several trips to Japan and China, many to the West Indies and the Panama Canal. In the winter of 1905-1906 he made his first inspection of Egypt and did a series of travel letters—first syndicated to newspapers and then published as a book, *In Pastures New*.

Wherever he traveled, he regarded prescribed "sights" as part of the price for seeing what interested him most, the way people live in strange places. His greatest joy was always the people, sometimes other Americans. To study them in a new environment was a pleasure that never lost its zest.

"You happen upon a cluster of Americans, stubbornly trying to 'do' Switzerland, or Japan, or Jamaica, according to the printed instructions. Are they New England or Mississippi Valley? Are they having a good time or merely serving a sentence? Has the daughter been away to school? Is mother really managing the expedition? Did father have a nervous collapse before leaving home, or is that hunted look the result of recreation? From what size town do they hail? What do they think of the natives hereabouts? And what do the natives hereabouts think of them?"

The Ade spirit of tolerance and understanding was always with him. Instead of being pained by the strange antics of others, he made excuses for them.

"Let it be admitted that the gabby lad with the smoke-room training can be an affliction when he lets himself go; but he is a good deal easier to take if you sit back, nonresistant, and hang on to your sense of humor. . . . Regard him and all other fellow travellers with a large tolerance and bountiful compassion. Ever remembering: that every man becomes erratic in his behavior when he is out of his own bailiwick and up against new problems.

"Every new traveller away from home is a victim of fear—just a little agitated and beating against the bars. That is why his manners and his mental processes become temporarily abnormal. One kind of traveller yields abjectly to this fear engendered by strange surroundings. He acknowledges the hopelessness of the situation and becomes dumb and unresisting. Another kind tries to hide his fear under a loud combativeness. . . . Are most travellers ill-mannered? No—just a little fussed-up by the consciousness that they are giving the party and someone is holding out on the refreshments. . . . The American away from home is said to be a braggart. That is one of those crystallized misconceptions, the same as the side-whiskers of the Englishman and the ruffled shirt of the Frenchman. When an American does speak up for his native land, perhaps he has been goaded beyond endurance. For every voluble one, three or four are tongue-tied and lonesome and completely out of war paint."

To the first-time tourist, he offered this advice: "If you have become so ossified by habit that you cannot put up with the manners and customs and transportation facilities and cooking and cocktails of the older civilizations, the thing for you to do is to stay at home and watch the trains go through."

As an example of tourist behavior George liked to tell this story about himself. In Rome he gave a dinner for a number of friends, including Booth Tarkington, Harry Leon Wilson and Julian

Street. It was in a private dining room at an excellent hotel and Julian Street afterward insisted that George had topped the Roman record for lavish entertaining previously held by Nero. About ten o'clock a young woman guest wished to return to her hotel near by, and George asked to be excused long enough to accompany her. After taking her as far as the elevator his curiosity prompted him to look into the bar. There he saw two or three other friends and paused to chat with them. The conversation became so interesting that he forgot everything else. Around midnight someone happened to ask him where he had dined. He said he had been to a most enjoyable dinner at which Booth Tarkington had told some wonderful stories.

"Who gave the dinner?" he was asked.

George stared for a moment as a thought bored its way into his memory. Then with a look of horror, "My God, *I* did!"

On some of his trips abroad George was accompanied by his Chicago friend, Orson Wells, an enormous man with a bald, dome-shaped head. They had much in common, for "Ort" Wells had spent his childhood in Lafayette, where he had been a newsboy, selling papers at a hotel corner. He became a telegraph operator in a brokerage office, associated with that daring speculator, John W. Gates. He learned from Gates the art of successful speculation and made himself a millionaire. Then he retired and was free and willing to go wherever George suggested. In 1910 they set out for a trip around the world. In India they took a long daylight ride from Agar to Benares. "Our railway compartment was open on all sides," wrote George, "and the white, floury, choking dust . . . enveloped us mile after mile. A killing heat sizzled the dry plains and lay in trembling waves above every desolate landscape. The dust had penetrated to every crevice of our beings. We sat there like two ashen ghosts gazing blankly at the endless monotony of gray stubble and miserable shacks and parched roadways. Finally . . . I ventured to break the silence. I wanted to cheer him up.

"I said, 'Mr. Wells, if I remember correctly, I met you one fine, cool, bracing day last autumn at a ball-game on the West Side. . . . I believe you were wearing a light overcoat. . . . We went back to the Athletic Club in a taxi and, after a pleasant steaming, we took the shower and jumped into the pool.'

"He gazed at me as if fascinated, and I took it that he wished me to continue. . . . 'After the swim we went to your room and there you took a drink of something. It had a spoon and a large piece of ice in it.'

"When the word 'ice' was mentioned, I saw a quiver of the massive frame and the nostrils began to dilate. I had no reason for keeping on, except that I was enjoying myself for the first time that day.

" 'I remember that it took you a long time that evening to decide what you wanted to eat,' I resumed. 'At first you thought of black bass. . . . Someone suggested a combination chop, with kidneys on the side, and another recommended grilled turkey bones, but you finally compromised on the old stand-by. You took one of those big, thick, juicy steaks.'

"I saw his lower jaw move up and down and he seemed to be endeavoring to speak, for his Adam's apple was bobbing convulsively behind the ample folds of his neck, but no sound came forth. He simply continued to stare at me. . . .

" 'What I am leading up to is this,' I explained. 'Just as you poured the mushroom sauce over your steak, I remember that you said you *would* like to travel in India. . . . Now, Mr. Wells, if you consider the time and place appropriate, I should like to offer my congratulations. You've got your wish.' "

In Hongkong the night of their arrival a hotel clerk had urged them to visit the gayest of the night spots. George was fascinated by the extreme British accent of the woman in charge. She overheard something about Indiana and asked if they knew Lafayette. When she learned who they were, she gave orders to serve them all the champagne they could drink without charge. It came out that she was the daughter of a boardinghouse keeper in Lafayette. As a young girl she had known of George Ade when he worked for a Lafayette newspaper. She had made her way to the Far East and there married an Englishman.

Receiving special consideration because of his fame or his personality was a fairly common occurrence in George's travels. On his way across Europe, heading homeward on that first trip around the world, he was interviewed in Berlin by Frederick William Wile, who sent to the London *Daily Mail* George's comments about the good service at the Hotel Adlon. When he reached the Adlon again two or three years later on his way to Russia, he found himself in the royal suite. "There's been a mistake here," he said; but it was no mistake. Herr Adlon insisted that he should have the best the hotel could offer—and free of charge.

On one of their West Indies cruises toward the end of 1914 George and Ort ate at the same table with a couple from Kenosha, Wisconsin, Mr. and Mrs. Richard Welles. When they were saying good-by, Mrs. Welles said she had enjoyed their company so much that if the child she was expecting in a few months should be a boy she intended to name it for them, George Orson. And that is how Orson Welles of motion pictures and radio got his name.

On another of his trips with Wells, George met a studious German who asked him if his works had been translated into German. Wells heard him solemnly telling the German passenger that some of his works had not even been translated into English.

George loved to go shopping in foreign places and usually brought home trunkloads of "loot" for which he had no need, and this may have inspired an essay in which he said: "The fun of spending money is to garner things for which we hanker, without being compelled to explain why. But the shopping pastime can be worked up into a dreadful mania for collecting non-essentials. The article we covet begins to shrink the moment the price-tag is removed."

Sometimes on his West Indies cruises he took guests with him, and to be a George Ade guest on a trip must have been an experience. One Ade friend has told of his astonishment at having George casually press a roll of bills into his hand—more than $200—saying, "You'll want a little money for shopping—half the fun on a trip." And then a week later when he suggested that it was time to replenish the pocket money, George was astonished that the guest had not yet seen anything he wanted to buy.

George could not bring himself to be economical when traveling, because he felt that, no matter what the expense, he was getting full value on the whole. When anything cost too much he would say, "What will it matter a hundred years from now?"—an expression he often used. On a boat bound for England he met a theatrical producer he knew who suggested that they share hotel rooms in London. The producer ordered a large suite, as he wanted to interview actors and singers, and had a piano brought in. His phone calls were many. When George found that he was expected to pay half of the charges for everything, he did not protest, just thought it was a good joke on him. Yet at home he would sometimes walk out of a grocery without buying if the proprietor tried to charge him a penny or two more than a current price; and once he went to court to fight a bill from a painter who had made an eighteen-dollar overcharge.

As previously mentioned, George's travels taught him that there is a limit to the amount of productive land in the world near the principal markets, and confirmed his belief that he was acting prudently to let brother Bill buy more land for him in the corn belt—which proved to be his safest investment. (During the inflationary period that followed the first World War, he was offered nearly a million dollars for his holdings.)

Another huge lesson that he learned from travel was that "back of the temples and cathedrals and the famous thoroughfares and show-places of every country there is always the same background —humanity in the mass, plain people, a myriad host of humble men, women and children, most of them toiling patiently for the smallest privilege of existence."

He summed up his general impressions of travel: "It may afford consolation to the large number of people who remain at home to know that only about five per cent of foreign travel is really worth while. . . . You pay for what you get, not in money alone, but in hardships, annoyances, and long periods of dumb, patient waiting.

"The blessedness of travel is that when the sun comes from behind the clouds and a new city begins to arise from the sea, we forget all the gloomy days on board ship, all the crampy rides in stuffy railway compartments, all the overcharges and vexations and harassments and get ready to tear ashore and explore a new wonderland.

"Who can forget the first hour of the first railway ride through rural England? The storybook pictures that you have seen all your life come true at last.

"In the first hour of 'rickshaw riding in Japan I saw so much that was funny and fantastic and nerve-kinking that at the end of the ride I wanted to pay the coolie for a year instead of an hour. And how about the first hour up the Grand Canal of Venice?

"Travel is hard work, and your true traveller is a mighty grumbler; but he goes on buoyed always by the hope of another 'first hour.' "

23

A Bachelor and His Family

"As a family man, I would have been a total loss, a devastating calamity." Yet in a way George Ade was about the "familiest" man one could imagine. He loved children, always took a deep interest in his nieces and nephews, and showed exceptional devotion to his father and mother. Regardless of rehearsals of a new play, he always contrived to be at Kentland with his father and mother on Thanksgiving day, to them a more significant family fete day than Christmas. When he came into great prosperity, his first thought was of what it could mean to his father and mother. A day or two after the opening of *The Sultan of Sulu* in Chicago, he sent for them and reserved for them the best suite at the Palmer House, putting them at their ease by saying that the manager was his friend and gave him a low rate. He knew that it would be hard for his mother to forget the days when she had to wash and dry the children's underwear while they slept. To protect her from shock he told the waiter not to show any menu but simply to suggest some dishes. He opened a charge account at Marshall Field's and urged his mother to go on a shopping frolic. He suggested that she refurnish the house. She roamed about the store until tired and her purchases consisted of three china plates to give to neighbors.

Then he did something that boys dream of doing, went back to the home town, picked out the best house that was for sale and bought it for his father and mother. He induced them to make a trip to Washington and New York. They attended *The College Widow*, but George felt sure that his father would enjoy most of all Ringling's circus at Madison Square Garden. It became known that George Ade's father and mother were in a box, and the clowns, most of them George's good friends, did their best acts in front of that box. John Ade did not realize that all the special attention was because of the fame of his son. He said they were lucky to have such good seats.

While in New York John Ade demonstrated his sense of humor. At the Herald Square Hotel, the head clerk, eager to show every courtesy to George Ade's father, walked over to chat with him as he sat in the lobby.

"This your first visit to New York?" asked the friendly clerk.

"No," replied George's father, "I was here once before—stayed a whole week. It was some time ago."

"Do you notice any changes?"

"Oh, yes. Indeed I do! The town is considerably larger. Quite a number of new buildings have been put up. As I go around I observe ever so many improvements. There's no question about it, the town has changed."

"How long since you were here before, Mr. Ade?"

"Seventy-two years," George's father casually replied.

"Even after father and mother had celebrated their golden wedding anniversary they refused to fold their hands, and they shied at luxuries. We children scolded mother because she would not turn the household duties over to a helper. That is, we scolded her to her face and bragged about her when she couldn't hear. We brought her fine things to wear and she put them away in tissue-paper and saved them for exhibition purposes."

Early in 1907 George's mother died. To give his father a change of scene, George took him on a trip to California. On the way back they stopped at Salt Lake City where George had friends. John Ade had a violent prejudice against the Mormons. George arranged that during a visit to the Mormon Temple the organist would play a special program of his father's favorite hymns. His friends selected a particularly pretty young Mormon girl for John Ade's escort. She was so kind and solicitous that John Ade took a great liking to her.

Back at their hotel George's father said, "George, all this has been a revelation to me. And wasn't that a sweet, lovely girl?"

"Yes," George told him, with a chuckle, "one of Brigham Young's grandchildren."

George insisted that they had received special courtesies because his father "looked just like a Mormon elder." With his white chin whiskers, black suit, white shirt, stiff white collar and no necktie, there was a resemblance.

George was a delegate to the Republican National Convention at Chicago in 1908 and he took his father with him, but he could find a seat for him only in the rear of the gallery. To his amazement, when he reached his own place on the main floor, there was his father not far away with the Arizona delegation. Then his father was invited to occupy a place of honor on the platform as a Frémont Republican. He ended by helping the secretary tabulate the vote. And, George insisted, "when Henry Cabot Lodge, the Chairman, was in doubt as to the procedure, father prompted him."

George often said that it was one of his happiest recollections that twenty years after his college days, his father came into a "postponed vindication" for sending him to Purdue, and that he was able to "slather" his father with money. When his father was eighty-one, George succeeded in persuading him to retire from the bank. "Just sign my name to checks," George told him, "for whatever money you need."

After he retired from the bank, John Ade was busier than ever, attending conventions, Chautauquas, circuses and all kinds of busy gatherings for the good of something or other. He was keen for political rallies and pitched horseshoes at every outing held by the Indiana Society of Chicago. J. M. Studebaker, of South Bend, was his regular partner. They won all their matches.

On the day his father completed his eighty-fifth year, in September 1913, George arranged for a celebration at Hazelden in his honor. "We had a ball game. My brother Will could not circle the bases because he was stiffened up with rheumatism, so father ran for him.

"On April 28, 1914, he was a delegate to the Republican Congressional Convention at Valparaiso. As chairman of the resolutions committee he drafted the platform and was sitting in the convention hall listening to the report of his committee. He fell asleep. His seat-mate tried to arouse him, but anyone might have known that father would not go to sleep in a Republican convention. He was dead.

"He and my mother were what they were, which was plenty good enough for this speckled world."

George's brother Joe, also a bachelor, was a "character." At one time he was a railway mail-clerk and almost foppish in his dress, given to fancy vests and expensive shirts. Then he was in a train wreck in which another man in the same car was killed. Joe was badly shaken up, and his mother dreaded to see him return to the railroad. George suggested putting Joe in charge of one of his farms.

From the time that Joe became a farmer, he forsook stylish haberdashery and went to the other extreme. Previously, he had been fairly particular about his grammar, but he gave that up too. People liked to hear him talk. Many said he was funnier than George. If he told a story that brought a laugh, he promptly told it over again.

It was not easy for Joe to prosper as a farmer, because he loved animals and hated to sell a steer or a hog when it was ready for the market. He always delayed selling and his feed bills ran up. He would buy canned food rather than kill one of his hens for the table. Among his favorite farm animals was a team of mules. They were a powerful team, but sometimes he hitched them to a light buggy. Once he invited a Hazelden guest to drive to Brook with him and the mule on the "haw" side balked for no evident reason. After ten or fifteen minutes of coaxing the mule to change its mind, Joe got mad. "I'll kill you," he yelled; "I don't know whether I'll shoot you or beat you to death, but I'll kill you." Then he got out and went to the mule's head and began to pat him. "You know I didn't mean that," he said. "Stand here as long as you want to."

In 1912 William Hodge, the actor, came to Hazelden for a visit. His purpose was to study Hoosiers, for he was to star in the part of a Hoosier in *The Man From Home* by Booth Tarkington and Harry Leon Wilson. The authors had intended the part for David Warfield, and George Tyler, the producer, wanted Nat Goodwin, but George Ade had talked so glowingly to Tarkington of what Hodge could do with the part that it resulted in his being engaged. He had made his reputation as an actor in down-East plays by James A. Herne, *Sag Harbor* and others, but George insisted that he would be a success in a Hoosier part if he spent a little time in Indiana to absorb some color. One afternoon Hodge told George of his rare find in Brook. He had overheard a farmer talking, he said, and if he only knew the man, so that he could talk with him for an hour or two, then he would have plenty of Hoosier atmosphere, for this farmer was the most rural type. George said they would drive in and find out who the fellow was and try to arrange to meet him. Of course the man turned out to be brother Joe.

George decided to make Joe independent by deeding him a life interest in a 360-acre farm. After he had sent for Joe and read to him the legal phrasing of the deed, he asked him if there was anything he did not understand. Joe said he'd like to hear the first part over again. When he started to go, Joe pulled a crumpled dollar bill from his pocket and laid it on the table.

"What's that for?" asked George.

"It's to pay you for everything," Joe told him. "That paper you read says it's for one dollar and other considerations, and—well, you know me. I never want to be under obligations to anybody."

As in their childhood, Joe, like George, felt little urge for regular church attendance, but their brother Will was active in the Methodist church. One day the presiding elder of the church came to see him and expressed a wish to meet his brother George. When he was introduced, he said to George, "I trust that you are as earnest a Christian as your brother Will."

"I don't know," George solemnly replied. "I think I stack up better alongside brother Joe."

Will Ade was opposed to the use of alcoholic liquor in any form. All his life he had been a total abstainer. One noon he dropped in at George's home for lunch. The dessert was plum pudding and as it was brought in George remembered that it was seasoned with brandy. Always a model host and not wishing to inflict anything distasteful on a guest, he tried to give a silent signal to his housekeeper, but it was too late. Will Ade ate it without remonstrance. Then he leaned back in his chair and looking at George, said, "I want to say something about this pudding." George, shamefaced, expected something harsh. After a momentary pause Will went on, "It's the best dessert I ever ate. Any chance for a second helping?"

That one of the most sought-after men of his time, who seemed instinctively a family man, should have contrived to remain a bachelor all his life naturally stirred curiosity. To interviewers George sometimes gave joking explanations. "At a time when I might have contemplated marriage, a license cost $2 and I never had the money. . . . I suppose I lived in a hall bedroom too long and became thoroughly undomesticated. On top of that maybe no woman would have had me." The American bachelor, he wrote, is not a woman hater. "When he comes into the presence of an attractive specimen of the more important sex he is not revolted. He is awe-stricken and rendered numb and dumb. . . . It isn't usually a lack of intense regard and reverence for womanhood that keeps the bachelor single. Often enough, it is lack of regard for himself as a fit companion for the goddess up there above him on the pedestal."

To a few intimates he would say, "I didn't marry because another man married my girl"—meaning Lillian Howard. Yet at other times he conceded that a marrying type of man, failing to make arrangements with one, finds another. "It seems useless to deny that the trick can be turned by any man—whose mental equipment enables him to decide that he should go into the house when it rains. Brigham Young, wearing throat whiskers, could assemble between thirty-five and forty at one time."

As Julian Street said, if George ever *had* married, "his wife would have been the best entertained woman on earth!"

24

The Country Squire

WHEN George Ade moved to Hazelden the neighbors soon found that he did not put on airs. A neighbor spoke of having talked with "one of the servants." George corrected him, saying, "I have no servants; we all just work there together." It was noted, too, that George was genuinely interested in everybody in the community. He went each day to a barbershop at Brook, shaving himself only on Sunday. He knew the barbershop was the place to hear what the neighbors were talking about. Someone remarked, "When George Ade asks you how your family is, he doesn't walk away without waiting for an answer. He really wants to know." Within a few weeks George's neighbors felt free to walk into his house without knocking. If someone rapped, or rang the bell, George would wonder: who's the stranger?

He began to give big parties and invited his neighbors for miles around. First a modest Fourth of July celebration, with lemonade, foot races, and skyrockets, then more elaborate affairs, for he liked to be Barnum and arrange a big show once in a while. "My reward...has been the sight of a large bunch of people undeniably having the time of their lives." His first elaborate affair was in September 1908. William H. Taft, Secretary of War, had been nominated for President. George had been a delegate to the convention and was on the committee to notify him. He conceived the idea that Taft should open his campaign at Hazelden. When he presented the idea to Will Hays, chairman of the speakers' bureau, at Indianapolis, Hays explained how impossible it would be. Taft would open his campaign in some large city. And yet, Hays thought, the audacity of the proposal warranted a little consideration, so he telephoned to Taft, who happened to be in Cincinnati. Hays did not know that Taft was one of George Ade's great admirers. He had been Governor of the Philippines at the time *The Sultan of Sulu* was produced, and it had delighted him. When Hays told him of Ade's invitation, he instantly replied, "I will go to the farm at Brook and see the Sultan of Sulu."

He made there the opening speech of his campaign. There were bands, circus seats in the front yard, two hundred luncheon guests, thousands of onlookers and twenty acres of buggies east of the house. To bring those who arrived by train at Brook, George provided a fleet of hay wagons.

George had planned to signal Taft's arrival by setting off some loud aerial bombs that could be heard above the music and the shouting. The catalogue said the bombs came a dozen in a box, so he ordered a box. A little while before the rally, he had one of these set off as a test to see if the mortar was set right. As the Taft party approached, George gave the signal and the boys set off the rest of the bombs. Among those on the Taft train was Colonel "Dan" Ransdell, a veteran Indiana Republican, for a long time Sergeant-at-Arms of the United States Senate. He called George to one side to compliment him on the way every detail of the demonstration showed careful thought.

"I was delighted," he said, "to note that you had studied the etiquette of the occasion and therefore gave the Secretary of War his proper salute of eleven guns." George didn't want to disappoint him by confessing that the eleven-gun salute had been accidental. He told him he had supposed everybody knew that a Secretary of War was entitled to eleven guns; but the Colonel said no, he was sure that George was one in a thousand!

In that 1908 campaign, George was invited to travel on a special train with Senator Albert J. Beveridge, making a speaking tour all over Indiana, starting from Chicago. George said he could not spare the time but would go as far as his own town of Brook. A number of distinguished newspaper correspondents—among them Sam Blythe—were in the Beveridge car, champagne flowed freely, and the conversation was amusing. George got off at Brook, as planned, and was waving good-by to his friends, but as the train was pulling out he changed his mind. "I can't miss this," he said, and jumped back on.

There were more big political rallies at Hazelden and numerous smaller parties. Probably no other country squire was ever so given to hospitality. The Indiana Society of Chicago asked George if it would be all right to drop in for dinner. Six hundred came, but George was prepared. He had sought the aid of women experienced in preparing church suppers. One hundred tables were under the big trees "and every table had a floral decoration and was completely equipped with receptacles and implements."

The Purdue Alumni of Chicago, and members of his college fraternity from all over Indiana and Chicago, were George's guests every year. One of his biggest parties was a Home-coming on July 4, 1919, for soldiers and sailors, with thousands of cars parked in his nearest pasture.

As if he were not giving enough parties himself, he started a golf club to give more. In 1910 he laid out a golf course, consisting of nine approach-and-putt holes, intended for his week-end guests. It did not seem neighborly to have its use limited, so he formed the Hazelden Country Club with about forty members from Brook and Kentland. Then they enlarged the course, which became about the best nine-hole golf course in the state. Membership grew to 150 with dues nominal. George paid the taxes as well as much of the upkeep. He built a clubhouse and encouraged the club to give big annual parties at his expense. Some of these parties, with famous golf professionals participating, were of national interest.

George was the club's president for life. It was close to his heart, for he believed it served a community purpose in promoting neighborliness and the benefits of outdoor sport. He encouraged the wives to take up golf and suggested that if the youngsters got jobs as caddies it would keep them out of poolrooms. He provided in his will that the land would finally belong to the club. From the first he insisted that there should never be any racial discrimination in the membership.

For Saturday night dances held regularly in summer he sometimes brought top-notch orchestras from Chicago. When "G.A.," as the neighbors called him, was sure that a party was going along all right, he would walk back to his house to go to bed and read.

One of George's childhood recollections was of never having enough ice cream; and such thoughts led to a series of children's picnics that became the most noteworthy of all the parties at Hazelden. At the first of these he had about eighty youngsters under twelve years of age to herd and feed and supply with lemonade, ice cream, noisemakers, gas balloons and day fireworks. After he had been host, annually, at four or five such parties, children began to come to them or be brought to them from adjoining states. Mothers living near Hazelden wrote to relatives as far away as Iowa suggesting that if they were planning to come with the children for a visit, it would be best to arrive at the time of Mr. Ade's party. Then a day or so before the big picnic, mothers would call up to say that relatives had come unexpectedly and would it be all right for *their* children to attend?

"We sent out five hundred invitations," George reported, "and got nearly eight hundred acceptances!" The children's picnics became too big even for George. Someone said that Hazelden seemed to be the amusement center of the United States! The last party began at ten in the morning and lasted until late afternoon. George had sent to Chicago for some of the best vaudeville entertainers, a professional master of ceremonies, a famous clown, a ventriloquist, a Punch-and-Judy show, an organ-grinder with a monkey, a magician, a tramp juggler and an acrobatic comedy team; another feature was a balloon ascension. Then there were swimming, diving, dancing, cracker-eating and beauty contests, besides ball games for "the championship of three counties" and some "surprise distributions." George did all the planning himself and made thorough inquiries about the kind of games youngsters of each age group liked best. He devoted much care to the selection of each item used and was especially painstaking about having cookies of the right flavor. He bought the best grade of toy balloons and had an expert come from Chicago with gas tanks to inflate them. Also, he had Red Cross nurses and a doctor on hand. Throughout the day he mingled with the children to make sure that all were happy, and it pleased him that most of his guests felt free to call him George. He said the fun *he* had was worth more than the party cost. As the *Newton County Enterprise* commented, "It is nice to have the facilities to stage such an affair, and still more wonderful to have the disposition to do so."

George sometimes took a hand, too, in providing entertainment over at Kentland. In his childhood circus day had been a memorable event; but with the growth of larger towns, the big traveling shows began to pass by Kentland. He used his influence to have the Hagenbeck-Wallace circus come there if the town would offer special inducements, free license, free lot, free water and no complimentary tickets. Then he wrote a letter to hundreds of people in the county, urging them to attend. Kentland had a population of about 1,200, but a total of 12,000 attended each of the afternoon and evening performances.

George was an exceptional host even at small parties held indoors. His invitations sometimes read: "Men who wish to show off may wear dinner coats or full dress." He discouraged real gambling, but gave Monte Carlo parties at which his guests played for high stakes with stage money, and the big winners and big losers got prizes.* As one who had done a reasonable share of experimenting with alcohol, he observed certain niceties regarding drinks for guests. For women he served cocktails of less alcoholic content than those for men, but always kept such precautionary discrimination a secret. If young people were among the guests, he told his helpers: "Remember that no one must ever have his first drink of strong liquor on these premises."

George came to know what people want to eat in the country. The first rule, he said, is to avoid hotel dishes and try to make dreams of home and mother come true; to combine quality with quantity.

"Fried chicken alone will make the party a success if the springers have been dispatched and dismembered on the morning of the day before, soaked in cold water and finally rolled in flour and fried slowly in sweet country butter and served moist and piping hot. This article of food has no point of resemblance to the vitrified and kiln-dried fowl served at many public eating places.

"Because of some idiotic edict of fashion, real gravy can no longer be found except in the country. We serve huge receptacles of genuine gravy in which the giblets jostle one another. The partakers are not only permitted to drown the mashed potatoes and blot up the overflow with the highly absorbent country biscuits but are actually urged, in a nice way, to do so. I should say that the first thing to do in the operation of a popular feeding resort is to suspend the rules.

---

* In his later years George Ade took no interest in card playing except solitaire. That he still understood poker was shown by the definition of it he wrote in an introduction to H. T. Webster's book of poker cartoons: "The only game in which courage so often triumphs over intelligence, guided by caution."

George Marion, stage director of Ade plays, as
painted in later life by A. G. Warshawsky.

Ort Wells, companion of George Ade's
many travels.

Ade and Madame Schumann-Heink, the opera singer.

Advising Purdue students about their 1941 revival of *The College Widow*.

"If I had to select an All-American menu for a large cluster of people out in the country in the summertime, it would run about as follows: fruit cocktail (if compounded by local experts with no hotel experience); fried chicken (prepared by women over thirty years of age); bona fide gravy; cole slaw, made of fresh young cabbage, smothered in a sharp cream sauce, and served at the freezing point; cottage cheese that has not been to market; fresh boiled beets (they sound unimportant, but you would be surprised); country biscuits, lined up in rows; cakes and cakes and cakes; pie, made of fresh fruits; regular ice cream; coffee, milk, or iced tea.

"Pie is maligned frequently. And yet hot cherry pie has caused some of our most prominent lady visitors to break down and cry."

George felt a pride in anyone in his neighborhood who had distinguished himself or who could be called a "character." He would "brag" about "Alvy" Harriman, of Brook, the best horseshoe pitcher at the State Fair; of "Biddie" Harrington, at Fowler, who always ordered *a* fried chicken instead of *some* fried chicken; of Fred Erb, in West Lafayette, who broke 100 glass balls with his shotgun "without missing ary one"; of "Hank" Granger, in Lake Township, who had developed a secret process for curing ham. He talked of driving over to a near-by town to get acquainted with a man reported to have written to Sears, Roebuck for a package of macaroni seed.

Tenants on the Ade farms thought of George as good neighbor rather than as landlord. On rare occasions he would drive about on an inspection tour of his farm buildings with Jim Rathbun, his nephew and for twenty-five years his farm manager. Jim did not altogether like to take George on such trips for he was always seeing improvements that should be made, and Jim wanted to make a good showing on the net income. George was more con-

cerned about dingy outbuildings surrounded by wreckage of
ancient implements than of mustard in the oats or failure of a tile
drain to carry away the water. If a tenant housewife expressed a
hope that in the spring they might have new wallpaper in the
front room, George was likely to say, "I think *all* the rooms should
be repapered." Or he might suggest that the house needed better
plumbing. He admitted that his enthusiasms regarding his farms
were more for things that cost money than for those that brought
in money. "My idea of a landlord," he said, "seems to be a combination of landscape gardener and interior decorator."

"Let's try to hold back enough farm income for taxes," Rathbun
would say.

"That's your worry," George would tell him. "You're my
squidge." That was a term he often used, after hearing it in a
comic opera in which Frank Daniels, playing the part of a king,
had a "squidge" to do all his worrying.

George himself was "squidge" to many people in trouble, and
they were not confined to his own locality. As Booth Tarkington
once said of him, George was "helplessly generous." He had a soft
spot for anyone ever connected with the stage and almost any actor
down on his luck could get money from him. For many years he
supported an old newspaper friend in failing health. Shortly
before he died, the man suggested to an acquaintance, on an adjoining cot in the hospital, that George might sometime give him
a helping hand, too. "Willed me to him," George commented,
when he began to receive appeals from the stranger; and he did
not refuse him.

Sometimes the demands upon him were for impressive sums. A
friend in another part of the state was in desperate need of $10,000.
He *had* to have it. After exhausting every other possible source,
he thought of George Ade and drove to Hazelden, arriving late at
night after George had gone to bed. The man's situation was so

serious that George let him have the ten thousand on his note, though sure that the note would always be worthless.

He could not resist even a dog in trouble. When a stray female dog happened along, thinking, George said, "that we were conducting a rescue mission—which we were," he sent her to be clipped, cleaned up and operated on "so that she would not be called upon again to assume the responsibilities of motherhood." He named her Sadie, after Sadie Thompson in *Rain,* "whose life had been a series of mistakes." Perhaps he summed up his feeling about people as well as dogs when he said, "Instinct may have told her that an old bachelor who had stubbed his own toe a couple of times would be forgiving."

Strangers who sensed George's tolerance for human shortcomings wrote to him in unusual emergencies. One man's letter said, "Owing to a rather indiscreet and highly unsuccessful love affair I find myself in a position where I have got to come across for damages or else be shown up in a poor light at home. Could you let me have a couple of hundred dollars for a month or two?" George sent the money.

Arrival of the morning mail was a major event in the daily routine at Hazelden, for George was forced to carry on an immense correspondence. Not counting the appeals for help, there came stacks of letters from strangers who thought of him as a friend, and he felt bound to answer any sensible letter he received. His replies, though usually dictated and done hastily, yet had a neighborly warmth. One letter writer mentioned casually that his wife had just had another baby. George wrote back to inquire the baby's sex and name. This interest was quite sincere.

Sometimes a question in a letter caused him to write something quite serious, in contrast to the Ade of the Fables. In reply to a college student's inquiry as to the characteristics of the ideal American college girl, he wrote: "As to her appearance, she should be well groomed and her style of wearing her hair should be up to date but not fussy. Her attire should be correct with no striving for extreme effects. She should avoid highly colored finger-nails. I am sure most men do not like them, but many girls persist in them. She should strive to make herself attractive but not worry too much about 'glamour.' Her interests should include modern literature, current events, social problems and a sensible relation between the sexes. I think she should be interested in good house-keeping and try to be sympathetic with the average man's point of view. She should strive for old-fashioned charm instead of the ability merely to do stunts. Her ambitions and outlook should include: a real desire to know a lot about the problems of modern society and she should strive to develop an individuality and a broadminded willingness to give a hearing to all the various programs which are advocated for modern women. Even if her ambitions do not include the duties of a housewife, I think she should prepare herself to become the head of a home, because matrimony is always more than a possibility."

In reply to a question from another inquirer, he wrote: "I do think the church is necessary in modern life because people cannot get the comforts and consolation and the promises for the future by scientific research or a study of the philosophies. Our churches inspire faith and arouse emotions which are useful to the well-being of the world and so, I think, they are necessary."

Regarding his opinion of jazz, he wrote: "The cruder forms of jazz, a collection of squeals, of squawks and wails against a con-cealed back-structure of melody, became unbearable to me soon after I began to hear it. . . . I suggest that every ragtime artist should be compelled to take an examination and secure a license before he is permitted to fool with a saxophone."

A man about to be released from a penitentiary wanted George to help him get a job with the Ringling circus. "I'm not a lawbreaker at heart," he wrote. "I was only thoughtless." George investigated and learned that the man's thoughtlessness had caused him to crack a few safes.

George's generous spirit showed itself in a letter to a New York newspaper which asked him to comment on a report that Theodore Dreiser, in the first edition of his novel *Sister Carrie,* had incorporated in a description of one of his principal characters the word picture of Cousin Gus in Ade's Fable of the Willing Performer. George had already noticed it but said nothing, believing that Dreiser had absorbed the description and used it with no thought of plagiarism. To the New York paper he wrote: "Most certainly I do not accuse Mr. Dreiser of plagiarism; I have a genuine admiration for him. . . . While some of us have been building chicken coops or possibly bungalows, Mr. Dreiser has been erecting skyscrapers. . . . If in building one of his massive structures he used a brick from my pile, goodness knows he was welcome to it, and no questions were asked or will be asked."

Even "crackpot" letters to George often got polite answers. A woman in Indianapolis wrote him at great length urging him to think more about saving his soul. He replied: "I am somewhat flabbergasted to receive your letter of nineteen pages. You are wasting a lot of penmanship on someone who does not deserve so much attention. You write a good hand and use good English and you seem to know your Scriptures. . . . I am quite sure that your interest in my behalf is sincere and unselfish and I am duly thankful, even if I am a little amazed and upset to receive a letter nineteen pages long."

She came right back at him, and then George wrote her: "I am wondering what I can do to cause you to desist in your strenuous efforts in behalf of my spiritual welfare. I have adopted my own way of life and my own tenets of belief and I fear that they cannot be changed even by your eloquent and persistent reasoning.

I must request you, as politely as possible, to refrain from these labors in my behalf. . . . I think it would be better simply to terminate our correspondence."

One of the few unforgiving letters that George ever wrote was to his former teacher in the far West, who had whipped him unjustly in his primary-school days. The teacher reminded him of the school episode. "I gave you the start on your career." George replied: "Instead of giving me a start, you raised welts on my legs, broke my heart and nearly ruined me."

One kind of letter which never got a reply, and which he never even read through, came from women who hated to think of his living alone and offered their companionship.

Besides all the strangers who wrote to express good wishes, many other Ade admirers came to Hazelden in person to pay their respects, rightly assuming that the Ade home would have no stiff formality. One morning shortly after the end of the first World War a young Army Colonel drove up. He told George Ade Davis, an Ade nephew who received him, that he was driving from California to Washington and had swung a little off his route in the hope of being permitted to shake hands with George Ade who had been one of his heroes since high school days. He and his boyhood hero had a good chat. The Colonel was Douglas MacArthur. (After MacArthur had become one of the great figures of World War II, George Ade would scratch his chin and smile and say, "I wonder if we made enough fuss over that fellow when he was here. But how were we to know what a great man he was!")

Much as he loved Hazelden and his kind of life there, George did not forget his own observation, "Early to bed and early to rise, and you'll meet very few prominent people." He did not recommend staying in the country too long at a stretch. "You may acquire peace of mind by listening to the breeze in the trees, but you will not get any man-size experiences out of botany. If you wish to keep tab on the human race you must go, once in a while, to where the interesting specimens are assembled."

As a compromise between life in Chicago and that of the rural townships, he began to spend his winters in Florida—that is, the winters when he was not traveling abroad—at first in hotels, and then, for many years, in a rented house at 1331 Fourteenth Street, Miami Beach. But when he received reports of the first signs of spring in the corn belt, he was always eager to resume the life of a country squire.

25

With Cheerful People

NATIVE of a community where everybody was rabidly partisan, and with experience as a reporter at national nominating conventions, George Ade could hardly have escaped keen interest in politics. He was all the more ready to take sides after he had formed a close friendship with President Theodore Roosevelt, thenceforth his greatest hero.* It was because of this heightened interest that he became a delegate to the convention that nominated Taft and was host at the big meeting when Taft opened his campaign.

George first met Roosevelt at a Gridiron Club dinner in the autumn of 1904. Roosevelt invited him to come the next week to dinner at his home in Oyster Bay. Almost from the moment of the guest's arrival Roosevelt quoted exuberantly from the books of Ade Fables, with a familiarity that suggested recent reading! Then Roosevelt began to ask questions. "What do they think out your way of So-and-So?" mentioning a well-known Hoosier Democrat. George remembered what a neighbor had said of this man, and replied: "Out our way we think he is the kind of man who would be taken along on a Sunday-school picnic for the purpose of putting up a swing for the children."

The President laughed until the tears came. Then he wanted advice. He pointed to a picture on the wall, a large halftone of Roosevelt, in a riding costume with high, close-fitting boots. The

---

* There was one possible exception, Benjamin Franklin. Ade often said he would give anything to have known him.

National Committee had printed the pictures for wide distribution, but advisers feared that the riding costume would cost thousands of votes in the Middle West. Anyone in that outfit would
be either an Anglo-maniac or a dude.

"What do you think?" asked the President.

"I think," said George, "that you are the one man who could
get away with it. It would be fatal to Henry Cabot Lodge. It
would be ridiculous for Bryan. It would be criminal for almost
any Congressman. But it is just the rig for you."

The advice proved good. There was no criticism of the pictures
and Roosevelt won by a big majority. George became a favorite
at the White House and the President always chuckled about the
man who was taken to the picnic to put up the swing.

On one of his trips to Washington George met his old friend
of Chicago newspaper days, Opie Read. Doing articles for the
Hearst newspapers, Read was to write an attack on Roosevelt.
George was at the White House for dinner that evening, and he
remarked to Roosevelt that Read was hoping to see him the next
day. Roosevelt pricked up his ears and asked questions. What
papers was Read writing for? Had he written any books?

Read had no trouble getting his appointment. When he reached
the President's office, Roosevelt greeted him with a "dee-light-ed"
and said he had always wanted to meet him because a character
in his novel, *The Jucklins,* had interested him. (He had, presumably, had it rushed to him from the Library of Congress.) Later,
when Ade met Read, Read mentioned the President and said, "Mr.
Hearst hasn't got enough money to get me to write anything
against that man!"

A regular Republican by upbringing, George broke away from
the regulars and joined Roosevelt's Bull Moose party in 1912. He
promoted a big rally at Hazelden. There was talk of running
him for governor. The next time George met his old friend and

neighbor from across the Illinois line, Joseph G. Cannon, Speaker of the House of Representatives, "Uncle Joe" upbraided him for his deflection. Shaking a bony finger at him, he said, "You are the unworthy son of a noble sire."

"I didn't get mad at him," George reported, "because I knew he was at least fifty per cent right. There was no question about the noble sire."

George's next political activity was in 1914 when he helped in the campaign of his brother Will who had been nominated for Congress on the Bull Moose ticket. But the district stayed Republican, and Will Ade lost to Will Wood.

In 1920 at a dinner in George's honor at the Lotos Club, in New York, Will Hays, then chairman of the Republican National Committee, said: "George Ade could be and would be nominated and elected Governor of Indiana any time he would say the word, and I speak with some authority and knowledge."

In 1924 George was host to the biggest crowd ever at Hazelden when his old friend, General Charles G. Dawes, made there the closing speech of his campaign for Vice-president.

In 1928 when Al Smith was running against Hoover, George resented the attacks on Smith because of his religion. In reply to a letter from Donald Freeman, of *Vanity Fair,* he wrote, "When I check up on the principal opposition to Governor Smith, I am tempted to vote for him because I do not wish at any time to be in the same camp with the mental dwarfs . . . who are raging against him. I think he would be a much pleasanter roommate than Herbert Hoover. . . . Al knows how to sing a song and to him the world is an alluring spectacle." Mr. Hoover, he added, "does not sing."

George was too conservative to like the New Deal, though he voted for Franklin D. Roosevelt for his first term. He never knew that F.D.R. was one of his great admirers. During the darkest

days of World War II, the President often read Ade Fables to some
of those who conferred with him in his study—remindful of
Lincoln's practice of reading from Artemus Ward at Cabinet
meetings.

Though he had no ambition for political office, George took
an important war job in World War I. For the Indiana Council of Defense he directed war publicity. He moved into the State
House in Indianapolis and worked day and night, determined, he
said, to keep the Germans out of Indiana. The newspapers were
flooded with so much propaganda that it was impossible to print
all. George proposed to condense the material into a column a
day. As a result the papers could print all that went out from
the Ade office, and Indiana ranked high in the performance of
every war service.

George wrote a series of pamphlets showing how each age group
could help, including the group six years of age and younger.
How could they help? "By observing the conduct of weak-kneed,
hysterical and complaining adults, and then being just as different
from them as possible. . . . Let the very young children set their
elders an example by remaining calm but determined." In addressing those between sixteen and twenty-one he referred to the
"mental calm in soldiers induced by the knowledge that all the
girls at home will postpone definite arrangements until the soldiers come back."

In September 1918 Ade and the Hazelden Country Club held a
golf tournament. They sold at astonishing prices permits to carry
the clubs of famous professional players and raised more than
$5,000 for the Red Cross. "Chick" Evans was to be the featured
golfer but was detained and George thought to substitute a little-
known player named Walter Hagen. The crowd seemed so disappointed that George told Hagen not to play; they would wait
for Evans. After Hagen a little later had won American golf

championships, George would bow his head and murmur, "To think that I once *benched* him!"

On July 4 of the next year he arranged for the great Homecoming at Hazelden for the soldiers and sailors, attended by 15,000.

He wrote and sent by first-class mail news bulletins to all Purdue students in the armed services and he also edited the Purdue monthly alumni magazine.

After the war he found himself on so many advisory committees that if he had listed them all, his *Who's Who* biography would have been one of the longest. "Promoting things," he said, "brings one into pleasant association with cheerful people."

The use of his country place as a community center led him to propose a plan for having county parks. He thought a tract a mile square should be set aside in each county for a combination park, forest preserve and recreation field. Most of the area should be left in its native condition and every plant and animal belonging to the region protected. "Maybe we can put this scheme over," he said, "if we surround it with a lot of restrictions and *verbotens*. If we could keep the thing closed on Sunday and not let anyone walk on the grass, I know a lot of good people who might be interested." His advocacy of county parks probably was an influence in promoting the Indiana state parks, now among the best in the country.

George advocated the establishment of a national holiday to be known as Returning Day, "the observance of the day to be the restoration to proper owners of everything borrowed during the preceding year, with special reference to books, umbrellas and garden implements." He was serious about this, but was handicapped by being known as a humorist.

Though he treated the subject with humor, from the time that the National Prohibition Amendment was enacted, George had been urging its repeal. He had strong convictions that prohibition was terribly dangerous as a precedent for forcing on the public the opinion of fanatical or intolerant minorities. "Take the matter of red underwear during the winter months," he wrote. "You say you have become accustomed to a union suit of linen mesh and that a two-piece red suit with pearl buttons is not only irksome but positively scratchy. Well, are you going to pit your judgment against the set opinions of the most moral citizens in the remote rural townships?"

His prize example of the working of laws to prohibit people from doing what they feel that they have a right to do was an incident when Indiana had an anticigarette law. An ape, named Consul the Great, was shown in a vaudeville act in a South Bend theater. The manager of the theater was fined $25 for permitting the ape, as part of his act, to smoke a cigarette!

He thought there was too much of a premium on the negative virtues. "The man who stands in the middle of the street and says, 'Let's get a rope and go and hang some one,' will find a hundred willing volunteers to help him, but the one who proposes a lot of hard manual labor for the good of the community will find himself standing alone, talking to himself. . . . Sometimes I feel that my plans for improving conditions never arrive anywhere because I am always an advocate of *doing* something instead of prohibiting something."

26

Paying His Fine to Society

WHILE still busy as a playwright in 1909 George Ade found himself giving time to two unsought jobs. For a year he had been a trustee of Purdue University. Then his college fraternity, without consulting him in advance, elected him Grand Consul, its national chief officer. He would have liked to avoid the extra work, but he accepted without a murmur. Sometimes when a man long out of college plunges into fraternity activities, he does so for business reasons; but not George Ade. He did not need prestige, nor a larger acquaintance, but he liked young people and did not wish to disappoint the boys. The office carried with it the task of directing a campaign to raise funds for a memorial building at Miami University where the fraternity was founded. He traveled over the Middle West calling upon those who might make sizable contributions, and the campaign was successful. A little later, after he had finished his term of office, he started a campaign to raise money for a new house for his fraternity at Purdue; but the brothers were slow in their responses and George, unwilling to let the project fail, provided most of the money.

In 1915 there was a fuss at Purdue between the alumni and the university administration, mainly about athletics and regulation of student enterprises. Always youthful in his outlook, George sided with the alumni and with the students. He said the control over the students might help to make good subordinates but not leaders. "You cannot teach a bird to fly," he said, "by tieing him to a limb."

For the benefit of those who considered football too "brutal," he proposed some new rules. One was that "any player who takes hold of an opposing player or who displays brusqueness or lack of refinement shall be put into a compartment on the side-lines known as the 'bone-yard' and he shall not be released until the captain of his team has answered ten comic questions without laughing."

After resigning from the Board of Trustees, George continued to be active in Purdue affairs, particularly after the university in 1921 got a new President, Dr. Edward C. Elliott, with whom he formed a lasting friendship. His resignation from the Purdue Board of Trustees had played its part in the passing of a law that three of the appointments to the Board of Trustees by the Governor of the State should be on recommendation of the alumni.

As the best-known alumnus of Purdue, he added much to the fame of his alma mater. His biggest material contribution to the university now helps to perpetuate his name. This came about in a surprising way. One day in 1928 George received a telephone call from his old friend of college days, Henry Vinton, then Judge of the Superior Court at Lafayette, who asked if he could come over to meet David Ross about something of importance. David Ross was a member of the Purdue Board of Trustees, a little later president of the Board and was Purdue's greatest benefactor. As a Purdue student he had never attracted much attention, but a few years after his graduation he invented an improved steering gear for automobiles that brought him an immense fortune. Like George he had remained a bachelor, and with no family obligations he had spent his money on Purdue. Somehow, Ross and Ade, living less than fifty miles apart, had never met. George was curious to know what was up, and he drove over to Lafayette the next day.

After Judge Vinton had introduced them, Ross told Ade that he wanted to take him to see something interesting. Accompanied by Vinton, they drove to a farm west of town. After crawling under a barbed-wire fence and climbing up a steep hillside covered with burdock and dogfennel, they came within view of a great oblong hole. Here, said Ross, was the place for a great ready-made stadium, a natural depression gouged out by glacial drift. Purdue could have a concrete bowl without having to move millions of cubic yards of dirt. "All we have to do," he said, "is to buy sixty-five acres of land before the owner finds out that he has a stadium on his premises."

"And how," asked George, "does all this concern me?"

Ross explained that he had brought him there because he thought he might like to help finance the enterprise.

George looked at the landscape for a few moments and then said the proposal interested him. He had never had much luck, he said, in getting others to follow *him* in promotions. "Simply to help someone else would be a great relief. So my answer is yes."

They shared equally in buying the land with the hope that some day the stadium would be built. Then these two men, who had never met until that day when they formed their partnership, decided not to wait but to go ahead with the stadium at once.* "We must have it completed," said George, "while we're still alive to see some of the games played in it." Besides it seemed a suitable way for two old bachelors "to pay their fines to society." They put up more money and got a lot of alumni to buy life seats at $200 apiece, and in November of the next year Ross and Ade were in the Ross-Ade Stadium at its dedication, with a home-coming football game in which Purdue defeated its ancient rival, Indiana University.

When the name Ross-Ade was first suggested for the stadium, George said he was utterly shameless about it. "Students who come

---

* Another account of this meeting is in *David Ross: Modern Pioneer,* by Fred C. Kelly.

here a few years from now will know nothing," he said, "about a fellow named Ade who wrote fables in slang, and plays, but if my name is . . . on that stadium, they'll be tipped off that someone named Ade was identified in some way with Purdue University. I'd like that." For a time, though, he was afraid Ross-Ade might sound too much like the name of a new drink!

When praised for his part in the achievement, George did not like to be looked upon as a noble benefactor. It was simply, he said, that he had never ceased to be a country boy and was still full of curiosity to see how it would feel to tackle a new job and watch it grow.

Not long after the dedication of the Ross-Ade Stadium in June 1926 George Ade, along with John T. McCutcheon, received an honorary degree at Purdue, L.H.D.—Doctor of Humane Letters, "As an appropriate recognition of his unremitting service in the upbuilding of this University, of his achievements as journalist, author, and playwright, of his distinctive interpretation of American life and manners, and of the joy he has added to the world." George was not blasé about the honor. Before the ceremonies began he whispered to the leader of the Purdue orchestra that he wished they would play his favorite tune, *Pomp and Circumstance,* to add drama to an important event in his life. A year later he got another honorary degree, L.L.D., at Indiana University. "But," he said, "I'll bet no one ever calls me Doctor."

27

Words Written and Spoken

By 1915 the name of George Ade began to appear on motion pictures. One of the Hollywood companies had bought a series of the Fables for short comedies. Use of the Fables for pictures helped Hollywood to break away from custard-pie-throwing as the main theme for comedy. When asked to put a price on them, George wrote, "I shall be glad to consider any insulting offer."

In the early twenties George did a series of full-length motion pictures for his friend Thomas Meighan. The first of these, *Our Leading Citizen,* he began with no plot but only the title, which for years he had been carrying in his head. Others for Meighan included *Back Home and Broke* and *Woman Proof.* Though all these were of a higher type than most of the Hollywood output, they were successful and each brought royalties of about $40,000. Of a number of other motion pictures he wrote, one was intended for Will Rogers and Marie Dressler, but Rogers was killed before the picture could be made.

George found it hard to stay away from playwriting and even when he was busiest in war work in 1917, he suggested to George M. Cohan a play in which the leading character would be Germany. A young man after living several years in Germany has returned to America, convinced that it is right not to be bound by scruples or written obligations. The play would be about this young man, perfectly groomed, well-mannered and highly educated, always smiling, polite and agreeable, using the people about him for his own purposes—"It must be shown that a good many easygoing, patient and good-natured people become exceedingly combative and fairly dangerous when they have been kicked too often in the same place. . . ." But the pressure of war work was too great for him to write the play. Four years later George discussed with the producer, John Golden, another idea for a play to be called *Keep Smiling,* in which the theme would be the fallacy of the Pollyanna motion that every human being should smile no matter what happens. "We want to demonstrate that the perpetual smiler is a nuisance; that the person who won't hit back on occasion is no fit companion for anyone." He finally wrote it as a piece of magazine fiction rather than as a play.

A friend suggested that the Fable of the *Two Mandolin Players* could be made into a one-act play. Within a day or so George wrote it. Then a request came from the magazine, *Country Gentleman.* He sent the playlet, though it had no relation to country gentlemen, aside from being written by one. The editor sent him $2,500. For months the magazine was besieged by requests for permission to produce the piece with home-talent casts. It is still being played by amateurs.

Another short playlet, *The Persecuted Wife,* written for a magazine in 1925, was used by a vaudeville team. It was a take-off on melodrama, showing the contrast between a heartless adventurer's treatment of his forsaken wife and child in two scenes, one in the '80's, the other forty years later.

George turned out an immense volume of magazine fiction and articles during his middle years of semi-retirement. The *Cosmopolitan* persuaded him to do a series of new Fables in Slang to be illustrated by John McCutcheon. He said he could not resist the sentimental satisfaction of collaborating once more with McCutcheon. These Fables were considerably longer than the earlier ones. The series was highly successful and demonstrated that Ade was still the shrewd observer of human behavior, but he never thought they were as good as his earlier ones. "A good fable should be short; it should be all kernel." He did a series of reminiscences for the same magazine during the three years beginning in 1925. Many of the quotations in this book are from that series.

A collection of slangless magazine essays published in the early '20's under the title, *Single Blessedness and Other Observations,* is today the most difficult of all Ade books to find in rare bookstores. Those who bought it hung onto it. After the book had been out of print for some years, George had so many requests for it from friends that he advertised for it in the book sections of newspapers, but that brought him only two copies at premium prices. Then he arranged with the publisher for the use of the plates for an edition of 200 copies which he autographed to give to friends. Copies are now practically unobtainable.

In one of the magazine articles he wrote after he quit most of his playwriting, George once more helped to "make" one of his friends. It was a short piece about Kin Hubbard, author of the sayings of Abe Martin, an imaginary character in Brown County, Indiana. For several years the Abe Martin feature, consisting of two unrelated sentences and a drawing, also by Hubbard, had been appearing in the Indianapolis *News.* Kin had offered it to newspaper syndicates but none was interested. The syndicate editors "knew" they couldn't sell it. They said it was too local to Indiana. But soon after the Ade boost of Hubbard appeared, the syndicates began to send him contracts to sign and before long Abe Martin was appearing daily in newspapers in almost every city of the United States.

A newspaper syndicate got George to revise his old Fables, bringing the slang and allusions down to date, and, beginning in November 1920, for about ten years the Fables once a week were a much advertised newspaper feature. They were still popular thirty years after their first appearance. For five or six years George also contributed about once a month to a series of weekly humorous articles syndicated under the heading, "Rogue's Gallery." In 1924 he suggested to his syndicate manager a weekly series to be called "Flowers for the Living," in which well-known writers would tell of important things done by prominent people still alive. The syndicate asked him to submit a list of the prominent people about whom he could write authoritatively. He began to jot down the names of the famous whom he knew intimately, and the list numbered several hundred. This was not surprising, for it is doubtful if anyone else knew so many people worth writing about. They were in every walk of life. One page of that list contained the names of John Ringling, the circus man; William A. Pinkerton, the detective; Lord Northcliffe, the London publisher; actors, writers, editors, lawyers, doctors, opera singers, statesmen, inventors, philanthropists, business men and leaders in sports. The list as a whole represented a kind of de luxe *Who's Who*. Unfortunately, George interpreted only a few of them.

Writing syndicate stuff, however, and being bound to deliver on schedule, had ceased to be fun. Least of all did George want to do any more Fables. In November 1926 he wrote to John Wheeler, head of the syndicate that was putting them out: "I have a feeling that I am not doing myself justice when I turn out this stuff under pressure and without enthusiasm. . . . What I want is my liberty now and at all times to do the work which appeals to me."

Yet, to oblige the syndicate, he kept at it for another four years!

George once said, "I do not choose to make speeches or listen to speeches." But he did make speeches. With a pleasing voice and a quality of humor that seemed at its best when spoken, he could hold an audience. If he had permitted himself to be booked by a lecture bureau, he could have collected another fortune.

At a Gridiron Club dinner in Washington in December 1925 he

began his speech as a guest of honor by saying: "When I learned that I had a chance to speak before the Gridiron Club, I was worried. I have been accustomed to reading my speeches. Someone said that anyone who read a speech before the Gridiron Club would not be accepted as an orator. So I wrote out enough talk to use up about five minutes and then I memorized it. I called in four friends and explained the situation and asked for advice. I told them I would read the speech and then I would recite it and then I wanted them to tell me what to do. So I read it and then I delivered it extemporaneously and asked them, 'What shall I do?' and they all said, 'Send a doctor's certificate.' "

In a talk to the Chamber of Commerce at Miami Beach, Florida, one of his suggestions was: "Your newspapers should stop printing reports about cold weather up north. It nearly breaks a man's heart to read that his wife's relatives up north are shoveling snow."

Some of his talks he devoted to hard sense with no attempt at humor. In an address to the National Editorial Association, made up of small-town editors, at Purdue University in 1933 he hinted that he had had a desire "to experiment with a paper serving a neighborhood well removed from the big city." Then he told them what he would do with such a paper. "Go out and interview the men and women of your own territory. Ask the women about their success in raising certain kinds of flowers. Print the news about the more attractive flower gardens. Keep up a constant drive for the beautification of your town. Pin a medal on every man or woman who does anything at any time to improve the looks of your town. . . .

"If I were editing the weekly newspaper of which I have been dreaming for years—I would ride out in the country and check up on the crops and give a few words of praise to the farmers who had their fields cleaned up, and their corn and oats and wheat a little ahead of the others. . . . Be friendly with advertisers but suppress no news to which your subscribers are entitled. At the same time I would preserve the honored tradition among country editors to keep out of the paper the current scandals which are whispered about and which help to break up homes and blast reputations. . . . I would print every week a list of the screened plays at all the movie theaters patronized by your subscribers. I would not only give the names of the plays but I would let the readers know in advance something about each play, whether it has been approved by the critics in the cities, whether it was clean or not, and what kind of general rating it had. . . . What happens in your community doesn't need to be important to be interesting. . . . If you are chatting about the home folks and the things in which they are interested, you will be highly regarded as a good editor."

After he escaped from the newspaper syndicate, when he was sixty-four years old, George intended to do no more writing except in behalf of some "cause" that interested him. But his Hoosier-born friend, Ray Long, had quit editing the *Cosmopolitan* to become a book publisher. National prohibition was still on, and Long suggested a reminiscent book for the benefit of those too young ever to have seen the old-time saloon; for those who saw it and remembered it with hatred; and for those who remembered it as an institution which to their way of thinking was not quite so bad as it was painted. The idea interested George and *The Old-Time Saloon,* published in 1931, was one of the most amusing books he ever wrote. Also it was a masterful job of reporting and of writing history, guided only by an extraordinary memory. Some of the chapters were: What Was a Saloon—and Why, The Free Lunch, What They Drank, Why People Behave So, The Bar-Keep, Song and Story and The Talk. It seemed as if no detail—neither the kinds of free lunch served, what the customers said to the bartender, nor even the verses of the sentimental songs sung—had faded from the memory of the close observer that was George Ade. The book had plenty of anecdotes, too. One was about Tom Heath of the vaudeville team of McIntyre and Heath who was chased out of an Irish saloon on St. Patrick's Day because he ate all the shamrock on the bar, thinking it was water cress.

"Defending the saloon is just as impossible," George wrote, "as defending Benedict Arnold, John Wilkes Booth, Guiteau, or Mr. Luetgart, of Chicago, who became annoyed one morning because his wife served cold coffee, and . . . ran her through a sausage machine. But it may not be extreme treason or distortion of history to say that some of the dealers possessed human qualities which distinguished them from the brute creation, and many a bar-keep had a sympathetic heart beating beneath his white, or once-white, jacket and his attitudes toward the problems of life were benign rather than cruel. . . . Drink had a way of transforming the timid shoe salesman into a noisy debater. . . . It encouraged the underdog to advertise his importance and relate his inmost grievances to anyone who would listen; and, usually, the bar-keep had to do the listening.

"At Christmas and New Year's the old-time saloon attained the heights of popularity, because the management wrote holiday greetings on the mirror, by the use of soap, decorated the dump with wreaths and provided free 'Tom and Jerry' for all the regulars. A huge bowl was in stage center. . . . A shaving-mug was filled half way up with the gooey confection—hot water was added and the foamy surface was flecked with nutmeg, after which came peace on earth and good will to men. . . . Any one who drank eight mugs of Tom and Jerry could arise next morning and see his breath. It was something like a search-light, only reddish in tinge. . . .

"Tom Moran had a famous place on Randolph street in Chicago. . . . Tom drew an occasional mug of beer with extreme reluctance but he absolutely refused to compromise the standing of his establishment by serving any kind of mixed drink. If one of the gentlemen in the line-up expressed a preference for a Gin Daisy or a Dry Martini, Tom simply requested him to leave quietly without creating any disturbance. . . .

"What was known as a 'gentleman's drink' never approached the rim. Probably an ounce and a half of dynamite in solution represented the portion which would not cause the clerk to give the buyer a hard look or gently inquire, 'Will you need a towel?' The implication was that preparations were under way for the taking of a bath. In the barrel-houses and out-and-out joints, it was taken for granted that the glass would be filled to the brim and the receptacle was of stingy capacity, but it had to be large enough to contain a real jolt or the trade might be lost to some competitor with a larger heart." .

The book was unsparing in showing the evil side of the old-time saloon but it also showed that there were daily habits, social customs and time-honored practices, tolerated for centuries, which could not be easily uprooted by taking roll calls in Congress and passing a law.

Not long after publication of *The Old-Time Saloon* national prohibition was on its way out. Perhaps the book played its part.

28

Love of Nonsense

WHEN George Ade read that a college English department was going to teach how to write humor, he said, "I wouldn't believe it if it weren't right here in the paper. What *is* humor and where is the dividing line between humor and two-reel comics, clowning over the radio, dialect stories, and soda-fountain wise-cracking?

"I have a fifteen-volume set," he went on, "which is supposed to contain the wit and humor of the world, for all time and all countries. Dozens of authors are quoted. Much of the 'wit and humor' could be set to music and used for any first-class funeral service. . . . The word 'humor' is much mistreated and misapplied. It is used to designate the Chautauqua attraction who tells a string of musty or moth-eaten stories. It is also used to describe great satirists."

Most American humor depends on exaggeration. Even Mark Twain was not above use of the tall story. Probably Ade's success came from his gift for detecting how absurd most of us can be. It was by the accuracy of his observations, his ability to see what was right under his nose and to show others what they had failed to notice, that he made millions laugh.

His own idea of high points in American humor was represented by Mark Twain, by Harry Leon Wilson's *Ruggles of Red Gap* and by Tarkington's stories of mischievous boyhood and of adolescence. He confessed that he had a great fondness for the kind of humor that is "sheer idiocy"—"nut" stuff, whether in writing or on the stage. For many years he was an admirer of

G. H. Derby who wrote under the pen name of "John Phoenix." Derby was an army officer stationed in California around 1850, and it was said that the War Department at Washington was annoyed by the outbursts of ridicule and humor and "goofiness" that crept into his reports. He appealed to Ade because he did not try to be funny by distortion of grammar and spelling, but "using correct grammar and Addisonian English wandered deliberately into the impossible and reversed all the laws of nature and wrote calmly and liberally the language of idiocy."

George was not ashamed of his fondness for nonsense, because, he insisted, it is a fact commonly overlooked that "only the high-brows, or the intelligentsia, or the people with mentalities attuned to the grasping of intricate propositions and the solving of difficult problems, can get the fullest enjoyment out of foolishness. Can you imagine a numbskull giggling over *Alice in Wonderland?* So far as the records show, Lewis Carroll, learned mathematician, with a frigid Victorian environment and surrounded on all sides by hard facts and iron-clad traditions, was one of the first to throw off the yoke and find relief in deliberate 'nut' comedy, meaning fiction which sounds as if it might have originated in an insane asylum instead of within the ivied walls of a venerable college. ... And all the sages and philosophers and wiseacres of the British Islands and other parts of the map consuming printed English, put aside George Eliot, Lord Disraeli and Thomas Hardy and chuckled over *Alice in Wonderland.*"

He thought that women more than men are likely to miss the fun of tomfooleries. His theory was that women somehow lack the kind of imagination to supply an intervening gap between cause and effect. He said that he had used one of Charlie Case's stories as a kind of acid test for a sense of humor, and that when he tried it on a number of supposedly intelligent women, all had failed to "get" it. The story went something like this: "Father and I were going home one night and to save time cut across a neighbor's back yard. While crossing the yard, Father stumbled over something in the dark, and out of curiosity he picked it up, but I couldn't tell what it was until we got home and struck a light. It turned out to be an armful of firewood."

"Once," George recalled, "I escorted two elderly women to a play-house and they were puzzled and irritated because 'Pete' Dailey kept on talking to an imaginary dog. They couldn't understand why the plump comedian should address so many confidential remarks to a dog when there wasn't any dog present. They would have been thrilled by 'Uncle Tom's Cabin,' or 'Ten Nights in a Bar-Room,' but they muffed the comedy gags and gazed at me in disapproval when I rocked around in my seat and laughed out loud at Mr. Dailey's insane antics."

Some of George's most vivid memories of stage scenes were of those which sounded the profoundest depths of silliness. He never forgot a one-act play by George V. Hobart, used in a "Music-Box Revue," with Willie Collier and other good comedians in the cast. "It was a conventional story dealing with the eternal triangle of a faithless wife, a deceived husband and a designing villain, leading up to murder and hysterics, but from the time the curtain went up, not one word of dialogue had anything to do with the action on the stage. When Willie Collier bade his wife an emotional farewell, he said, 'The square of the hypothenuse of a right-angled triangle is equal to the sums of the squares of the other two sides.' When the home-breaker was making love to the deceitful wife, he bounded one or two of the important States and named their principal products and, if I am not mistaken, when Hugh Cameron, as a man-servant, discovered the body of the lover, he leaned over it and exclaimed, horror stricken, 'Ashtabula, Ohio!' It was a nightmare of idiocy and one of the most enjoyable skits ever put into a review."

The meaninglessness of a speech by William Rock in one of Richard Carle's musical shows struck George as funny and it stayed in his memory: "Eepha-sopha-los! Eepha-sopha-dill! Eepha-sopha-lopha-sopha, eepha-sopha lill."

Having recalled that, George would smile and say: "Think of a man, big enough to haul a dray, deliberately remembering such stuff after forty years."

Crazy songs amused him, such as the one done by Nora Bayes, that began: "Hurrah! Hurrah! My father's goin' to be hung. Hurrah! Hurrah! I'm foolish but I'm young."

Another song that he liked was conceived by Booth Tarkington in the days when both were often at the Lambs Club in New York. It was a burlesque on one of the popular sob songs of the period.

> The court room it was crowded.
> All the witnesses were there.
> The judge he sat a-frowning
> In his highly cooshioned chair.
> They were trying an old lady
> For the stealing of a horse.
> They had hauled her to the station.
> They had dragged her there by force.
>
> Then up rose a handsome lawyer
> But would not geeve his name.
> He defended thees old lady
> And well he done the same.
> The verdeect was 'not geelty."
> Tears stood in the jury's eyes
> When the unknown lawyer heared it,
> Then says he to their surprise:
>
> She was my mother once
> In days so long ago.
> I'll not dee-sairt her now

Her lots have fell so low.
I've had other moth-urrs seence
To take me by the hand,
But I'll not deesairt thees one
Just because I'm rich and grand.

It had been his "blessed privilege," George often recalled, to go behind the scenes at Weber and Fields Music Hall once in a while and meet Lew Fields, Joe Weber, "Pete" Dailey, David Warfield, De Wolf Hopper, Willie Collier, Louis Mann, Sam Bernard, John T. Kelly and others of that remarkable galaxy, besides such women celebrities as Lillian Russell and Marie Dressler. Of course, all these were not in the cast at the same time, but there was always an impressive list of stars and the talk and comedy in the dressing rooms was as funny as the show itself. The whole establishment was so small that the male stars dressed in one large room, and all of them were addicted to exchanging the kind of nonsense that George Ade loved. The prize of the outfit, he thought, was John T. Kelly. One evening he heard him talking the following dialogue, taking both characters, while putting on his make-up:

Hello there!
How do you do?
Don't you know me?
Your face is familiar but I can't place you. Don't tell me. I'll make you in a minute.
You ought to know me.
Certainly I know you, but you look different since you shaved off the brush—the skilligans—the chinchillas.
I never wore whiskers in my life.
When I met you at the Coates House, in Kansas City, didn't you have a full beard, way down to here?
No, sir, I promised my mother I'd never wear a beard.
Well, I give up. Who are you?
I'm your brother Waldo.

George noticed that the others in the dressing room merely grinned and made expressive gestures indicating that if a man wanted to have a silly spell it was none of their business.

"Nut" humor, George thought, should be considered a blessing. "Don't you become sated once in a while with the irrevocable 'laws' of nature? Don't you have a vast respect for an insurgent who decides to disregard the laws of nature, the rules of logic, the traditions of etiquette, and all other regulations which hamper and restrict the human race?"

Probably he enjoyed the humor of feigned dementia all the more because it was a variety that he, in his own writing, never attempted.

29

Riley, Friend Extraordinary

GEORGE ADE was a wonderfully good listener, paying
the closest attention, and never impatient to tell *his* story. One
always knew when he had something to say. If he was wearing
his hat, he made an unconscious gesture of pulling the brim a
little lower on one side. He did the same thing as he came to the
point of his story. If he was bareheaded, he might catch someone's eye, smile, and raise an index finger, as much as to say, "I'd
like to tell one." It would seem natural to think of him in front
of the fireplace at Hazelden, with friends listening to his stories;
but for some reason he almost never sat near the fireplace. He
seemed most expansive leaning back in his desk chair in his office.
If he was not in a storytelling mood, there was no use in trying
to draw him out. But if ready with something worth telling, he
did not need a large audience. With only one friend to listen, he
might be at his best.

Sometimes he would say, "Let's play our little game. Here's a
copy of *Who's Who*. Open it at random and see if I can't find some
names on the pages exposed of people I know well enough to tell
more about them." And he never failed to find at least two or
three about whom he knew something interesting. Once the
page contained the name of Judge Kenesaw Landis, one of his
best friends. "No innocent man ever needed to be afraid to come
before Landis when he was on the Federal bench," he began. But
one day Landis was amazed to hear a defendant admit, on the
witness stand, that he had burned all the papers which might

John T. McCutcheon is amused by George Ade's dinner speech about the "good old days."

Shortly after Ade's death a Liberty ship was named for Ade. The *George Ade* had a brave career, suffered several enemy hits and was finally sunk in the Pacific.

throw light on an alleged attempt to conceal assets from a group of creditors.

"Why did you burn those papers?" Landis asked.

"I was noivous."

"Are you nervous now?"

"I don't know."

"I'll find out."

Landis descended from his perch, took out his watch and seriously counted the defendant's pulse.

"No, you don't seem to be nervous," he said, "but you have every reason to be, for in about ten minutes you're going to jail."

One day George's recollections of various celebrities prompted a question. "You've been everywhere and known everybody. Who was the most interesting person you ever met?"

George chuckled. "Oh, that's an easy one. The most unusual, the most amusing, the most interesting beyond all comparison was James Whitcomb Riley. He was the most lovable, the most altogether different person I ever knew."

Then he talked about Riley for a long time. Riley had often been a guest at Hazelden and had formed a habit of sitting under a certain big hickory tree, which came to be known as the Riley tree.

"Some one called him the 'typical' Hoosier," George said, "but he was not the type. If all Hoosiers had been like Riley, then Indiana would have been Mount Olympus rolled out flat.

"He was the best storyteller I ever heard because his character impersonations were vivid and accurate and convincing beyond all belief. Sir Henry Irving was right when he said that Riley would have been one of the few truly great character actors of the English speaking stage.

"Take his well-known verses, 'Good-bye, Jim, take keer o' yourself.' I have heard them recited by Sol Smith Russell, Maurice

Barrymore, David Warfield and other stars of the theater. They put into their renditions the skill of the trained reader, every trick of the actor's trade, and each gave to the reading the strength and warmth of a genuine personality, but after you heard Riley recite those wonderful verses, which revealed the genuine Hoosier, saturated with sentiment but ashamed to be sentimental—and you felt the lump coming into your throat and your eyes began to fill, you knew that our friend had gifts and graces which I really believe were not given to any other man of his generation. He was the best platform entertainer of his time—and yet he dreaded those public appearances and always suspected that he was about to fail. Once I heard him say, 'Every morning when I wake up the first thought that comes to me is: This is the day they get on to me.'

"He kept himself in the poet's mood by excluding from his life's program most of the activities which we regard as important. The world of politics and propaganda, golf, baseball, bridge whist, collecting bills, selling goods, rushing to the bank, putting ads in the paper, calling committees together—it was a region into which he never ventured and he smiled and wondered to see his friends so busy with things which did not matter in the least.

"Riley," George went on, "shrank from idle and promiscuous friendships. He made his own ratings and never consulted the social register. He was given to long and intimate confabulations with a Negro barber, whom he patronized for many years and who always showed a devouring interest in the stories brought to him by Riley. These stories concerned a certain Frank who lived at Fortville, Indiana—also his wife Minnie, a most courageous and resourceful Amazon. Frank and Minnie were of the adventurous sort, taking many railway journeys, adopting unusual trades and professions, going on perilous expeditions and running into all sorts of romantic experiences. Of course they had no existence except in the bubbling imagination of Riley, but he continued the fascinating serial, with the two as central characters, year after year—just for the satisfaction of pleasing one humble listener.

"He talked with a soothing drawl and employed the dramatic pause with rare effect. He could squint his eyes and twist his mouth and perk his head with all the superb artistry of a Coquelin. His stories were different from any others in the world because, I really believe, he made up most of them as he went along. I never heard him tell a story which anyone else had told before. He would start a rambling narrative about some fool friends of his somewhere off in Indiana and would go along inventing dialogue and elaborating details and weaving a most fantastic and amusing tale out of nothing whatsoever.

"Riley had a lot of stories which were pointless unless the listeners happened to be those who love the right kind of nonsense. And I don't think Riley ever told these stories unless he knew all about the listeners.

"We were talking one day about the futility and foolishness of the ordinary games and pastimes and someone asked him if he had ever played chess. Without answering the question he proceeded to tell a story.

"He said that the captain of an ocean liner walked along the deck the second day out, greeting the passengers, who were curled up on their steamer chairs. It was a pleasant morning after a stormy night and the captain was cheerily congratulating everyone on the weather and complimenting the ladies, and whenever he paused to address a group he would ask the question: 'Does anyone here play chess?'

"It seemed that no one on deck *did* play chess. The captain went into the smoke room and gave a breezy 'Good morning' to the men. He wanted to know if any one of them played chess.

There was a pause and then a man over in the corner, who was reading a book, spoke up and said he played once in a while.

" 'Would you mind having a game with me?' " the captain asked.

"The passenger would be delighted. So a steward brought out the board and all of the kings and queens and castles and bishops and other queer 'men' used in the game, and after the board was all set the two players faced each other and the captain said, 'I challenged you and I think it is only fair that you should have the first play.'

"The passenger promptly made a long, sweeping and diagonal move with one of the wooden pieces. Just as he made the move the captain said, 'Aha!' and then he sat for five minutes with both elbows on the table and his head supported by his hands, studying the situation.

"Then he asked the steward to bring him a cigar. He lighted the cigar and smoked for another five minutes.

"Then he got up and took off his coat and hung it up. Then he took off his cuffs. He used metal clips to hold his cuffs on and it required some time for him to get the cuffs off and attach them to the lapel of his coat.

"Then he came back and looked at the board for another five minutes and finally said, 'Well, that *beats* me!'

"One morning Mr. Riley started to walk downtown. As he came to the first corner the policeman saluted him and said:

" 'This is a fine morning, Mr. Riley.' Mr. Riley didn't contradict him.

"As he passed the grocery and market his old friend wearing an apron accosted him and told him that the weather was highly satisfactory.

"As he continued on his way various small boys and eminent

citizens and lady friends hailed him, because he carried his halo with him in Indianapolis and couldn't get away from it.

"Between his house and the Bobbs-Merrill store fifty people informed him that the weather was beautiful.

"Finally he walked into the office of Will Bobbs and sat down and Mr. Bobbs was glad to see him and said, 'Well, this is a lovely morning.'

"Riley could stand it no longer. He shouted, so you could hear him all over the store: 'It *must* be! Everybody speaks very highly of it.'

"It always seemed to some of us that Riley's best story was the one about Wes and his trombone. I have told this story to people who laughed immoderately and to others who waited for the finish after it was all over.

"The story went that down in Greenfield, while Riley was painting signs, there lived an ambitious young fellow named Wesley Hanchfield. For several years he had played the second alto in the town band. He was content with the second alto until he went on an excursion to Indianapolis and attended a performance of Dupree and Benedict's Minstrels, and then he saw and heard, for the first time, a slide-trombone. From that day his guiding ambition was to own the same kind of slide-trombone.

"He sent to Elkhart and got a catalog and saved up and finally he got enough money together and bought one of the most beautiful and most expensive 'slip horns' anyone ever saw. It was silver on the outside, with scroll-work engraved on it, and the inside of the bell was gold-plated.

"After Mr. Hanchfield received his trombone he decided that he should have a case for it. It was such a valuable instrument that he didn't want to get it all nicked and dented while they were riding around in the band-wagon to fairs and rallies. He went to the tinner and had him make a special tin box. By the time the tinner got through he had turned out something of very unusual appearance. Any container which conforms to the eccentricities and irregularities of a slide-trombone has to be something out of the ordinary.

"Mr. Hanchfield brought the case to Riley and had him paint it and then grain it, in imitation of rosewood, and also letter on the outside the name:

WESLEY HANCHFIELD

"After the paint was dry, Wesley came in and looked at the job and said: 'Jim, that is the blamedest-looking thing I ever saw. I know that every fellow that sees that box will want to know what's on the inside. It's goin' to save a lot of talk if we put the name of the instrument right on the box and then I won't have to answer so many fool questions.'

"So Riley did some more lettering, with the following result:

WESLEY HANCHFIELD

TROMBONE

"Wes stood looking over Riley's shoulder and when Riley had completed the lettering, he said, 'Well, Jim, as long as we've gone this far, I guess we might as well put on the rest.'

" 'What's that?'

"Then he said, 'Indiana.'

"That is really the end of the story and will serve as an explanation of why Mr. Hanchfield attracted considerable attention whenever he turned out with the band boys, carrying a metallic box of weird design, on which was painted:

WESLEY HANCHFIELD

TROMBONE

INDIANA"

This was the kind of story George Ade loved to hear and to tell. He appreciated them, as he appreciated Riley, because of his feeling for "character."

30

Life Had Been Good

In June 1939 when George Ade was seventy-three years old, a cyclone knocked over most of the grove of great oaks at Hazelden that had caused him to build there. He was distressed. "What happens to me doesn't matter, but I wish those old trees could have been spared."

He sent for experts to salvage the trees they could, and his first order was for them to try to save the Riley tree, which had been damaged, the hickory tree that had been James Whitcomb Riley's favorite.

From then on, though he loved Hazelden as much as ever, he no longer showed the same interest in its care. He seemed to look upon the passing of those patriarchal trees as symbolic.

He showed no fear or dread of death, though he had no faith in a better life beyond. To him a future life had never been convincingly proved.

He knew that life had been good to him. "I feel that I have been fortunate in arriving on earth just when things were beginning to happen. As a member of the reception committee I have greeted the telephone, the electric light, the airplane, motor cars, moving pictures, radio, concrete highways, electric refrigeration, air conditioning, woman suffrage, television, and a lot of interesting by-products. . . . It's a great world and most of the people are worth knowing. I am glad to have been among those present."

On the evening of his seventy-fifth birthday he was about to leave his Florida home with his friend and business manager, Jim Rathbun, to go out to dinner. Then he said, "Wait a minute. I think it's just time for a news program on the radio." It so happened that the news broadcaster was another Hoosier, Edwin C. Hill. Instead of the usual news report Hill announced he wanted to take time to pay a birthday tribute to a great American, George Ade. When he turned from the radio, George had tears in his eyes. "It's nice not to be forgotten."

A year later he was remembered in another way. The pupils at every public school in his native Newton county sent him birthday post cards. He found himself swamped by nearly one thousand greetings. At once he had prepared cards of thanks to send in reply—every one to bear his signature.

"Why not use a facsimile signature?" a friend suggested. "It will be no small job to write your name a thousand times."

"Nevertheless," George said, "that's what I shall do. Surely, every kid that sent me good wishes is entitled to the courtesy of an acknowledgment signed by my own fist."

On his seventy-seventh birthday he wrote, "I am taking it with a grin and an outward show of indifference, but I am not hanging out any banners, shooting off any rockets, or giving three cheers."

A few months later in June 1943 he became ill while attending a dinner at the Hazelden Country Club. He was able to walk with assistance to his car, but he had suffered a paralytic stroke. It affected his left side but did not impair his speech.

The next morning Jim Rathbun put in a long distance call to Dr. E. C. Elliott, President of Purdue University, to tell him the sad news. Elliott's line was being held for another long distance call, the operator said, and it turned out that Elliott's call was to George Ade. He wanted to notify George of the death that morning of David Ross, George's associate in promoting the Ross-Ade Stadium.

George remained bedfast and when winter came he was too ill to be taken to Florida. He characteristically adjusted himself to the situation and uttered no word of complaint. Then it developed that he could not stay in his own home during the winter, for wartime rationing did not allow enough fuel oil for his furnace. A small furnished house in the near-by village of Brook happened to be available, and it was there that he spent the rest of his life. He never lost his cheerfulness or his humor. His memory was as good as ever and he amused himself, while lying helpless, by recalling events of childhood. One day he remarked to Katie Krue, his housekeeper: "I believe I can go up one side of the main street over in Kentland, and down the other side, and give in the right order every business place that was there when I was a kid, and name the clerks who worked in each store." He could, too.

On May 16, 1944, George Ade died at the age of seventy-eight. Three days later, as members of his family listened to George's old friends, John T. McCutcheon, Judge Kenesaw M. Landis and Dr. E. C. Elliott talking about him in an informal way, some of them recalled another occasion when they were together in that same room, the dining room, hearing good talk. They could remember the date because it was the day after the ceremonies at the unveiling of the George Ade portrait in the Kentland High school. George had invited them to a family dinner, served at noon. After dinner they had sat about the table, entertained by George in his best storytelling mood. Now they were in the same room, at the same hour, same date, May 19, four years later, with good talk *about* George.

At one time George had intended to be buried at Hazelden, but because of the uncertainty about the future use of the property he decided to have his final resting place with the rest of his family, and was buried in the Ade lot in Kentland.

George left his house to the decision of trustees, who gave it with ten landscaped acres to Newton county for a George Ade Memorial Hospital. His library, manuscripts and papers and most of his art objects he gave to Purdue University. In dividing his farms among relatives, he put into his will this comment: "I think it proper to declare . . . that one purpose in parceling out the lands . . . is to insure a number of relatively small holdings rather than to keep my landed estate intact. I believe it to be good public policy to divide the land of a farming community among many owners, and I believe that the interests of the community are best served when the various tracts are finally owned by the farmers who cultivate them."

Will historians a century from now read George Ade? If they read his *Stories of the Streets and of the Town* (microfilm copies of which have been made), his Fables and his plays, they can learn of the common talk and thoughts and pretenses of the period. The more observant historian would discover that Ade had an enduring influence on the American language; that with Ade the language became less rigid and more human. He might find that Ade, as much as any other American of his time, taught us to know and enjoy and be tolerant of one another.

His philosophy was apparent in his essay, "The Yankee's Prayer:"

"Help me to get things straight. Give me an outlook on the whole world. . . . Let me read history aright and learn that a people can seldom be made happy and prosperous by . . . ponderous legislation. Assist me and my associates to look to ourselves and not to Congress. Give me patience and tolerance and the strength to brace myself against sudden and hysterical and gusty changes of popular feeling. Let me not construe the rule of the majority into a fool axiom that the majority is always right. Cause me to bear in mind that in every age of which we have record, an unpopular minority advocated measures which later on were accepted by the majority. Protect me against labels and member-ships and binding obligations which will submerge me as an individual. Save me from being enslaved or hampered by catch phrases. May I never take orders which will make me a coward in the sight of my conscience. Let it not be said of me that I 'belong' to a political party. Lead me to an understanding of the new meaning of 'service.' Help me to believe that the man prospers best and longest who is concerned as to the welfare of the people about him. Compel me to see that our organization is a huge experiment in co-operation and not a scramble for prizes."

INDEX

INDEX